The Investment Checklist

The Investment Checklist

THE ART OF IN-DEPTH RESEARCH

Michael Shearn

WILEY

John Wiley & Sons, Inc.

Published by John Wiley & Sons, Inc., Hoboken, New Jersey.
Published simultaneously in Canada.

For general information on our other products and services or for technical support, please contact our Customer Care Department within the United States at (800) 762–2974, outside the United States at (317) 572–3993, or fax (317) 572–4002.

Wiley also publishes its books in a variety of electronic formats. Some content that appears in print may not be available in electronic books. For more information about Wiley products, visit our web site at www.wiley.com.

Library of Congress Cataloging-in-Publication Data:

Shearn, Michael, 1975–
    The investment checklist : the art of in-depth research / Michael Shearn.
        p.   cm.
    Includes index.
        ISBN 978–0–470–89185–8 (cloth); ISBN 978–1–118–14943–0 (ebk);
    ISBN 978–1–118–14944–7 (ebk); ISBN 978–1–118–14945–4 (ebk)
        1. Investment analysis.   2. Portfolio management.   3. Investments.
I. Title.
    HG4529.S47   2011
    332.63'2042—dc23
                                                                        2011021446
Printed in the United States of America

SKY10087873_101524

*For my wonderful wife, loving parents,
and beautiful daughters.*

Contents

Preface

This book can help you make better investment decisions by helping you truly understand the companies you're investing in.

If you're like most investors, you make mistakes when you rush into an investment idea without doing the proper work to understand the value of a business. By rushing, you are essentially *betting on probabilities* that certain assumptions will work out, instead of basing your investment decision on *real analysis.*

Too often, investors buy stocks by relying on recommendations from other investors, or on hunches, or because of isolated facts they've heard or read about a business. When you make your purchase decisions on these factors and do not take the time to thoroughly understand the businesses you are buying, you're more prone to make investment mistakes. Your decision-making then becomes dangerous because you don't really know enough, and you're relying on *other people* and the information (or misinformation) they provide about a particular stock. Instead, your investment purchases should be based on understanding the value of a business through *in-depth research.* If you truly understand the value of a business, then you will be in a position to recognize investment opportunities and can more easily make buy or sell decisions.

Don't be daunted by the idea of in-depth research. This book makes the research *manageable* (more about that in a minute). Also, I'm sure you do research all the time before you spend your hard-earned money: For example, think about any major purchase you've made in your life—whether it's a house, or a car, or an expensive piece of jewelry or electronics. Before you spent all that money on whatever it was, you probably spent some time researching to make sure your money would be well spent. If you were buying a house, you (or your realtor) researched the price of other houses in that neighborhood and other amenities that would make that house desirable (e.g., the school system, ease of commuting, neighborhood parks or pools or tennis courts or shopping, etc.). The more you know about your purchase, the more easily you will be able to recognize a good deal. The same is true when buying or selling a stock. The more you understand the dynamics of a business and the people operating it, the better the odds that you will be able to recognize a good deal on a business.

Many professional investors believe that in-depth research is a waste of time. To them, great investment decisions boil down to a few simple factors, such as an extremely low stock price. I used to subscribe to this theory myself, but over time, I discovered *I was wrong*. As I came to appreciate that the value of a business cannot be condensed into a few simple factors, I searched for books that would teach me how to value a business and invest intelligently in stocks. I was looking for a *practical* book instead of one that focused on broad concepts. In spite of the fact that there are hundreds of books written on the subject of investing, I honestly couldn't find *one* that truly helped me.

My instinct after failing to find a good investing framework was to over-research potential investments. I often ended up reading everything I could get my hands on about a potential investment. As a result, I subjected myself to information overload and was unable to recognize good information. I also kept repeating investment mistakes, such as paying too much for a business or partnering with the wrong management team.

So I set out to establish a systematic process to force me to think through my investment ideas more carefully and help me avoid repeating the same investment mistakes. Over the past 10 years, I began to use checklists of questions I needed to answer to make informed investment decisions—questions that would guide me in learning about a business's competitive position, customer positioning, and management strength. To come up with the questions, I studied the past mistakes I had made investing, and I read many books about the common mistakes made by investors and executives. I interviewed private equity managers, venture capitalists, entrepreneurs, chief executive officers (CEOs), hedge fund managers, mutual fund managers, and private investors to help me prepare a more comprehensive list of questions. During the stock market decline in 2008 and 2009, I made significant improvements to the checklists as the decline exposed weaknesses in my investment process.

As I used the checklists, I discovered that if I could answer the majority of the questions on the checklist, I could more easily value the business by minimizing the number of assumptions I was making about a business's future prospects. If I was unable to answer a question on the checklist (such as "are its managers honest?"), then I could identify the potential risks I was taking in an investment and the areas that I needed to spend more time researching.

My ultimate goal was to understand how well I understood an investment by the questions I was able to answer—and those I was *unable* to answer, which is often even more important. With some companies, I found that the more I read about them, the more questions I had about how the company operated—and I realized this was an indicator that I didn't really understand that business! For example, I spent a lot of time researching mortgage insurers in 2007 before the credit crisis began. Yet the more time I spent, the more questions I had. I never had enough information to be able to calculate a reasonable range of valuations for the businesses. I felt I was answering too many of the questions with *assumptions* rather than backing these assumptions with evidence. I therefore determined I was not in a position to value those businesses and I didn't invest in them. That red flag saved me a lot of money!

The result of all my research is this book, which describes the checklists I've used in my own investing over the past 10 years.

How This Book Can Help You

The Investment Checklist is for anyone who's investing in stocks, at any level—if you're just starting out and thinking about what you want to invest in, or if you already have a portfolio (of any size) that you want to manage better and watch your money grow (after all, no-one wants to watch their investments *lose* money, shrink, or disappear altogether!). That said, this book *isn't* for stock traders (aka *day traders*) or people who invest only for short-term gains.

Instead, this book is for anyone who wants to learn how to *value* a business and invest for the long term: I wrote it to help you learn what you need to know about specific companies you're considering investing in, and to help you evaluate whether or not those companies are *worth* investing in.

Before you read any further, consider these questions about *you* and your approach to investing (and be honest): You're not sharing these answers with anyone else!:

- Do you check stock prices frequently?
- Do falling stock prices make your stomach churn?
- Do you react quickly to positive or negative news announcements about the companies whose stock you own?
- Do you ever feel you're under time pressure to make buy or sell decisions?
- Do you have high portfolio turnover? Are you buying and selling shares often?
- Do you feel you need to defend your investments when others challenge you?

If you answered "yes" to *any* of the above questions, this book can help you make better investment decisions, by helping you research more effectively so you'll truly understand how a business operates and is managed. As I developed my checklists, the benefits of creating a concise and easy-to-use framework became apparent. In short, the exercise of going through *The Investment Checklist* lowers your risk by increasing your knowledge of a business. Here's how the checklists in this book can help you:

- *The checklist will help you filter out the noise and instead focus on information that is most important and relevant.* There is an unending stream of information available; don't get bogged down in information overload, as I did when I first started investing. This book tells you what information you really need and where to find it.
- *The majority of the questions can be answered by information that is relatively easy to find.* You can find most of the information to answer the checklist questions in publicly available Securities and Exchange Commission (SEC) documents or articles written about management and the business.
- *The questions should help you understand the business as if you're the business owner and help move you away from thinking of stocks as pieces of paper.* The checklist questions force you to think about the fundamentals of the business rather than just its stock price. Worrying about things such as fluctuations in

the stock market (which are outside your control anyway!) is a waste of time. Instead, you will be able to identify the main factors that drive the value of the business, most of the risks the business can encounter, and the things that can go wrong.

- *The checklist will help you take a long-term view of your investments.* Most people tend to remember recent events more easily. The checklist requires that you answer questions using a long time span, which helps protect you from overvaluing more recent pieces of information. Researching a business over a long period of time allows us to sort through things rationally and puts us in a position to better interpret information.
- *The checklist is useful for compiling information that goes against your investment thesis.* It is human nature to overweight information that supports your investment thesis and underweight information that is contrary to your investment thesis. The checklist questions help you ensure you're accepting (or at least recognizing) divergent facts about the business.
- *The checklist will help you improve sell decisions.* Knowing when to sell an investment is one of the most difficult decisions you have to make. Most sell decisions are based on judgment, feel, or instinct. The checklist helps you learn when to sell by helping you identify when the fundamentals of a business, such as the quality of the business or management team, begin to change.

How This Book Is Organized

The three most common investing mistakes relate to the price you pay, the management team you essentially join when you invest in a company, and your failure to understand the future economics of the business you're considering investing in. The questions in this book can help you minimize these mistakes by helping you gain a deeper understanding of how a business operates:

- Chapter 1 outlines a search strategy that will improve your odds of finding investment ideas that are worth researching further.
- Chapter 2 helps you understand the basics of a business: What it does, how it earns money, how it evolved over time, and in what geographic locations it earns its money.

- Chapter 3 demonstrates the importance of understanding the business from the customer's perspective rather than your own. These insights will help you learn how important a business is to the customers it serves.
- Chapter 4 helps you evaluate the strengths and weaknesses of a business. These are the questions that will help you evaluate whether or not a business has a sustainable competitive advantage, the competitive landscape, and the industry it operates in.
- Chapter 5 helps you understand the operational and financial health of a business. You'll look at key risks facing the business, how inflation affects it, and whether its balance sheet is weak or strong.
- Chapter 6 looks at the distribution of earnings (cash flow) of a business. You'll learn how to assess whether the company's accounting practices are conservative or liberal (so you can avoid a company like, for example, the now-defunct Enron), the type of revenue it generates, whether the company makes money consistently or in cycles, and whether or not it's resistant to recessions.
- Chapter 7 is the first of three chapters that show you how to understand the quality of the management team. You'll look at what type of manager they are, how they rose to lead the business, how they are compensated, and other background information.
- Chapter 8 helps you gain insight into the competence of a company's senior management. You'll look at how they handle daily operations as well as long-term strategy, how they treat employees, and how they think about costs.
- Chapter 9 helps you assess the management of a company by looking at their positive—and negative—traits: How they think, whether they're self-promoting, and other critical factors. Remember, when you buy stock in a company, you're essentially going into business with the managers who run that company, so you want to know as much about them as you can!
- Chapter 10 demonstrates how you can evaluate the future growth opportunities of a business. You'll look at whether it's growing organically or by merging with or acquiring other companies, whether historical growth has been profitable,

and how quickly it's growing and whether management is growing in a disciplined way.

- Finally, Chapter 11 looks specifically at mergers and acquisitions, to determine whether those completed in the past have been successful and how management makes the decision to merge with or acquire another company.

Each chapter offers countless examples of businesses I've researched, considered investing in, actually invested in, or decided not to invest in. These examples tell you in detail how my checklist helped me make investment decisions, and they'll show you how you can make better investment decisions for your own portfolio. In addition, each chapter ends with "Key Points to Keep in Mind," so you can zero in on the critical factors in each set of questions.

Now, let's get started by learning how to generate investment ideas!

Acknowledgments

This book would not have been written without the encouragement and help of Judd Kahn and Bill Falloon who championed this book from the earliest proposal. No one deserves more thanks than my partner Ann Webb. Her willingness to make everything she touches a success is forever appreciated. Ruth Mills simplified the book-writing process for me and I can't imagine finishing this book without her. Dr. Sandy Leeds was a true devil's advocate. Those who have Sandy in their corner, both students and friends, are very fortunate. My friend Jeff "Falcon" Sokol helped ground the book and at the earliest stages attempted to convince me not to endeavor in this project. As such, all critics need to talk to Jeff about improving his powers of persuasion. I want to thank my mentor and intellectual coach John "Chico" Newman who always provides practical advice.

I would also like to thank the following for their contributions to the book: Bob Aylward, Ciccio Azzolini, Ron Baron, Peter Bevelin, Dr. Paul Bobrowski, Jean-Philippe Bouchard, Dr. John Delaney, Pat Dorsey, Matt Dreith, Ryan Floyd, Meg Freeborn, Ben Gaddis, Francesco Gagliardi, Dave and Sherry Gold, Bob Graham, Todd Green, David Hampton, Norman Hecht, Casey Hoffman, K.K., Paul Larson, Brad Leonard, Steve Lister, Chris Lozano, John Mackey, Denise Mayorga, Bob Miles, Vincent Nordhaus, Francois Rochon, Robert Silberman, Paul Sonkin, Jim Sud, Seng Hock Tan, Lee Valkenaar, and Matthew Weiss.

On a personal note, a heartfelt thank you to the most important people in my life. My parents have never wavered in their support of my ventures. Their patience allowed me to find my own path. Most of all I thank my wife for her steadfast love, support, and guidance. And I want to give a special dedication to my beautiful girls who have forever changed my life in the most wonderful way.

1

How to Generate Investment Ideas

There are many ways you can generate investment ideas, some qualitative, some quantitative. *Quantitative* methods include looking at specific financial or operating metrics, whereas *qualitative* methods rely on more subjective characteristics, such as management strength, corporate culture, or competitive advantages. Whether you are running a complicated stock screen or simply getting ideas from other investors, all methods have their own advantages, limitations, and risks. Ultimately, the best method of generating ideas for you is the one that gives you the largest number of opportunities.

This chapter explores why stocks become undervalued, how to generate investment ideas, how to filter these ideas, and how to keep track of them. These steps are critical to creating a pool of stock ideas.

How Investment Opportunities Are Created

You can't manufacture investment opportunities. Instead, you need to be patient, and you have to be ready for the right opportunities. It is important to understand that good investment ideas are rare, and consistent success in the stock market is elusive. Those investors who believe that they can make money year after year in the stock market are setting themselves up for disappointment. Most investors are far too optimistic: They often think they've found great ideas when they haven't.

In contrast, investors with the best long-term track records have made most of their money with just a handful of investment ideas. For example, Warren Buffett states that his investment success is due to fewer than 20 ideas, such as the *Washington Post* newspaper,

Coca-Cola, and GEICO. In short, you need to mentally prepare yourself in advance with the idea that you will not have many outstanding investments in your lifetime. Most investments you make will produce mediocre results, but a few can provide outstanding results.

The best investment opportunities usually come in big waves, such as when entire markets decline. There have been several recent examples: the Asian financial crisis of 1997 to 1998, the Internet bubble ending in 2000, and the recession starting in 2007. There were many buying opportunities in 2008 when the S&P 500 dropped 36 percent. This was caused by forced selling. The market sell-off was exacerbated by the indiscriminate selling of stocks by money managers who were forced to sell stocks to fund client redemptions. Even if these money managers knew these stocks were undervalued, they had no choice but to sell. This forced selling created artificially low prices—which created a rare opportunity for investors.

Other kinds of forced selling include situations when stocks are thrown out of an index because they no longer meet the minimum standards to remain in an index. Many investment managers who exclusively invest in stocks found in a particular index (such as the S&P 500) are forced to sell when the stock moves out of the index. Spin-offs (where a business divests a subsidiary) create a similar situation when the business that is spun off does not fit the investing criteria of an investment manager. Forced selling decreases prices—which creates opportunities.

Besides broad market sell-offs that create forced selling, the stock market has a way of magnifying different types of business and industry-wide risk that cause the stock prices of businesses to drop. To learn which area of the stock market is in greatest distress, look for those areas where capital is scarce. Scarcity of capital creates less competition for assets, which decreases prices. Ask yourself, *what areas of the stock market are investors fleeing, and why?*

You may want to begin by looking at the percentage change in prices of certain industries found in common indices such as the materials, energy, or financials subset of the S&P Composite 1500. For example, the price performance for components of the S&P Composite 1500 from April 23, 2010 to June 7, 2010 showed that:

- Materials were down 18 percent
- Energy was down 17 percent
- Utilities were down 9 percent

With that information, you might start researching the materials industry, looking for stocks that have significantly dropped in price. Ideally, you want to identify those stocks where the baby has been thrown out with the bathwater—and then rescue that baby!

Most stock price drops are due to some type of uncertainty about the business, and there are many possible reasons:

- Litigation fears
- Accounting irregularities
- Accusations of fraud
- Health concerns (such as swine flu)
- Execution problems due to a flawed strategy
- Management concerns
- Executive departures
- Government intervention or regulation
- Loss of a customer
- Technological changes
- Credit rating downgrades
- Competitor announcements
- Or a myriad of other reasons

In most of these cases, investors automatically assume the worst-case scenario and tend to sell stocks first and ask questions later. Once the reality starts to set in that the ultimate outcome will not be as bad as expected, then stock prices adjust and typically rise. Ideally, you want to identify those areas where the outlook is most pessimistic and *identify whether the sources of pessimism are temporary or permanent.* Let's look at an example.

Case Study: Investors' Pessimism about Heartland Payment Systems Proved Unfounded

In 2009, Heartland Payment Systems found itself in what appeared to be a disastrous scenario. Heartland helps small and mid-sized merchants with credit-card transactions, providing the physical card machine and payment-processing services that enable customers to use credit and debit cards in retail stores. In 2008, computer hackers installed spyware on Heartland's network and had gained access to the systems that process Visa, MasterCard, Discover, and American Express transactions.

After discovering the problem, Heartland announced details concerning the breach, including the number of months the spyware might have gathered card numbers and the number of transactions that the company usually processed. Framing it as potentially the largest data breach in history, the *New York Times* noted that 600 million or more card accounts were vulnerable, and quoted a data security analyst who said that there could be as much as *$500 million* in losses and other expenses if you added it all up. Early estimates were that Heartland would have to pay $2 per card for MC/Visa to reissue each affected card. The result? Investors quickly sold the stock. The price plummeted from $18 per share before the breach was announced (on January 6, 2009) to as low as $3.78 per share on March 9, 2009.

However, other investors with a solid base of research on the company and industry knew several things that helped them take advantage of this situation:

- First, they focused on Heartland's transaction count of 100 million transactions per month, and they recognized that not all of those would be from unique accounts. People tend to go the same places more than once. Later, more conservative estimates of stolen cards emerged at about 140 million cards, instead of 600 million.
- Second, there was publicly available information about a similar case involving retailers TJ Maxx and Marshalls that had been settled recently. In that case, the average settlement per account to the issuing banks to replace cards was about 70¢ per card.

In 2010, Heartland agreed to pay MasterCard, Visa, and American Express $105 million—not the $500 million that was originally estimated by news sources. This amount, which averaged 81¢ per card, was similar to the recent TJ Maxx and Marshalls case. More important for investors was the fact that this was a far cry from the first potential loss estimates. Investors who already held stock in Heartland shouldn't have immediately sold the stock on the news. They would have been *rewarded* if they had purchased *more* of the stock to decrease their cost basis. Also, investors who didn't already own Heartland stock should have bought at this time because this one-time event was nowhere near as devastating as the sources in the press made it out to be. After investors realized that the liability from the breach was lower than they anticipated, the stock price recovered to more than $13 per share several months later (by the end of 2010).

In sum, if you had purchased the stock after the breach was announced, *you could have tripled your investment!*

Be Wary of Exciting New Trends that Turn out to Be Fads

You must also learn to identify those areas of the stock market that are benefiting from abundant sources of capital, which drives up prices, so you can be careful investing in them. Wall Street is good at pitching stories, and investors tend to get excited by what they believe is an important new trend. However, many of these exciting major trends turn out to be fads that are based on speculation, rather than fundamentals. Let's look at a couple of examples.

In the 1960s, investors bid up the stocks of conglomerates that were increasing their earnings through acquisitions. Businesses such as James Ling's LTV (Ling-Temco-Vought), bought unrelated businesses to increase and diversify their revenue streams. Growing quickly, they used their high stock prices to purchase other businesses. LTV acquired company after company, growing from the 204th largest industrial company in 1965 to the *14th largest* in 1969— only four years later!

Yet by 1970, under the pressure of enormous debt, antitrust threat, and a generally bearish market, LTV's stock had plummeted, as did the stock of several of the other recently ballooned conglomerates. From a high in 1968 of $136 per share to a 1970s low of $7 per share, LTV ended up selling many of its acquisitions at clearance prices.[1]

The 1990s gave us another kind of speculative boom, what we now call the Internet bubble. Technology stocks provided rates of return that dwarfed their actual growth or profits (if they had any profit at all). For example, computer manufacturer and services company Sun Microsystems was once valued as high as 10 times revenues when its stock traded for $64 per share. CEO Scott McNealy recalls that heady period: "At 10 times revenues, to give you a 10-year payback, I have to pay you 100 percent of revenues for 10 straight years in dividends." McNealy noted that his assumptions include a few major obstacles such as getting shareholder approval for such a plan and not paying any expenses or taxes. Furthermore, McNealy noted that Sun Microsystems would also have to maintain its revenue run rate without investing in any R&D. McNealy asked, "Now, having done that, would any of you like to buy my stock at $64? Do you realize how ridiculous those basic assumptions are?"[2]

How to Spot Investment Bubbles

To understand where current bubbles exist, ask, "Where is a lot of money being made very quickly?" Look at the *Forbes* magazine list of billionaires. What industries are the new billionaires coming from? For example, in the early 1980s, the *Forbes* list was populated mainly by individuals in the oil and gas industry. Also, monitor initial public offerings (IPOs) coming to market. Are the IPOs that are quickly rising in price concentrated in a certain industry, as Internet stocks were during the technology boom of 1998 to 2000?

When capital is abundant, it searches for other similar businesses to duplicate success. The IPOs of technology businesses caused many other technology businesses to be formed and seek to go public. Here are a few signs of a bubble:

- Lots of available capital
- Higher levels of leverage
- Decreased discipline from lenders as they try to get higher returns than through conventional lending guidelines
- Decreased responsibility for the borrower, combining high leverage and looser lending terms

One of the lessons from the 1980s real estate boom/bust was that there was a grace period in which everybody had money in their pockets and they did not have to worry about whether tenants would occupy the buildings or whether the assumptions about future cash flows were going to be proven correct. Buildings were built on a speculative basis, as lenders were in essence throwing money at developers to build new projects and did not worry if the builders had tenants to occupy these buildings. Eventually, there was an oversupply of real estate, which caused prices for real estate to drop. Lenders and developers found themselves with many empty properties, and there were many bankruptcies during this period. This just goes to show that areas where there is an abundance of capital are usually poor hunting grounds for great investments. Investors who got caught up in the hype of the 1980s real estate boom or technology bubble of the late 1990s ultimately ended up losing most of their capital.

Now that you know more about how to generally look for investment ideas, the following sections of this chapter describe a few more formalized ways to begin looking for investment ideas.

Using Stock Screens

A stock screen is a tool investors use to filter stocks, using preselected criteria. For example, if you're an investor looking for cheap stocks, you could enter a set of filters such as: "companies that have enterprise value to earnings before interest, taxes, depreciation, and amortization (EBITDA) ratios of less than five times that also have market capitalizations over $100 million."

This produces a list of businesses that fit the limits you've just set.

There are many different types of screening tools available. Services range from free services to those with high-end fees, with features and coverage varying by service. The higher-fee services cover a greater number of businesses, including microcap stocks and international stocks, and they often come bundled with a range of analytical tools that can help you further refine searches, such as "search for businesses with more than $100 million in revenues that have CEOs over the age of 60."

One of the main limitations of stock screens is that they use Generally Accepted Accounting Principles (GAAP) accounting numbers, which rarely present a realistic financial picture of a business. For example, if you are looking at a multiple of last year's earnings, this can be misleading if the company reported a big loss in the prior year. Investors often need to adjust GAAP earnings to understand the real earnings of a business.

For example, in 2006 and 2007, the average trailing 12-month price/earnings ratio (P/E) for retailer 99 Cent Only Stores was more than 90 times.[3] After adjusting the earnings for special charges 99 Cent Only Stores took in those two years, I learned that the adjusted P/E was closer to 12 times rather than the 90 times being reported.

On a standard stock screen, many of my best investments showed up as having a P/E ratio of more than 50 times because GAAP accounted for such factors as restructuring costs that reduced earnings. After I made GAAP adjustments, I found that these ostensibly high price-to-earnings-ratio businesses were really trading at only five times earnings, not 50. Had I relied exclusively on stock screens, I would have missed many of my best investments.

For example, when I was researching the stock of Four Seasons Hotels, which had dropped in price after the September 11 terrorist attacks, its P/E ratio was 85 times earnings. Four Seasons had just taken several restructuring charges, which reduced the earnings of the business. After adjusting the earnings of the business for these restructuring charges (which were due to GAAP standards rather than actual cash charges), the P/E ratio was closer to 10 times earnings. Had my firm relied on a stock screen, we would have never found this investment, which doubled in price in a short period of time.

Keeping an Eye on New-Lows Lists

Newspapers and websites can provide other idea sources like new-lows listings. For example, the online site for the *Wall Street Journal* offers daily and historical new-lows listing of U.S. stocks—that is, those reaching new 52-week price lows on the NYSE, AMEX, and NASDAQ.

Also, Value Line regularly publishes stock listings such as those that have:

- The widest discounts from book value
- The greatest percentage price changes over the previous 13 weeks
- High 3- to 5-year price appreciation potential
- Current P/E multiples and price-to-net working capital ratios that are in the bottom quartile of the Value Line universe

Paul Sonkin, manager of the Hummingbird Value Fund (a micro-cap fund), uses stock screens and new-lows lists, but he believes these tools are misused by investors 99 percent of the time. According to Sonkin, ". . . a lot of investors will put together a screen of low price-to-book or low price-to-earnings stocks, but usually 90 percent of the companies on the screen are cheap for a good reason. Many stay on these lists for a long time."[4] Sonkin believes the proper way to use a screen or new-lows list is to run them on a weekly basis and look for *new* companies that appear on the list. This way, you are able to separate the companies that deserve to be there from those that may only be suffering from a temporary problem.

My firm has benefited from tracking new-lows lists. For example, I missed an opportunity to invest in Apollo Group, the for-profit higher-education business known as the University of Phoenix, in 2001, when the stock price was near $20 per share. By the end of 2001, the stock price rose to more than $30 per share, and by the middle of 2004, it rose to $100 per share.

Although I missed the opportunity to invest in 2001, I continued to research Apollo Group by attending industry conferences, listening to conference calls, and keeping up with SEC filings. Five years later, I was able to act decisively when the stock price dropped from $60 per share at the beginning of 2006 to $35 per share on November 14, 2006 due to an options backdating scandal. I was able to discover the opportunity because I was continually monitoring the new-lows lists and saw that Apollo Group's stock price had dropped. Also, because I had consistently followed the business over a long period, I knew investors were overreacting to the scandal. By the beginning of January, the stock was trading for more than $40 per share and by July it appreciated to $60 per share. Had I not prepared in advance and monitored new-lows lists, I would have missed the small window of opportunity to make this investment.

Reading Newsletters, Alert Services, Online Recommendations, and Media Recommendations

There are many publications that tout stocks. It is better to stick to those services that are fact-based, such as *Bankruptcy Week* or *Distressed Company Alert,* rather than those services that are more interested in selling subscriptions by marketing high rates of returns to their subscribers. Fact-based publications are those where no opinion is attached and instead corporate events are chronicled. Be aware of self-serving recommendations and less-than-transparent presentations of results. Some newsletters will exclude certain stocks they have recommended in the past when presenting their overall rates of returns, and instead present only those that have done well.

Using Value Line

Value Line is a great source for you to build knowledge on certain businesses or industries. It presents much critical information on a single page. A typical stock report shows 10 years of financial information, including sales, operating margin, depreciation, net profit margin, income tax rate, working capital, long-term debt, and shareholder equity. It also shows historical returns, such as return on total capital, return on shareholder equity, and return on common equity. There is also a quick write-up of significant developments over the last quarter as well as a historical stock chart.

Each week, a new issue comes out highlighting a group of stocks within an industry, such as auto and truck, precision instruments, electric utilities, or medical supplies. I read each issue from beginning to end looking for new ideas. This also builds my understanding of new businesses and industries. I borrowed this idea from Charlie Munger, Vice Chairman of Berkshire Hathaway, who mentioned at an annual meeting that he leafs through these reports regularly to learn more about different types of businesses as well as to find opportunities. The main limitation of this source is that its publications cover only 3,500 stocks, and not all 9,000 publicly traded stocks in the United States.

Following Other Investment Managers

Many investors (professionals included) generate ideas by closely tracking the holdings of well-known investment managers with above-average track records. There always seems to be a hot group of investors that others follow, although most aren't followed for long. These are usually investors who have had recent success, so the media constantly reports their new holdings.

The problem with following others is that most of these great records were generated by *past* investments, and investors wrongly conclude that *existing and future* investments will have similar results. Many of these investors fall in and out of favor (for example, when investors began to question the investment wisdom of Warren Buffett when he was telling investors to avoid high-priced Internet stocks in 1999), and it is typically when they are out of favor that you should be following their holdings. Investors who manage the largest amounts (i.e., more than $100 million) have to disclose their investments each quarter in an SEC 13-F filing, so following them is straightforward (albeit slightly delayed).

Early in my career, I occasionally sourced investment ideas from these managers. When the filings came out, I would be excited to discover that the investment managers I admired had made some new investments or significantly increased their position in a stock.

If it was an investment idea I understood, this excitement translated into higher conviction, sometimes causing me to cut corners on my own research.

There are several disadvantages to following other investment managers:

- Most great investment track records come from a limited number of investments. For every 10 investments a successful investment manager makes, only one will appreciate substantially, contributing outsize returns to the investment record, while the others will either mildly perform or underperform.
- You typically will not know the reason why a certain investment manager is buying or selling a stock. Perhaps the investment manager is suffering from investment redemptions and he or she needs to sell stocks.
- No matter how good they are, all investment managers will make mistakes, and you may be following them into such a mistake.
- Investment managers change their strategies. Recognize that the strategies the investment manager followed in the past to generate the superior investment record is not necessarily the strategy the investment manager is following *today*.

Therefore, in the end, be careful about following the ideas of other investors.

Casually Reading the Business Press

You can generate ideas from the business press by regularly reading publications such as *Barron's*, the *Wall Street Journal*, the *Financial Times*, *Forbes*, and *Fortune*. Consider subscribing to trade journals as well, such as *American Banker* (if you are interested in financial-services stocks) or *Las Vegas Review-Journal* (if you are interested in casino stocks).

As you read the articles, you'll not only ground yourself in industry basics, but you'll uncover descriptions of management teams you'd like to invest with. The best investment ideas usually come from those businesses that are in distress. Focus on those articles that are not success stories but those about distress, to give you better odds of finding a well-priced investment.

For example, First Manhattan senior managing director Todd Green remembers how he first became interested in the diversified industrial conglomerate Tyler Corporation. Green read an article in *Forbes* (in 1990) where CEO Joseph McKinney said he would not consider doing a leveraged buyout (LBO) because this would put him on the opposite side of the table from shareholders. This was during the days of a serious amount of LBO activity, and the comment signaled to Green that the CEO had the right attitude regarding the alignment of shareholders and management interests. Green purchased the stock on April 26, 1991 at $3.07 per share and sold it on June 8, 1998 at $9.99 per share, a compound rate of return of more than 18 percent.[5]

Buying Shares to Track a Business

You can buy a few shares in a stock that meets your criteria to force yourself to follow the business. By purchasing a very small piece of a business, you've guaranteed that you will not forget the business, and that you'll have consistent reminders about that business. Paul Sonkin of the Hummingbird Value Fund calls this his *grab bag*. In his personal account, Sonkin has purchased one share of more than 300 companies. In the mail each day, he usually receives something from some of the companies. He has followed some of the companies for many years, and he uses this method as a way of filling his in-box with companies that he has already screened as being interesting.

For example, Sonkin was able to invest in Control Chief Holdings, a manufacturer and marketer of wireless remote control equipment primarily used in the railway industry, which was trading for $250 per share. Sonkin had followed the business over some time and learned that the business had more than $147 per share in net cash and estimated that it had $25 per share in earnings power. Therefore, at an enterprise value of $103 per share, Sonkin bought the stock at four times normalized net income, an extremely low price.[6]

Don't Ignore Your Existing Investment Portfolio

Admittedly, it is more exciting to discover opportunities outside of your portfolio, but it's not necessarily more beneficial. Many investors forget to look at their existing portfolio for ideas. Often, your best opportunities are right in front of you. If a stock you hold drops in price, this may represent the best investment opportunity for you, especially compared to a stock you know less well.

For example, when the S&P 500 dropped 36 percent in 2008, there was an abundance of opportunities. Instead of attempting to analyze many of the new opportunities being offered, my firm decided to analyze our own portfolio holdings that were trading at significantly lower prices than they had just weeks or months before. At one point, our core holding Whole Foods Market traded at close to four times enterprise value to free cash flow, which means we could have bought the whole business (including debt net of cash) and paid for it in four years out of existing depressed free cash flow. We ended up buying more of our existing holdings, such as Whole Foods Market, which helped us generate a net return that was far superior to the S&P 500. Had we analyzed new potential holdings, we probably would not have increased our existing holdings and not generated an excess return.

Research Upcoming IPOs

You can regularly research IPOs, spin-offs, and stocks of companies that are exiting bankruptcy, all of which are new businesses to the stock market. You can subscribe to various services that will alert you to these new entrants, such as Gemfinder's *Spinoff & Reorganization Report*. Once alerted, you should read the prospectus that accompanies an IPO, spin-off, or stock exiting bankruptcy, because these are especially rich in information and are much more useful than a standard 10-K filing. The biggest advantage of tracking these businesses is that there is not a public price to influence you. You can calculate a reasonable valuation range for the business in advance, and then compare your value to the business's trading price.

For example, I analyzed pediatric nutrition business Mead Johnson Nutrition before it was spun-off from parent Bristol-Myers Squibb. Because, there was not a public price to influence me, I determined that the stock was worth $40 per share and that I should buy it at any price below $30 per share. When the price of the spin-off was set at $27 per share in February 2009, I purchased the stock, which quickly increased to $43.70 at the end of 2009. Had I not prepared in advance, I would have missed this opportunity.

How to Filter Your Investment Ideas

So far in this chapter, I have shown a few of the ways you can gather investment ideas. The rest of this chapter demonstrates ways to filter these results and begin evaluating investment candidates that you may want to include in your set of potential investments.

Criteria Is a Filter

When filtering through the many investment opportunities the stock market is offering at any given time, it is important for you to establish criteria of the types of businesses and management teams you are searching for. These criteria serve as a filter, so you don't have to review thousands of investment opportunities and therefore can reject investment ideas quickly. If you have ever purchased a home, when you first started looking, you were probably overwhelmed by the number of houses that were available. At some point, you probably began to establish criteria for the types of houses and areas you were interested in, and this helped you narrow the list of houses that were potential candidates for purchase. The investment criteria you develop will work in the same way.

Your criteria can be as simple as looking for a simplified business with a large market opportunity, managed by a great management team, and trading at a low price. You can also set criteria of what you do *not* want to invest in. For example, you may want to avoid businesses that have a high dependency on commodity resources, such as exploration and production (E&P) businesses, because oil prices are difficult to forecast. By articulating and following strict criteria, you can put the odds of making a successful investment in your favor.

Table 1.1 is something you might want to consider using in order to make comparisons among different types of businesses. You can list what your preferences are for a business, such as these:

- A recurring revenue stream
- A business with high organic growth prospects (i.e., growth that is *not* accomplished by acquiring or merging with other businesses)
- Management that has a long tenure at the business
- A competitive moat

Table 1.1 Sample Criteria Checklist

Name of Company	Recurring Revenue	Long Runway	Proven Management	Franchise	Strong Financials	High ROIC	Limited Competition	Low Capital Expenditures	Diversified Customer Base	Strong Balance Sheet	Total
					Potential Holdings						
Discount, Variety Store	√	√	√	—	√	√	√	√	√	√	9
Personal Financial Services	√	√	—	√	√	√	√	√	√	√	9
Education & Training Services	X	—	—	√	√	√	√	√	√	√	7
Online Travel	—	—	X	√	√	√	√	√	√	√	7
Asset Management	√	√	√	√	√	√	√	√	√	√	10
Sporting Goods Store	√	√	√	√	—	—	√	—	√	—	6

KEY: √ = Possesses, X = Does Not Possess, — = Don't Know

- Strong existing or potential financial characteristics, such as high free-cash flow
- High existing or potential returns on invested capital
- Limited competition
- Low capital-expenditure requirements
- A diversified customer base
- A strong balance sheet

A check mark indicates that the business possesses a certain attribute, such as a high return on invested capital, whereas the X mark indicates that it does not. You can make a simple tally of how many attributes the business exhibits. This serves as a scoring system and helps you compare different businesses from different industries.

Evaluating the business in each of these 10 areas will help you understand the tradeoffs you are making when investing in a particular business. Perhaps you found an investment with a strong competitive advantage, yet the business has limited future growth prospects: Using the criteria in Table 1.1 clarifies the advantages and disadvantages of such a business as well as its potential dangers. The more closely a business meets your stringent criteria, the less risk you are taking. For example, it is easier to monitor a business with limited competition rather than one that has a lot of competition. If a business meets only four or five of your criteria, you can usually pass on the business, as most investment mistakes are made when you stretch your criteria.

Once a business meets your criteria, it is important to track it. You may want to create a spreadsheet where you list the businesses that meet your criteria, similar to the example in Table 1.2. It is essentially a formal watch list of businesses and can range from a few ideas to hundreds of ideas.

Once you add an investment to your list, you should begin learning about the business and management team, and track the valuation of the business using financial metrics such as free cash flow (FCF) yield or total enterprise value (TEV) to earnings before interest and taxes (EBIT) to alert you if a business drops in value. Because of the GAAP issues mentioned earlier, you may want to avoid using valuation metrics such as price-to-earnings ratios. Also, you don't need to update these spreadsheets yourself; instead, there are various services you can use to update the numbers on a daily basis, such as Bloomberg or Standard & Poor's Capital IQ.

Table 1.2 Inventory of Ideas

Name	Ticker	TEV/EBIT	TEV/ EBITDA	TEV/ Normalized Earnings	Pre-Tax Earnings Yield	Debt to EBITDA	EBIT/ Interest Exp	FCF Yield EV	FCF Yield Market	Dividend Yield (%) EV	Last market Price	Free Cash-Flow Estimate	Target Price	Stock Price vs. Target
Western Union Co.	WU	10.1x	8.9x	18	9.9%	2.2x	8x	6.77%	7.47%	1.30%	$18.73	$1.40	$20.51	91%
Whole Foods Market, Inc.	WFM	19.1x	11.9x	32	5.2%	0.7x	14x	4.14%	4.14%	0.00%	$49.71	$2.06	$34.76	143%
Dell Inc.	DELL	6.0x	4.6x	10	16.8%	1.4x	17x	12.92%	9.69%	0.00%	$13.41	$1.30	$20.09	67%
Penn National Gaming	PENN	13.5x	8.3x	37	7.6%	3.9x	2.5x	6.56%	10.94%	0.00%	$34.72	$3.80	$25.00	139%
Morningstar Inc.	MORN	19.9x	15.0x	32	5.0%	0.0x	0.00x	4.62%	4.03%	0.40%	$52.64	$2.12	$30.00	175%
Moody's Corp.	MCO	9.0x	8.3x	16	11.0%	1.5x	15x	6.13%	6.58%	1.60%	$27.35	$1.80	$20.00	137%
Strayer Education	STRA	9.4x	8.7x	15	10.7%	0.0x	0.00x	4.83%	4.42%	2.70%	$158.26	$7.00	$160.00	99%

Source: Capital IQ, December 14, 2010
KEY: TEV = Total Enterprise Value; EBITDA = Earnings Before Interest, Taxes, Depreciation, and Amortization; FCF = Free Cash Flow

Valuation Is a Filter

The one thing you can't fix after making an investment is the price you pay, so it is critical to remain disciplined on price. Your future rate of return will be determined by the price you pay for the business. This is why you should only consider those investments that are trading at a low price. The following case study gives you an example of how investment manager Brad Leonard generated high returns for his investors by paying low prices.

Brad Leonard founded BML Capital Management, LLC in 2004. He has compounded capital at a rate of 26.94 percent, net after fees from 2004 to 2010, compared to 3.87 percent, net for the S&P 500. He credits this record to being disciplined about paying low prices for stocks. He typically pays three times enterprise value (EV) to EBITDA for a stock, and he prefers to buy businesses that do not need a lot of capital expenditures to maintain their businesses and those that have little to no debt. In 2009, when the stock market was declining, Leonard was buying stocks at one to two times EBITDA. Leonard says, "When you are paying one or two times EV EBITDA, not much needs to go right. If the business survives, you win. As long as the business does not end, you don't need to make a lot of great assumptions in your analysis. If instead I were paying a 5 percent earnings yield (earnings divided by market capitalization) on depressed earnings, it would not really be that cheap."

For example, Leonard first began buying Kirkland's, a home décor retailer, at $1.70 per share in the fall of 2007. Shortly thereafter, the stock price declined to $0.70 per share (when the stock market declined by more than 36 percent in 2008). As Leonard was buying Kirkland's, the fundamentals of the business continued to improve. After reporting negative comparable store sales in the fourth quarter of 2007, Kirkland's same-store sales turned positive in the first two quarters of 2008. Cash flows, comparable store sales, and margins all continued to improve, yet the stock price continued to decline. Leonard stepped on the gas even more in his purchases. He said, "Every quarter, the results of Kirkland's would improve, and it seemed that no one cared. At this time, I thought it was likely the company would post around $20 million in EBITDA, so in essence, I was buying the stock around 1 to 2 times EV to EBITDA." The stock eventually recovered to around $2 per share by 2008, and by 2009, it was trading at more than $20 per share. Leonard's disciplined buying was well rewarded.[7]

Using a Spreadsheet to Track Potential and Existing Holdings

There are many advantages to using a spreadsheet to track your potential and existing holdings. First, the discipline of placing newly developed investment ideas in a spreadsheet lets the novelty of the new idea wear off, and it helps you counter your natural desire to act on impulse and buy a stock. You will not feel as if you are about to miss the opportunity of a lifetime because you have many choices to invest in. Most of us look for stocks that are cheap and then study the business and assess management. By the time you are up to speed on the business and ready to buy, the opportunity is gone. After this happens a few times, you will begin to feel a sense of urgency whenever you spot a new investment idea. You might be tempted to short-cut your research process so that you will not miss another opportunity.

Having such a spreadsheet, however, allows you to optimize the use of your time by allowing you to concentrate on those opportunities with the greatest upside potential and lowest downside risk. Instead of *scrambling* to analyze the many investment opportunities being offered to you by the stock market, you can *carefully choose* from the best opportunities in your spreadsheet.

The greatest advantage to maintaining an inventory of existing and potential investments is the ability to make comparisons. If you are comparing your existing holdings with hundreds of potential investment opportunities rather than a limited set, you increase the probability of making good investments and avoiding bad ones. The more comparisons you can make in your spreadsheet, the higher the probability of uncovering an investment idea. In addition, those comparisons will increase your awareness of areas of the stock market and individual stocks that are out of favor. You can gradually build your spreadsheet over time or proactively build it— two approaches that I'll discuss in the final sections of this chapter.

Gradually Building a Spreadsheet of Potential Investments

When you do not have investment opportunities that you are ready to act on, you can use your time to prepare for future opportunities. When you identify a unique business or superior management team, add the business to your inventory of ideas or watch list, regardless of its current valuation. This is the secret sauce to investing intelligently, because it allows you to *act decisively* when a good opportunity is in front of you, and it prevents you from *acting imprudently* when you first have the idea or insight. In essence, you are letting time work in your favor.

Be Proactive

One of the biggest advantages of investing in public markets is that you can identify every business in your investable universe. You have the ability to review more than 9,000 publicly traded businesses one by one. You can look for those businesses that meet your criteria. Exclude those businesses that you do not believe you can accurately value because this will help you get through the list at a quicker pace. This will help you narrow down the number of businesses you consider investing in from 9,000 to a more manageable several hundred.

Once you have some ideas of the companies you're considering investing in, there are a couple of preliminary questions you should ask yourself before getting into the nitty-gritty of researching those businesses. Turn to Chapter 2 to discover the first several questions of *The Investment Checklist.*

Key Points to Keep in Mind

- You will not have many outstanding investments in your lifetime.
- Investment opportunities are created when capital is scarce. Capital becomes scarce when one or more of the following events occurs:
  - An entire market declines
  - There is forced selling from a stock being thrown out of an index or if it is spun off
  - There is some type of uncertainty about a business that causes investors to sell their stock
- If you use stock screens to identify investment ideas, understand that you may miss many investment opportunities because most screens are based on GAAP accounting numbers which may under- or overstate the earnings of a business.
- Be careful when following investment managers in their investment ideas.
- Use specific criteria to filter out the investment ideas you don't like.
- Create an inventory of ideas to track potential investments that meet your criteria on a continual basis in order to prepare for future opportunities.

2

Understanding the Business—The Basics

Once you know you are interested in a particular business and ready to begin your research, you should take a structured approach to evaluating that business. This chapter tells you how to nail down the most basic questions you encounter when analyzing a new company: What does it really do, and how does it make money? Sometimes this is easy, but I've certainly been surprised at times. If you have a solid understanding of what a company does and can explain it simply, you are less likely to waste time on tangential issues as you go into more depth.

Essentially, you want to understand the company as it is today by looking at how it evolved. I believe that history goes to the heart of why a company is successful: Was it really good? Or was it just really lucky?

After gathering the basic information on a business, we'll turn our attention to the special case of evaluating a company's success in foreign markets. For most companies, globalization has created interconnected markets, which creates a new research task for you. Even if the company you're researching is still mostly a domestic operator today, you want to evaluate the company's profitability and commitment to foreign markets.

Let's start by considering whether or not you're even *interested* in learning about a particular business, and then imagine yourself in the shoes of the company's CEO. Let's take a closer look at these questions.

☐ 1. Do I want to spend a lot of time learning about this business?

Before you begin to analyze a business, ask yourself if you are interested in learning more about it. If not, you probably won't have sufficient interest to do in-depth research and as a result, you may make an uninformed investment decision. You can't truly understand a business in a couple of weeks. It takes a long time, years in most cases, to truly understand how a business operates and to determine the competence and integrity of a management team. It is a continuous process, and if your interest begins to wane in a couple of weeks, you will not have the stamina to continue to learn about the business over the long term.

If you are just beginning to invest, it is best for you to analyze one business over a long period of time. Too often, even professional analysts spend their time analyzing too many businesses, and they never develop the ability to fully understand the value of a business (i.e., they don't see the whole picture).

For example, at the beginning of my investment career, I spent six months analyzing TV ratings company Nielsen Media Research. I spent my time interviewing more than 80 percent of Nielsen Media Research's customer base, and I developed an in-depth understanding of the business. As a result, I was in a good position to value the business.

As you begin to read about the business, ask yourself how steep your learning curve will have to be to understand a particular business. If you find that it is extremely difficult for you to evaluate the business or that you are simply not interested, this is a sign you might want to pass on the investment. Most of us can eventually understand a complex business if we invest enough time, but our understanding may ultimately still be shallow. Instead of over-investing in a process that yields less return, try to develop a deeper understanding of businesses you genuinely care about.

Too many investment firms assign investment ideas to their analysts without considering whether those analysts will enjoy researching the business or industry. If the analyst is not interested in learning about the business, he or she may never uncover useful insights. It is common sense that you are less likely to succeed at something you are not interested in, yet investors force themselves to study such businesses.

For example, I remember researching a bank recommended by an investor with a long track record of successfully investing in bank stocks. As I read through the 10-K form, I quickly found that I did not enjoy learning about the bank. Although I forced myself to continue to read about the bank, I found myself looking for distractions. My lack of interest caused me to lose momentum in my analysis. I waited for inspiration to continue reading and sometimes would find it, although it was short lived. Because I was uninterested in the business, I was unable to conduct a thorough analysis.

In contrast, retail held instant fascination for me. If there was a term I did not understand, I researched its meaning or how it was calculated. I searched for articles and books on how to identify an efficient retailer, took classes to learn more about retail operations, and started going to industry conferences. Thoroughly engaged and stimulated, I found that few things distracted me. I recall cutting phone conversations short so I could get back to learning more about retail. My passion for retail gave me the drive to constantly learn more about the industry and put me in a better position to evaluate opportunities within this sector.

However, there's an element of risk to this passion: Personally liking a product or service can lead you to believe that others will like it as well. For example, it's hard to objectively weigh criticism of your favorite restaurant: Because your own experience has been different, you may even discount a negative report. My own passion for retail has caused me to lose discipline at times, as I overlooked negative attributes and instead focused on the positive ones. Whether positive or negative, be aware that your personal preferences may negatively influence your investment decisions.

☐ **2. How would you evaluate this business if you were to become its CEO?**

The goal of any long-term investor should be to have the greatest understanding of the underlying economics of a business and know how those can change. Ideally, you should research the business as though you would be taking over the business in the next few months as chief executive officer (CEO). That is exactly what Robert Silberman, CEO of Strayer Education, did.

I interviewed Silberman at a Strayer University campus opening in Austin, Texas. The opportunity to take over as CEO of Strayer came about when one of Silberman's friends, Bob Grusky, called Silberman and told him that the private equity firm he was starting, New Mountain, had identified Strayer as a company they wanted to invest in. New Mountain was buying out the former Strayer CEO, who was set to retire. Grusky and his partners needed someone to come in as CEO and asked Silberman to join the company.

Silberman's first reaction was, "How can you own a university?" He had never heard of the business model before this phone call. At the time, Silberman was the chief operating officer (COO) of Cal Energy, which was owned by Berkshire Hathaway. Before formally accepting the position, Silberman spent the next five months completing an in-depth research study of the for-profit education industry and Strayer Education.

From March to July 2000, Silberman researched the history of for-profit education and the education sector in the United States. In particular, he wanted to understand the role of private capital in this sector.

Silberman told me, "One of the advantages of running an international energy company is that you are on airplanes a lot—I had all these 13-hour flights. After a few hours of sleep and taking care of my other responsibilities, I was able to really dive in on an uninterrupted basis. And the more I looked at this as a business, the more excited I got. The renewable energy business that I was in had incredible capital requirements, very low returns on capital, and all sorts of extraneous risks such as technological risks, political risk, and currency risk. The education sector in this country, at the post-secondary level, was the exact opposite. It had low capital requirements, very high demand, very limited supply, and if you really ran a great university with a good reputation, a very wide moat."

Silberman read broad histories of higher education in the United States and then focused on the for-profit sector. His analysis included macroeconomic factors and sector-level data. He identified and studied other companies in the industry that were publicly traded, and finally, he researched Strayer.

He studied the industry's history in order to understand how the for-profit education industry had developed, and he analyzed the factors that had driven the accelerated growth of the industry over the last 20 to 25 years. To study the public companies, he read 10-Ks and 10-Qs, annual reports, and analyst reports from competing education companies, such as Apollo Group, DeVry, and ITT Corp. Silberman analyzed reams of statistical data about the for-profit customer. He wanted to understand who went to for-profit colleges and who did not. He looked at the outcomes for the customer by analyzing data about the earning potential for someone who had a college degree.

Silberman learned that the earnings potential for college graduates was high and rising as the U.S. economy shifted away from its manufacturing base, where a high-school degree and limited technical training had been enough to support a middle-class lifestyle. As the United States moved toward a knowledge- and service-based economy, achieving a middle-class lifestyle with only a high-school degree was getting tougher. The gap in earnings between educated and non-educated people was growing wider and creating intense demand for higher education. Furthermore, the supply was essentially fixed.

As part of his due diligence, Silberman visited Strayer's campuses in Washington, D.C., and he wandered into classrooms, where he pretended to be a student. As he saw professors and working adult students interact, he sensed how intense the students' desire was to complete their degrees. He could see that the educational experience was life-changing.

Silberman explains, "Take a 35 year old, with only a high-school degree, who has been working either as a pink-collar, blue-collar, or underutilized white-collar [employee] for 15 years. Their earning power and ability to maintain a middle class lifestyle has become more difficult. When they attend college, it is an absolute game changer."

Silberman remembers flying in to Washington, D.C., for a Monday evening class. It was fall, and the Washington Redskins were playing that night. Having grown up in the D.C. area, he understood how important it was to watch the Redskins play. Meeting just once a week, the class usually went from 5:30 to 10 P.M. Around 9 P.M., the professor started wrapping up and told students he was giving them "a Redskins break" that night. The students nearly started a small riot in protest. Silberman thought about what a serious contrast this was with his own college experience and how thrilled he was when a professor let him out early. At Strayer, however, many of these students were paying out of their own pockets for this education. They knew they needed it, and they didn't want to go home and watch football. They wanted to finish the class.

Silberman's research made him excited about the for-profit education industry as a whole, and especially excited about Strayer Education. It was a great platform—it had been around for more than 100 years, and it had achieved regional accreditation. He saw great financial characteristics, too: a motivated customer base and a big market. By the middle of summer 2000, Silberman told his Cal Energy boss that he was leaving to run Strayer.

Fast forward to 2009: Silberman's efforts to intimately understand Strayer Education have paid off. Since Silberman assumed stewardship of Strayer in 2001, revenue, operating income, and earnings per share have grown at compounded rates of 24 percent, 23 percent, and 22 percent, respectively, at the end of 2009. Under Silberman, Strayer Education has been a true compound machine. The stock price increased from $30 per share at the beginning of March 2001 to $215 per share by the end of 2009.[1]

In essence, Silberman went through the process of answering key questions from the checklist. Silberman developed an understanding of how the for-profit education industry developed; the types of customers that typically enroll in for-profit universities and the benefits these customers receive; and he visited campuses to understand firsthand the value of the education to the student. This is the same process that an investor should use in order to analyze a business.

☐ 3. Can you describe how the business operates, in your own words?

To understand how a business operates, read the business description found in the 10-K. Item 1 of the 10-K provides an overview of the business and a detailed description of all of the following:

- Each of the business's segments
- Distribution channels
- Marketing strategies
- Manufacturing activities
- Regulatory requirements
- Extensive management discussions of strategies and risks facing the business
- Industry size and trends
- Insight into the competitive environment

After reading this section carefully, write in your own words how the business operates. How does the business manufacture products or produce its services? How does it distribute these goods and services to the customer? Try to visualize how a product or service is delivered.

Next, visit the website of the business to better understand what the products or services look like. Your goal is to be able to explain how the business operates to a friend who has limited business knowledge. By writing it in your own words, you will gain a deeper understanding of how the business operates than you would by reading the text and taking light notes.

For example, after reading Item 1 of the Form 10-K for company VCA Antech, which is 10 pages long, I summarized the business description as follows:

- VCA Antech operates 471 animal hospitals in 40 states that offer pet physicals, dental care, neutering, spaying, and specialty surgeries. These hospitals represent 75 percent of 2008 revenue. The industry is composed of 22,000 companion animal hospitals operating at the end of 2006.
- Each hospital employs a staff of between 10 and 30 full-time equivalent employees, which typically includes administrative and technical support personnel, three to five veterinarians, and a hospital manager.
- Customers choose an animal hospital based on convenient hours and recommendations from friends.
- In addition, it operates 44 veterinary diagnostic labs, which represented 21 percent of 2008 revenue, where 16,000 customers send blood, tissue, and urine samples for testing.
- In 1999, the company operated 194 animal hospitals and 13 labs and then mainly grew through acquisitions:
  - 2004: 67 animal hospitals;
  - 2005: 46 animal hospitals;
  - 2007: 44 animal hospitals.
- Main industry association survey indicates that 63 percent of U.S. households own at least one pet.
- A source of growth is technology migrating from the human healthcare sector into practice of veterinary medicine so pets have more treatment options.
- 99 percent of customers pay in cash at the time of visit.

- The business markets through targeted demographic mailings regarding specific pet health issues.
- The business employed 9,000 full-time-equivalent employees in 2008.[2]

If you are having a difficult time understanding a business, ask what the customer's world would look like without the product or service. For example, if you were analyzing Internet media delivery company Akamai Technologies and could not find a simple way to summarize how the business operates, ask yourself, "What does the Internet world look like without Akamai Technologies?" In a world without Akamai Technologies, it would take longer to download video to your computer. Content providers such as movie rental company Netflix would be unreliable and would have to charge more to deliver movies.

Another method you can use to simplify a business description is to find an analogy that best explains how the business operates. For example, Akamai Technologies is similar to an air traffic control tower. Akamai Technology's software routes data from its customer, such as online video website YouTube, to the closest server on Akamai's network. The control tower charges a fee to the producer (YouTube), and gets the plane (the video) to its destination faster.

☐ 4. How does the business make money?

At first glance, this sounds like a simple question to ask, but it is critical for you to summarize how a business generates earnings. *If you can't understand how a business makes money, then you should not invest in it.*

Many investors fall into the trap of investing in businesses where they do not understand how the business generates earnings. For example, if you had asked most investors in insurance firm American International Group (AIG) how the firm generated earnings, they would have given you vague answers. Even the top managers of the business had difficulty understanding each of the different pieces of the business and how they contributed to the total earnings of the firm. As AIG moved from its core insurance business into esoteric financial instruments (such as credit default swaps), it became more opaque, offering little visibility into its future earnings. New businesses, such as International Lease Finance and the Financial

Products group were not easy to understand. Most investors bought into the *past reputation* of AIG and *its historical performance*, without understanding how these new business lines contributed to the earnings and risk of the business. Later, AIG entered bankruptcy due to losses sustained by these new business lines.

You want to summarize how a business makes money much like Robert Silberman, CEO of Strayer Education, did in his 2001 shareholder letter:

> Strayer's revenue comes from tuition payments and fees paid by, or on behalf of, Strayer University students. That revenue comes in essentially three forms. Roughly half is paid through federally insured student loans by banks, approximately 20 percent is paid directly to Strayer by corporations or institutions on behalf of their employees who attend Strayer, and the remainder is paid by students through their own sources of credit. Strayer's expenses include salaries paid to the faculty at the university who perform the teaching duties, salaries paid to the administrative and admissions staff who manage the campuses and recruit the students, and salaries paid to the corporate staff who manage the company's affairs. Expenses also include lease payments for the campus buildings we lease and depreciation for the campus buildings we own, as well as advertising and marketing costs which serve to attract prospective students to Strayer. Finally, our expenses include supplies such as books, paper, pencils, desks, chairs, and computers necessary to support the educational process. Some of the furniture and electronic equipment is capitalized on our balance sheet and the expense is recorded as amortization over the period we expect the equipment to last, in accordance with generally accepted accounting principles.

☐ 5. How has the business evolved over time?

A historical perspective on a business provides both a deeper understanding and useful insight into its competitive advantage. You can better understand if the success of the business is due to managerial brilliance or simply being at the right place at the right time. If the business you are researching has a particularly complex story or has made many acquisitions, answering this question is especially useful.

The first place to start is the company's website. Most businesses will include a timeline or history of how their business evolved. Write in your own words a short summary of the history of the business.

Another great source, typically found at a library, is the *International Directory of Company Histories* published by Gale, which profiles more than 8,500 companies. Each entry is usually a few pages long and includes citations of news and magazine stories for follow-up reading. It will give you the complete background and history of a company, including merger and acquisition activity over time and key dates.

If both of these sources yield limited insight, then gathering and reading the business description using at least 10 years of 10-Ks can be useful. Print out the business descriptions and read them, starting with the first year. Summarize in your own words how the business evolved by noting acquisitions made and new product developments from year to year. You can then read articles written for the past 10 years about the business to help you fill in the gaps in your understanding of how the business evolved.

☐ 6. In what foreign markets does the business operate, and what are the risks of operating in these countries?

Over the last few decades, the global economy has become more interconnected. It is difficult to believe that before World War II, the U.S. economy was the largest in the world, and both China and India represented only a small percentage of the world economy. U.S. businesses now sell more of their products and services to other countries, and these sales are becoming a larger percentage of revenues for many of them. As a result, it has become increasingly important to learn more about the foreign markets in which a business derives its earnings.

When a business first enters a foreign market, revenues may grow quickly, which signals to investors that the product or service will be successful. Most management teams will highlight this revenue growth in their annual reports or other financial filings. It is dangerous to project these high initial growth rates into the future, however, because growth in new markets will, of course, stabilize at some point.

To determine whether a business will be successful in a foreign market, you must determine how committed a management team is to growing in a foreign market. Many management teams overestimate the potential of new foreign markets, and after they sustain losses, they reduce their commitment to these markets. As a result, the business does not replicate the success it has in domestic markets. You need to understand if the management team is prepared to commit enough resources to sustain their growth in that particular market. Just as in domestic markets, the more customers are comfortable and familiar with an existing product or service, the more difficult it is to persuade them to change brands. To build brand awareness, a business must commit to a sustained presence and invest for the long term.

For example, Peter Brabeck, CEO of Nestlé, said that to have sustainable profits, he had to be willing to invest for the long-term even if it had a negative impact on the short-term. He noted that "the financial community" often thought in timeframes of between six months and a year, so it was tough explaining to them what it really meant to build a business in Korea, China, or Russia, where it takes five to 10 years to reach profitability. Brabeck recalled his decision to stay in Russia during the Russian crisis, saying that if he had thought only about short-term profits, Nestlé would have withdrawn "...like everybody else." He said, "It very clearly had an impact on my profit margins, but in 18 months, we doubled our market share in confectionary."[3]

To understand how committed the top executives are to growing in foreign markets, you need to answer the questions discussed in the next subsections:

- How long has the business been operating in the foreign market?
- Is the business investing in research and development (R&D) to adapt its products to the specific tastes of the customers in a foreign market?
- Has the management team assigned a specific regional manager to emerging markets?

How Long Has the Business Been Operating in the Foreign Market?

Scan historical press releases and articles found in news archival services to learn when the business expanded into each foreign market and the reasons behind the expansion. For example, if a business states that it operates in Europe, find out which countries it operates in, and determine why the business chose those particular countries. Also, when dealing in Europe, keep in mind that it is not a cohesive market. Each European country can be considered a unique set of customers.

Is the Business Investing in R&D to Adapt Its Products to the Specific Tastes of the Customers in a Foreign Market?

Few products are so globally appealing that a business can market them around the world without adapting them. Exceptions are products like Microsoft's Windows 7: Microsoft made only minor tweaks to its software before selling it to more than 100 countries. Boeing's airplanes also travel well without design change, and nearly 80 percent of Boeing's sales for commercial airplanes in 2010 came from international customers.[4] But these are exceptions. It is difficult for most businesses to sell the same product or service it sells in one market to all markets without adapting in some way.

Urban Outfitters, owner of Anthropologie women's apparel stores, started its European business by first setting up a local design and merchandising unit in London so that it could tailor goods to European tastes. This increased overhead costs and delayed profitability in Europe, but it helped Urban Outfitters successfully expand throughout Europe. These European stores now account for more than 10 percent of revenue and have close to the same operating margins as those based in the U.S.[5]

Similarly, to better familiarize itself with local markets, Nokia established R&D centers in China and India. As a result, Nokia built a phone that was specialized to the needs of customers in India: It had a built-in flashlight, alarm clock, and radio, all of which help customers during blackouts. Nokia also learned that its poorer customers shared phones, so it built handsets with multiple address books.[6]

In contrast, when Wal-Mart expanded into Germany and Korea, it did not adapt its stores to local customs and tastes. It ended up withdrawing from these two countries in 2006 to stem its losses.[7]

Has the Management Team Assigned a Specific Regional Manager to Emerging Markets?

It is a red flag when a regional manager oversees both emerging and developed markets, such as the head of Europe overseeing

Africa. The reason for this is that these are two different markets that need different strategies and oversight.

For example, for most of its history, Nestlé SA has assigned an executive in charge of emerging markets, rather than having an executive oversee both developed and emerging markets. This has contributed to the success that Nestlé had in emerging markets: As of 2010, 32 percent of sales came from these markets.[8]

Is Revenue Growth Translating into Profit Growth?

You need to determine whether revenue growth is translating into profit growth over the long term in a foreign market. The amount of disclosure for revenues and operating profits earned in international markets varies from company to company. Most businesses break down their revenues and assets by geographic region in the footnotes to the 10-K, but few will disclose enough information to allow you to assess whether the business is increasing its profitability in foreign markets. If the company does not provide adequate information, such as the operating profits earned from certain geographic regions, be cautious. This means that management is probably not generating excess profits in these foreign markets.

For example, in its 2009 10-K, Western Union broke down its revenue between the United States, Mexico, and International. The International section is not further broken down into separate countries or regions, so it is difficult to understand how much operating profit Western Union generates in various geographic regions.

In contrast, Coca-Cola breaks out its revenues and operating income by continent: Eurasia & Africa, Europe, Latin America, North America, and the Pacific. It also separates capital expenditures and identifiable assets for each of these regions, which allows you to calculate financial metrics, such as return on invested capital.

If a business does not break out its operating income by region, you can sometimes determine whether international expansion has been profitable by comparing historical financial statements of the business before it expanded into foreign markets to recent financial statements. Review the financial margins before the expansion and then after the expansion. Has the operating margin over this period increased or decreased? You will need to assume that the core domestic business has not deteriorated or improved during this time or if it has changed, you will need to make the proper adjustments. Keep in mind that when a business enters a new market, it typically has a higher cost structure, earning less in new geographic regions than in more mature markets. You can also read press releases and articles and speak with the investor relations department of a business to help you obtain more insights.

What Are the Risks to a Company's Foreign Earnings?

Foreign earnings are impacted by many factors that are often outside of the control of the business. These include country risks (the political and social climate as well as local customs and regulation), and currency fluctuations. In other words, there is a risk that a business will lose money in a foreign market due to external factors. Let's take a closer look at each type of risk.

Country Risks   You need to understand the risks of doing business in each of the countries where a business earns more than 10 percent of its revenue. For example, Brazil has a complicated tax code and archaic employment laws. (The cost of hiring someone is usually about 100 percent of that person's base salary, per month, in addition to the base salary.) Apple does not have any stores in Brazil, even though Brazil is one of the fastest-growing consumer markets in the world: When CEO Steve Jobs was asked why he did not operate in Brazil, he said the "crazy, super-high tax policies" were too much for his company.[9]

Be careful extrapolating the past success of a business in a foreign market into the future. You need to consider that the government policies for foreign investment can easily change. Many foreign businesses operating in China have had high revenue growth in that market. When China first began to open its economy to foreign businesses, it needed foreign capital, so it encouraged multinationals to do business in the country with many incentives and benefits. As China's reliance on foreign capital has decreased, it is imposing tougher rules on multinationals. Some business executives have suggested that the Chinese government is reassessing its long-standing emphasis on opening its economy to foreign business and is instead favoring state-owned enterprises (SOEs). By instituting tougher government policies and regulations for multinationals, the Chinese government is intensifying domestic competition.

For example, state-run media in China reported that the government plans to increase the market share for domestic car manufacturers to more than 50 percent of passenger vehicles by 2015, from 44 percent in 2009. This will hurt non-domestic carmakers, such as Volkswagen AG and General Motors, who have benefited from the growth in demand for cars in China and have reported high revenue growth rates there in the past.[10]

Another example of Chinese protectionism is in the wind-turbine industry. Although foreign technology in wind turbines is superior, foreign market share has dropped from 75 percent in 2004 to 14 percent in 2009, with no foreign turbine maker winning a national bidding project since 2005.[11]

There are many resources you can use to understand the difficulties of doing business in specific foreign markets. You can often learn more about the risks of operating in a particular country through the World Bank, which publishes a *Doing Business Report*, which ranks countries according to the ease of doing business in them. Brazil, for example, ranked 127 out of 183 countries in 2009.

You can also use resources such as Business Monitor International's (BMI) *Country Risk Reports* to get an understanding of the business environment for a particular country. These typically cover political and macroeconomic issues and industry and operational risks in each country.

Currency Risks   One risk to international earnings is changes in the currency rate. For example, if you have a plant in Canada that manufactures a product and sells it to the United States, then the costs for the plant are in Canadian dollars and sales are in U.S. dollars. If the U.S. dollar depreciates against the Canadian dollar, the margins of the business will decrease because each dollar is now worth less when converted to Canadian currency.

Most businesses protect their exposure to changes in currencies by hedging, which allows a business to lock in predetermined foreign-exchange prices for future costs or revenues. The forward contract (where companies can lock in an exchange rate ahead of time) is the most common type of tool used to reduce the impact of currency fluctuations. You need to determine how a business protects itself against currency changes and how it hedges. The notes to the financial filings will often reveal how a business hedges its currencies. You can also read articles about how the business hedges its currency.

For example, by reading an article, my firm learned that Lincoln Electric (a manufacturer and reseller of welding and cutting products worldwide) has a policy in place whereby it hedges at least half of its exposure to another currency once that exposure exceeds a predefined threshold.[12] By learning more about how a business hedges its currencies, you can measure the amount of exposure it has to currency movements.

Many times, a business will disclose the exposure it has to various currencies. For example, Louis Vuitton Moët Hennessy (LVMH, which makes and sells luxury goods and spirits) breaks out its sources of revenue denominated in foreign currency in its 2009 annual report:

- Euro 30 percent
- U.S. dollar 27 percent
- Other currencies 28 percent
- Yen 10 percent
- Hong Kong dollar 5 percent

Even though LVMH hedges most of its currency exposure, this information may give you additional insights.

Most businesses will report the impact of changes in currency in their public filings. Most of the time, the impact is low due to hedging. For example, watchmaker Swatch Group's 2009 annual report shows that foreign currencies negatively impacted sales by Swiss Franc (CHF) 105 million or –1.8 percent, mainly in the second half of 2009.

If a business reinvests the revenue it earns in a foreign country back in the same currency, then it will not need to hedge. This is often referred to as a *natural hedge*. For example, Brookfield Asset Management (a global asset manager focused on property, renewable power, and infrastructure assets) does not hedge its exposure to currencies because it often reinvests the money it earns from foreign countries back into the same country. This reduces its exposure to currency movements.

Key Points to Keep in Mind

Understand How the Business Makes Money

- If you can't understand how a business makes money, then you should not invest in it.
- You will gain a deeper understanding of a business if you learn how the business has evolved over time.
- If you are having a difficult time understanding a business, ask what the customer's world would look like without its products or services.
- To simplify a business description, find an analogy that best explains how the business operates.

Evaluate Current and Potential Foreign Markets

- When a business first enters a foreign market, it often experiences high initial revenue growth rates. Projecting such growth into the future is usually a mistake because new markets will, of course, stabilize at some point.
- A management team that is committed to a foreign market invests for the long term, adapts its products to the specific tastes of that market by investing in R&D, and assigns a specific regional manager to emerging markets.
- A management team needs to be prepared to commit enough resources in order to sustain growth in a foreign market.

Understanding the Business—from the Customer Perspective

Customers are the lifeblood of a business. In fact, the quality of a business is determined by the quality of its customers. At the end of the day, they are the stakeholders who determine the fate of a business. If customers are not satisfied with a business, they will eventually find alternatives, or an entrepreneur will create an alternative if one does not exist. The more you can understand a business from the customer's perspective, the better position you will be in to value that business, because satisfied customers are the best predictor of future earnings for a business. As Dave and Sherry Gold, co-founders of dollar store retailer 99 Cent Only Stores, often say, "The customer is CEO."

One of the main pitfalls in researching a business is viewing the business from your *own* perspective, instead of viewing the business from the customer's perspective. This is one of the areas where investors make the most mistakes. Most investors allow their personal likes and dislikes to influence their analysis of a business. If you really like Nike tennis shoes, for example, then you will look at Nike's business in a more favorable light. Try to disregard how you feel about a business: What you personally like is irrelevant to investing.

To begin thinking like the customers and to understand how they interact with the product or service on a day-to-day basis, you need to interview real customers. You need to determine why they shop at a business or use its services and, most important, if they will continue to buy products and services from the business.

For example, when I first researched 99 Cent Only Stores, I paid for the items of more than 50 customers in order to solicit their feedback on why they shopped at the store. 99 Cent Only Stores carries a variety of items, but it's really more of a grocery store. It often sells brand-name products that it can obtain at discount prices because manufacturers discontinue certain products, change labels, or make other changes that make an older version of the product obsolete. For example, they might sell candy bars that have movie advertising or tie-ins: The candy bar is still good, but the movie is no longer playing in theaters. My goal was to understand how customers made the decision to shop at 99 Cent Only Stores, rather than trying to guess why they shopped at the store.

As part of my research, I visited 120 out of the 150 total stores. It took about four months, as I ended up visiting about 10 stores each day in California, Nevada, Texas, and Arizona. Because the stores tend to be fairly close together, it was reasonably easy to visit so many locations. Although I didn't interview customers at every store I visited, I did take the time to speak with as many as five or 10 each day.

First, I picked store locations that represented different ethnicities and economic groups, to make sure I was interviewing a diverse and complete customer base. Once in the stores, I looked for people purchasing more than 20 items, which indicated to me that they shopped at the store frequently. Then I approached them and told them that I was researching how customers shopped at 99 Cent Only Stores and that if they agreed to a short interview about their purchases, then I would buy 10 items for them. I was looking for any patterns in their responses about why and how often they shopped at the store. I also asked them what would change their opinion about shopping there.

I learned that most customers shopped at the store because they could buy smaller package sizes and thus increase the variety of their grocery purchases. These customers were on a tight budget, so if they shopped regularly in grocery stores or other retailers, they would be forced to buy fewer items to meet their budget. By shopping at 99 Cent Only Stores, they were able to stretch their budgets. This information helped me understand the true competitive advantage of 99 Cent Only Stores. Once I understood the competitive advantage, I could then carefully monitor any threats to that advantage, such as competitors offering smaller packaging sizes or the company offering less variety.

Interestingly, Wall Street analysts spend very little time viewing the business from the customer's perspective. More time is spent constructing detailed financial models and talking to the management team than trying to understand the business from the customer's viewpoint. The main reason for this is that it takes a lot of time to locate and interview customers, whereas most management teams are readily accessible to Wall Street analysts.

☐ 7. Who is the core customer of the business?

You need to determine who the core customer of the business is. Many times, a small percentage of customers will represent a large percentage of revenues for a business. For example, the management team at Whole Foods Market used to disclose that it believed 75 percent of purchases were made by 25 percent of the customers who shopped exclusively at the store. My firm conducted its own due diligence by speaking with customers, suppliers, customer demographic information services, and competitors, and we learned that this was generally true. This information helped us continue to buy more stock in Whole Foods Market when the economy entered into a recession in 2007 and the stock price dropped from $37 per share at the beginning of 2008 to as low as $8 per share in November 2008.

At the time, many other investors believed that Whole Foods Market was a high-priced grocer and that its customers would abandon the store in search of lower prices. However, because my firm had taken the time to understand the core customer of the business, we believed these loyal customers who shopped exclusively at Whole Foods Market would not move to competitors, but instead they might simply decrease the number of items they purchased. Within a year, we got confirmation of this, as Whole Foods Market disclosed that sales had not dropped as much as investors had anticipated, and the stock price recovered to more than $30 per share. By identifying the core customer of a business, you will be able to gain an in-depth understanding of a business, and you will be in a position to carefully monitor customer trends.

As you begin to learn more about the business's core customers, you want to understand how the business caters to them or whether it attempts to cater to too many types of customers. For example, electronics retailer Best Buy attempts to figure out which customers make them the most money and then segments them. It has names for each type of customer, such as "Barry," an affluent tech enthusiast, and "Buzz," a young gadget fiend. By segmenting its customers into different categories, Best Buy is able to tailor its inventory to a particular location based on the composition of customer types in that area. For example, to attract Barry, Best Buy has created a separate department for home-theater systems that has specialists who can answer most questions on the products. Best Buy also trains its employees to recognize these customers so that the employees can encourage them to spend more at the store or come back more often.[1]

Paccar is a manufacturer of heavy trucks that is a great example of a company that has built its product around its core customer, the owner operator. Owner operators buy the truck they drive and spend most of their time in it. They work for themselves, either contracting directly with shippers or subcontracting with big truck companies. Owner operators care about quality first, and want amenities, such as noise-proofed sleeper cabins with luxury-grade bedding and interiors. They also want the truck to look sharp, and Paccar makes its Peterbilt and Kenworth brand trucks with exterior features to please this customer. Paccar also backs up the driver with service features, such as roadside assistance and a quick spare parts network. Because owner operators want this level of quality and service, they are less price sensitive, and they will pay 10 percent more for these brands.

In comparison, Paccar's competitors sell to large truck-leasing businesses or customers that operate large fleets. Because these customers buy in bulk, they can negotiate lower prices. By choosing a customer base that is more fragmented and discerning, Paccar avoids selling its trucks at a lower price, which allows it to earn higher profits compared to its competitors.[2]

□   8. Is the customer base concentrated or diversified?

A business that earns its revenues from a diversified customer base has less risk than one with a concentrated customer base. If a business is dependent on few customers, then these customers can influence the price a business charges for its goods or services, and the loss of one customer can have severe financial consequences.

For example, there are thousands of auto suppliers, yet only a couple dozen giant automakers. Therefore, if even the most diversified auto supplier lost a couple of automaker clients, it would be difficult to make up this business elsewhere, as there are only so many giant automakers. The auto supplier might either go bankrupt or lose a significant amount of its revenues.

If a business has revenues from one customer that exceed 10 percent of total revenues, then the amount of revenues from each of these customers must be disclosed in the 10-K as well as the name of the customer. For example, the June 30, 2010 10-K for American Woodmark, a cabinet manufacturer states:

> During the last fiscal year, American Woodmark had two primary customers, The Home Depot and Lowe's Companies, Inc., which together accounted for approximately 71 percent of the Company's sales in its fiscal year ended April 30, 2010. The loss of either customer would have a material adverse effect on the Company.

If a business has a more diversified customer base, the business probably won't even mention this as a risk. Instead, it may state that it is *not* dependent on a small number of customers.

Also, you need to watch for trends in customer concentration. For example, clothing maker Liz Claiborne became more exposed to specific retailers as many department stores went out of business. This has increased Liz Claiborne's dependence on a few customers, such as Macy's, which now represents a large percentage of Liz Claiborne's sales.[3]

☐ 9. Is it easy or difficult to convince customers to buy the products or services?

Think about businesses that use aggressive sales tactics, such as time pressure, to sell their products or services. You will often see these businesses advertise, "Sign up now or lose the opportunity of a lifetime." If a business needs to rely on these aggressive sales tactics, then the product or service is not being sold based on its merits but instead on the ingenuity of the salespeople. Businesses that rely on high-pressure sales tactics to sell their products or services typically do not have sustainable business models and are typically not good for the customer.

☐ 10. What is the customer retention rate for the business?

Determine whether a business is retaining its customers or if it is constantly turning them over (churning them). The longer a customer is retained by a business, the more profitable that business becomes. Most of us acknowledge that it is more expensive to gain a new customer than to retain a valued one. Another reason: A loyal customer base generates more predictable sales, which can improve profits. Customers also often serve as advocates for the business, which brings in new customers and more sales. In the long run, the businesses that spend time cultivating long-term relationships with their customers are more likely to succeed.

The customer retention rate is the most common metric for tracking customer longevity. It is usually offered as a percentage, which tells you from period to period how many customers are sticking around. Unfortunately, you will only be able to calculate or track customer retention rates for certain types of businesses, such as those that earn recurring revenues from subscriptions or franchise fees. For example, FactSet Research Systems, a financial research solutions provider, disclosed (in its 10-K from August 31, 2010) that its customer retention rate was 90 percent, compared to 87 percent the year before.

Also, if businesses that earn their revenues through subscription models do not disclose their customer retention rates, this should serve as a red flag. This may indicate they have low retention rates, making it a poor-quality investment.

One method you can use to estimate customer retention rates is to monitor the number of customers who are enrolled in loyalty programs. If a business has a loyalty program, it will often disclose the number of members that are enrolled in the program in the 10-K. Customers who enroll in loyalty programs are typically repeat customers.

For example, in its December 31, 2009, 10-K, Western Union said it had more than 13 million active cardholders in its Gold Card loyalty program, a 10-fold increase since the program was launched in 2003. Watch for declining loyalty program numbers as well, as this can serve as an indicator that customer retention is declining.

You should also find out if the business is making investments to retain customers. You can often ask the investor relations department of a business this question, or you can gain insights by reading historical articles written about the business. For example, when I researched Tesco, a leading U.K.-based grocer, I read many articles about Tesco's commitment to retaining customers. In order to learn more about its customers, Tesco began issuing a loyalty card. Tesco's card, like most, is used to track customer behavior, including stores visited, products purchased, and even method of payment. Tesco uses the results of its analysis to inform its product development and selection, which helps it satisfy local tastes when it moves into new areas.[4]

It is also helpful to interview the sales staff of a business to understand if there is an incentive to retain existing customers. You do not need to talk to many salespeople, as your goal is simply to understand how their incentive structure relates to customer retention. It is easy to locate most salespeople because their contact information is typically found on a website. Call or e-mail them and tell them you would like a few minutes of their time and that you would be happy to share your research with them. You can also call or e-mail investor relations and ask them this question.

You want to learn if the salespeople are rewarded for retaining customers. Do they receive a commission both at the time they make a sale and when the customer renews? Or do they receive a commission only when they make a sale? For example, insurance agents typically are given a commission each time a customer *renews* an insurance policy with the existing insurance underwriter. Therefore, insurance agents have an incentive to retain customers. What do you think would happen if an insurance agent were given a commission only at the time they sold an insurance policy to a customer? They would need to go out and constantly find new customers, and all of their time and effort would be devoted to that goal. This is why insurance businesses pay commissions both when customers purchase policies and when they renew policies, providing incentives to agents to retain customers.

One final factor to consider as you evaluate the customer retention rate is whether a business is selective about the types of customers it will do business with. If they are selective, consider it a good sign. If certain customers are more profitable because they are easier to attract or easier to retain, look for the high-quality businesses that focus on these more profitable customers.

For example financial research provider FactSet prefers selling its services to multi-manager asset-management firms rather than single-manager asset-management firms. FactSet believes that sales to related customers under the same roof are naturally much easier to make than sales to entirely new prospects, who are less familiar with the quality of the company's products and the level of support it offers its users. By selling to multi-manager firms, FactSet can sell more products to related customers, instead of having to make single-user sales, which are more difficult to make.

☐ 11. What are the signs a business is customer oriented?

The more frequently a business interacts with customers, the more critical it is to keep those customers happy. If a business interacts less frequently with customers, customer satisfaction is less important. For example, how often do you replace your dishwasher? Probably not often, so a bad customer experience may be less important than the performance of the dishwasher over a long period.

Ask yourself if the business is easy to do business with. Think about your experience with different businesses: Don't you prefer to frequent those businesses that are easy to do business with? Of course! For example, if you buy a television at Costco and it doesn't work, you can easily return it without many questions being asked. You do not have to go through a process of locating a supervisor to explain why you are returning the item or spend a lot of time with lengthy paperwork.

In contrast, think about a time when a company offered you a rebate when you purchased a product or service. Completing the many steps required to receive the rebate probably reduced the pleasure or satisfaction of saving that amount of money. Or remember the last time you spent five minutes in an automated telephone system trying to figure out how to get connected to a human customer-service agent.

You need to determine if a business has a customer-service-oriented culture. It is important because customers are not loyal to those businesses with poor customer service. One study recently found that 40 percent of customers who have bad experiences stop doing business with the company.[5]

Find out if the business solves customer problems quickly and easily. You can do this by learning whether a business gives its customer service agents enough authority to solve customer issues or whether customers have to go through a bureaucracy to get their problems solved. Does the business hire knowledgeable employees or does it outsource its customer service centers to other countries?

You are looking for examples either in articles written about a business or customer interviews that demonstrate the business is customer oriented. For example:

- Costco Wholesale has a practice of refusing to mark up its prices on any products by more than 15 percent.[6] In fact, when commodity prices began to fall on many products, Costco quickly cut its prices, whereas other retailers took advantage of the situation, keeping their prices high. CEO Jim Sinegal said, "It is easy to raise prices. It benefits you today, but will hurt you tomorrow. The practice of taking advantage of customers will eventually alienate them."[7]
- Southwest Airlines doesn't charge customers to check two bags, whereas other airlines have resorted to charging for bags to offset reductions in revenue. This policy has helped Southwest Airlines increase its customer loads and revenues per seat as customers have moved to Southwest from other airlines.[8]

Two other great resources are the J.D. Power & Associates customer satisfaction rankings and the American Customer Satisfaction Index (ACSI), developed by the University of Michigan National Quality Research Center. The ACSI measures the customer satisfaction with goods and services purchased from about 200 companies in more than 40 industries, along with some public sector organizations as well. It is based on interviews with more than 65,000 U.S. consumers each year, and it covers a big chunk of the total goods and services produced and imported. In fact, the University of Michigan National Quality Research Center estimates that the organizations it studies produce 43 percent of U.S. gross domestic product (GDP).

Some of the findings from their analysis of more than 16 years of data are that customer satisfaction is a leading indicator of company financial performance, and many of the companies with high customer-satisfaction scores produce higher stock returns than the S&P 500 index. Furthermore, they've found that the cash flows of businesses that rate high on customer service are less volatile than other businesses.[9]

How Does Management Stay Close to Customers?

You can evaluate how customer oriented a business is by observing how management maintains its connection to customers. The further management gets from understanding their customers' needs at a business, the higher the probability the business will fail.

Read the biographies from the proxy statements to determine how long the CEO or top executive officers have served a particular customer base. For example, Cisco's CEO John Chambers rose through the company ranks in customer-facing functions; as a result, he understands the importance of the customer experience. If he had instead risen through the finance, engineering, or manufacturing departments, then it is likely he would not place as much weight on the customer experience.

John Mackey, founder and co-CEO of Whole Foods Market, and Dave and Sherry Gold, co-founders of 99 Cent Only Stores, are both natural customers of their respective businesses. Mackey founded an organic grocery store because he liked to eat organic food, and Dave and Sherry Gold co-founded a discount retailer because they always liked to find bargains.

Here are a few examples of how CEOs stay close to their customers. Look for similar examples at the business you are analyzing:

Jim Cabela, co-founder of hunting and outdoor retail chain Cabelas, stays close to customers by personally reading all of the customer comment cards sent to headquarters from each of the stores. He then follows up on the customer comments with the appropriate manager or employee of the store.[10]

Howard Lester, who bought Williams-Sonoma (an upscale housewares and furniture retailer) in 1978, is another CEO who reads every customer letter and comment card. Lester did not measure the success of the business solely on metrics such as inventory turns, but instead on customer metrics, such as "How many customers did we fail to satisfy yesterday?"[11]

Finally, here are a few examples of how a business remains close to customers and attempts to view the products from the customer perspective. You will often see articles written about how businesses stay close to customers. Here are a couple of examples of the kind of detail you will find in case studies or other articles:

At Procter & Gamble, the managers who were responsible for the Max Factor and Cover Girl brands spent a week living on the budget of a low-income consumer. This gave the managers insight into the lives of these customers, especially how they budget to purchase personal items.[12]

Intuit, the tax-preparation-software company, often studies customers actually using their products at home or work to learn more about how they really use it.[13]

☐ 12. What pain does the business alleviate for the customer?

One of the most common questions venture capitalists ask a prospective start-up is, "What pain does your business alleviate?" The venture capitalists want to understand what problems the entrepreneurs are solving and what customer needs the business is filling. If a business does not fill a need or solve a customer's problems, then it will fail. Here are two examples of companies that solve a particular customer problem:

- Stericycle, a medical waste disposal company, helps physicians and other medical providers avoid potential liabilities that come from the disposal of medical syringes and other medical waste.
- ADP, a payroll and human resource management provider, eliminates the needs to hire in-house employees to handle payroll administration.

Just as these businesses are solving customer problems, you need to identify the problems that are being solved by the businesses you are analyzing.

☐ 13. To what degree is the customer dependent on the products or services from the business?

To answer this question, you need to determine if the product or service is "need to have" or "nice to have" for the customer. The more a customer *needs* to have a product or service, the less the earnings of a business will fluctuate. The more discretionary a product or service is, the more earnings will fluctuate.

A business whose customers *depend* on the product or service has a significant advantage. Think of this as a continuum:

- **Need to have.** On one extreme are products manufactured by Medtronic, which builds medical devices that people literally can't live without, such as implantable pacemakers.
- **Need to have, but not immediately.** In the middle are products or services that can be deferred but at some point need to be purchased, such as car maintenance. After all, if you don't change the oil in your car, the motor will eventually fail.
- **Nice to have, but not critical.** At the other extreme are discretionary products and services, on which customers are less dependent. These items are products or services that a consumer can defer purchasing for a long time (and may not even purchase at all), such as jewelry, a new car, a new house, or travel.

Do not make the assumption that a discretionary business or industry will always lose sales in tough times, however. For example, many luxury retailers—such as Louis Vuitton Moët Hennessy or Compagnie Financière Richemont SA, which owns Cartier, Montblanc, Alfred Dunhill, and Van Cleef & Arpels—were thought to be sensitive to business cycles, and their stock prices fell when the recession began in 2007. However, the stock prices of these two companies quickly rebounded as their core customers, who are ultra-wealthy, continued their spending habits, and sales did not drop as much as was anticipated.

☐ **14. If the business disappeared tomorrow, what impact would this have on the customer base?**

To understand how much customers depend on a business, ask what the customer would do if the business disappeared tomorrow. Think about what you would do if your favorite retailer disappeared. Where else could you go and why? Is it easy to find alternatives?

For example, when I interviewed customers of ratings firms Moody's and Standard & Poor's, I spoke with customers ranging from insurance bond departments to hedge funds, and I asked them what they would do if the ratings agencies disappeared tomorrow. Most answered that they would have an extremely difficult time buying new bonds and that it would severely disrupt their daily life. In other words, most of the customers were dependent on the service these ratings firms provide.

Key Points to Keep in Mind

- The quality of a business is determined by the quality of its customers.
- One of the main pitfalls in researching a business lies in viewing the business from your *own* perspective, instead of viewing the business from the customer perspective.
- A business that earns its revenues from a diversified customer base has less risk than one with a concentrated customer base.
- The more frequently a business interacts with customers, the more critical it is for it to have high customer satisfaction. You can learn if a business has a customer-oriented culture through research studies produced by J.D. Power & Associates or the American Customer Satisfaction Index (ACSI).
- If a business is out of touch with customers, or is failing to meet their needs or solve their problems, it will eventually fail.
- The more a customer *needs* to have a product or service, the less the earnings of a business will fluctuate. To understand how much customers depend on a business, ask what customers would do if the business disappeared tomorrow.

4

Evaluating the Strengths and Weaknesses of a Business and Industry

In addition to understanding a business from the perspective of its customers, it's also extremely important for you to analyze the strengths and weaknesses of a business in the context of its competitive environment. The stronger the business's competitive position, the higher the probability that it will be able to sustain its current earnings as well as grow them in the future. After all, a competitive advantage represents long-term protection from a company's competitors. Think of it as being in a wrestling match when you're 50 pounds heavier than your opponent.

Once you have established whether the company has a competitive advantage, you want to know if the industry is a good one. In some industries, it's relatively easy for a business to get a good return on its investment, but in other industries, the historical returns are negative. If the industry is difficult or unprofitable, you'll find it harder to make money on your investment, even if you manage to pick the best company out of tens or hundreds of others in that industry.

Finally, you want to understand how industry supply chains work. Good supplier relations can improve efficiency and reliability of source goods, so I'll walk you through how to evaluate supplier relationships, supply chain efficiency, and sources of supply chain risk.

Let's begin by evaluating whether a business has a sustainable competitive advantage.

☐ 15. Does the business have a *sustainable* competitive advantage and what is its source?

It is critical to determine whether a business has long-term protection from competitors, also called a sustainable competitive advantage. What's critical to long-term success and the ability of a business to grow and remain profitable is if that advantage is *sustainable*, such as when a business is protected by government regulation. If you are unable to determine whether a business has a sustainable competitive advantage, then it is difficult for you to commit to a long-term investment in a business.

When you do find an advantaged business, it is critical for you to determine the strength and staying power of its competitive advantage. Therefore, when you're analyzing a business, you should always ask these two questions:

- How easily can someone else copy or replace this advantage?
- How quickly might they do it?

The more sustainable the advantage, the more a company is worth because the company can protect its profitability over a longer period of time. Pat Dorsey, former director of research at Morningstar and author of *The Little Book that Builds Wealth* states:

> The way I think about the linkage between moats (competitive advantages) and intrinsic value is that moats add the most value to businesses that have lots of reinvestment opportunities within their moats. A business that has a large set of investment opportunities "inside the moat" has a much higher intrinsic value than a business without competitively advantaged reinvestment opportunities because the former compounds cash flow at a very high rate, whereas the latter is forced to use cash for sub-optimal opportunities.
>
> Microsoft's moat, for example, may give an investor a reasonable degree of confidence that the return on capital of the core business will persist, but it adds very little value due to the maturity of the company's core business—cash that is generated just sits on the balance sheet, or is invested "outside the moat" in areas like search (i.e. Bing). By contrast, the moats around businesses like Fastenal or C.H. Robinson—both

of which operate in fragmented industries—add tremendous intrinsic value because cash can be reinvested in the core business at a very high incremental rate of return. This relationship between growth, moats, and intrinsic value is central to understanding when it's truly worth paying up for a business.[1]

This section helps you identify the sources of competitive advantage and gives you real-world examples of competitive advantages that are either expanding or deteriorating. Let's start by identifying common sources of competitive advantages.

Common Sources of Competitive Advantages

To help you identify the sources of competitive advantage, I've borrowed several concepts from financial-services company Morningstar, which uses these concepts as the foundation of its stock analysis. Dorsey distills the sources of competitive advantage into four categories (Dorsey combines brand loyalty, patents, and regulatory licenses into one category titled *intangible assets*) which I have broken down into six categories:

1. Network economics
2. Brand loyalty
3. Patents
4. Regulatory licenses
5. Switching costs
6. Cost advantages stemming from scale, location, or access to a unique asset

Let's take a closer look at each source.

Source #1: Network Economics   One of the strongest sources of competitive advantage is network economics. If a product or service becomes more valuable if more customers use it, then the business benefits from network economics. When telephones first came out, not everyone had one, but as more people acquired telephones, the network became more valuable. The customer was part of the service itself (another node on the network), which meant an increased ability to connect to more people.

The same has been true for Facebook: When it was just for college students, it had less value to non-students. As it has grown to include non-students, it has become more valuable to older adults. More customers (of the right type) again resulted in more connection and access, and more value.

Timeshare exchange company Interval Leisure is another example of a company that benefits from network economics. When someone buys a timeshare, that person usually wants to be able to trade his or her specific week of vacation for other times and locations. Interval provides a network to timeshare owners for these trades. Owners pay an upfront fee to join Interval, and then they have access to all other timeshare traders in the network. More customers means more places and times to choose from. Interval's network benefit is also important to another of its customers, the timeshare developer, who knows that it is much easier to sell a timeshare (and retain its own customers) if it is part of such a network.

To monitor network advantages, you need to closely track the number and quality of users. If you see the number of users increasing but more valuable users moving to another network, this might indicate a deteriorating advantage.

Example of an Expanding Advantage   Money-transfer business Western Union has been increasing the number of locations in its network. In 2002, Western Union had 151,000 locations, but by the end of 2009, it had grown to 410,000 locations. More important, it is not so much the quantity of locations but the *quality* of those locations. Western Union has been able to sign exclusive five-year agreements with some of the world's most desirable agents—(i.e., supermarkets, convenience store chains, postal systems, or banks). The most desirable agents are, of course, those that generate the most traffic. This makes Western Union's network more valuable to customers who want to send or receive money, because there are more locations where they can do this. The more customers Western Union has, the more valuable Western Union is to its agents, because Western Union is able to deliver more customers to agents, compared to its competitors.

In contrast, Western Union's closest competitor is MoneyGram International, which has 200,000 locations (less than half of Western Union's 410,000 locations), and it processes only one-fourth of the total customer dollars that Western Union does. Its network is weaker because it offers its agents fewer customer dollars, and it offers its customers fewer quality locations.[2]

Example of a Deteriorating Advantage   A network effect is not always sustainable. Can you guess which was the first third-party charge card developed in the United States? Most of you will answer American Express, Discover, Visa, or MasterCard, which together represent the majority of current spending on credit cards. However, the correct answer is Diners Club, which spawned a new industry when it launched the third-party charge-card business in the 1950s. It possessed the highest number of both merchants and users; in fact, it was so successful that at one time, American Express even considered selling its charge-card business to Diners Club![3]

However, an influx of competitors in the following decades relegated Diners Club to only a small corner of the market. Diners Club rivals focused successfully on building their networks by signing up new merchants and customers. Diners Club stuck to its traditional roots as a charge card, whereas bankcards that extended credit offered more appeal and utility to the masses. Competitors seized this opportunity by increasing the number of customers (offering them free cards), which then allowed them to attract the best merchants. If you had closely monitored the numbers of cardholders, merchants, and transaction volume as competitors battled Diners Club, you would have been able to see the deterioration in Diners Club's network, beginning as early as a couple of years after its first major competitor jumped in.

Other examples of deteriorating networks might include social-networking website MySpace. Although it was the most popular social networking site in the United States, it was quickly surpassed by late-entrant Facebook. In December 2008, Facebook had fewer than 60 million users, whereas MySpace had close to 80 million users. Yet only a year later, in December 2009, Facebook had more than 100 million users (a gain of 40 million), whereas MySpace had close to 60 million users (a loss of 20 million).[4]

Source #2: Brand Loyalty   A brand can give a business tremendous advantage over competitors when customers remain loyal to the brand and when a business can charge a premium price for the brand. This often results in pricing power for the business. The degree to which brand strength will lead to a competitive advantage varies by the type of product or service. For example, bath and shower accessories have less brand loyalty than beverages.

Start by asking what the brand stands for with customers. Certain brand names are synonymous with user experience—for example:

- Four Seasons Hotels' brand means that the customer will receive unrivaled service. As a result, it can charge a higher rate for its hotels.
- Nordstrom is also well known for its unparalleled customer service such as its return policy, which lets customers return any item at any store.
- Starbucks is best known for supplying premium coffees in an inviting atmosphere.

To build a brand, businesses must continually strengthen the brand in the minds of consumers. Once a business stops investing in its brand, it is likely the value of the brand will decline. You can start to see this when management begins to cut development, marketing, and promotion to save expenses. This causes the brand's long-term identity to suffer at the expense of these short-term savings.

In other situations, management will discount the price of its products in order to sell its excess inventory, which can cause the value of a brand to deteriorate in the minds of customers. For example, luxury handbag maker Louis Vuitton is able to consistently charge a higher price for its handbags compared to its competitor Gucci because Louis Vuitton will destroy overruns rather than sell them through discount channels.[5] In contrast, Gucci discounts its inventory more frequently. Yves Carcelle, chief executive officer (CEO) of Louis Vuitton, says, "We're never on sale. All the rest discount. Us, never. When a customer invests in one of our products, they don't expect to see it discounted three weeks later, so we don't do it."[6]

Tommy Hilfiger is another company that suffered when it diluted its brand. For many years, Tommy Hilfiger had crafted an upscale image in its red, white, and blue flag and crest logo. But the brand became diluted when the company made it widely accessible to middle-class consumers (whereas before it had been accessible to that market only on an occasional basis). This caused it to lose its status as an aspirational brand. It also began to move from its traditional preppy style to a hip-hop image, which helped increase sales from $847 million in fiscal year 1998 to $1.9 billion in fiscal 2000 but eventually alienated many of its customers. The stock price peaked on July 1999 at $40 per share but dropped to $16.60 per share by the time the company was taken private on May 10, 2006.[7]

Recently, private-label products (PLs) have proven to be an enormous threat to previously strong national brands in groceries, household goods, and over-the-counter drug segments. According to the Private Label Manufacturers Association, "store brands now account for nearly one of every four items sold in U.S. supermarkets, drug chains, and mass merchandisers." In the United States and many other countries, labeling requirements allow for easy comparison of certain items, such as food and drugs. The cost of production, marketing, and promotion is often less for these private-label items, and retailers benefit because they get higher margins from selling them. In some cases, national brands have had to lower prices to stay competitive.

Many PLs are not just cheaper, lower-quality versions. With the introduction of PLs at several price points and quality levels (especially premium levels), these multiple-tiered products have gained substantial market share: In fact, a 2010 Nielsen study showed private label store brands had captured 17 percent of the market share in the United States.[8] Private labels now sell more mouthwash and dishwasher soap than Colgate and more food wrap and trash bags than Clorox (which makes Glad).[9] However, some products are less affected than others. The same 2010 Nielsen study also found that private-label market share ranged from a high of 40 percent in dairy to less than 1 percent for alcoholic beverages.

Source #3: Patents Patents can be a source of protection because they legally protect the products or services of a business from competitors over a 17- to 20-year period. The best way to determine whether a patent is valuable is to understand if it has any commercial value, as evidenced by any product or licensing revenues. Not surprisingly, drug companies have extremely valuable patents: For example, Pfizer's set of patents for Lipitor is the basis for a quarter of its sales, about $11 billion. Almost all of chipset designer Qualcomm's $10.9 billion in 2009 revenues are related to its patents on code-division multiple access (CDMA) and 3G cell phone network technology.[10]

The easier patents to research and understand are those in the pharmaceutical industry, because there is a lot of information as to the potential market size of a drug. The more difficult patents to evaluate are those based on technology. For example, Tessera Technologies has patented a technology that enables devices such as laptops and mobile phones to pack more silicon inside their products. It is difficult to analyze how many of these devices will be manufactured in the future and which ones will employ Tessera's technology.

Although they provide protection, patents have a finite life, and you need to be cautious not to assign too much value to them. Paul Bobrowski, dean at the College of Business at Auburn University, once joked that a patent was as valuable as his patent leather shoes. David Freedman, a reporter for *Inc.* magazine, explains, "The problem is that a long period of patent protection is not useful because a newer technology will displace it. Therefore, the more innovation there is or more technological changes there are in an industry, the less value a patent will have as a source of protection [of a sustainable competitive advantage]."[11]

Source #4: Regulatory Licenses   Regulatory licenses and approvals can also create sustainable competitive advantages by limiting competition. For example, Western Union benefits from laws and restrictions designed to inhibit money laundering.

If the source of advantage is regulatory, spend your time closely monitoring legislative threats from the entity that regulates it, whether it is in Washington or in state or local government offices. Closely monitor lobbyists who influence legislation by visiting the websites of groups that either generally support or oppose the industry or by reading articles written about what impact new laws or legislative changes have on an industry.

First, determine whether the license or approval is regulated by the state, local, or federal government or a combination. Next, determine what types of power each regulatory entity exerts on the business, such as the ability to regulate the price charged for goods or services or the number of units a business can sell. The competitive advantage's strength depends on how much power the regulatory entity has over pricing. If the regulatory entity controls the prices a business can charge customers, then the competitive advantage is weaker. Dorsey uses the example of a utility, which is regulated in the price it can charge customers. He then contrasts this to a pharmaceutical company where the Food and

Drug Administration (FDA) concerns itself with the safety of drugs it regulates, but it does not control the prices that a business can charge for them.

Regional casino Penn National Gaming is regulated by each state in which it operates. To evaluate the competitive threats to Penn National Gaming, you would need to watch legislative trends by state. The state legislature typically approves gaming for each state, then the licensing of casinos is monitored by each state through gaming boards (such as the Ohio State Racing Commission, Pennsylvania Gaming Control Board, or Maine Gaming Control Board). These boards approve the total number of slots or table games that are allowed within a certain geographical region of the state. The board also sets the amount of the *slot-win percentage* (which is the amount it is allowed to win from customers): For example, 6 percent to 10 percent of slot handle. The state also sets the tax rate on gaming revenue that casinos collect. For example, Maryland levies a 67 percent tax on gaming revenue, whereas Nevada levies a 6.5 percent tax. If the state decides to either reduce the amount of slot-win percentage or raise the tax rate, this would decrease the profitability of Penn National Gaming.

On the other hand, profitability can increase if a state approves new slots or table games for existing casinos, as West Virginia did when it allowed Penn National Gaming to add table games to its casino there. If a state is considering increasing the tax rate or allowing more gambling units, this information is found with the regulatory board. You need to closely monitor the licensing entities in these states for any proposed changes to understand what impact, either positive or negative, the changes will have on profitability.

Businesses regulated at the federal level have more risk in one respect, which is that a single rule change can affect the entire business. Most locally or state-regulated businesses would only have a percentage of business affected by each change.

For example, the for-profit education industry is regulated by the federal government through the U.S. Department of Education (ED). The ED sets the standards that need to be followed by this industry. A single rule change could have disastrous effects on the future profitability of the industry. For example, the ED is setting standards that must be met for the students of a for-profit institution to qualify to receive federal student loans, which represents more than 70 percent of the revenues of each institution. In 2009, the ED considered not extending loans to for-profit colleges if they failed to meet these standards. These changes could have disastrous effects for some for-profit colleges.

Source #5: Switching Costs   Why would you not buy a cheaper product of the same quality or a better product for the same price? The answer is that there may be an additional cost associated with changing products, or a reduction in the benefit you stand to receive. These are often called *switching costs*, like those you incur if you change cell phone providers.

The strength level of switching costs is determined by how embedded the product or service is with the customer or the amount of training needed to use it. Think about how much training you face when learning new software: If you have to retrain yourself or your employees when changing products, you've encountered a switching cost.

For example, Bloomberg, a high-end provider of financial and trading information, has embedded its services with customers through a lot of training, so it does not make sense for those customers to switch and invest the time to learn another product. The savings of switching to a lower-priced competitor would be outweighed by the additional training time. Also, because many of its customers are traders, the benefit of switching to a less costly service to save maybe a few thousand dollars a year is small in comparison to the size of the transactions they are making. Finally, there is also some chance of making an error as customers learn any new system.

In order to learn if the protection provided by switching costs is deteriorating or improving, you need to closely monitor a company's customer-retention rates. For example, Blackboard is a leading provider of software applications and services to educational institutions. Its software enhances the learning experience by allowing students to interact with teachers, classmates, and course materials outside of the traditional classroom environment. Blackboard's products are used daily by students, parents, and administrators, and the software is deeply embedded within a school's other information systems. For example, a professor may assign digital material on a class website. This embeddedness, or *stickiness*, is reflected in Blackboard's high customer retention rates. At greater than 90 percent for most of its products,[12] Blackboard's customer retention is roughly five times larger than the company's closest competitor. If this retention rate begins to drop, however, this might signal that Blackboard's competitive advantage is eroding.

Source #6: Cost Advantages   Cost advantages include such factors as economies of scale and advantageous locations. The more structural a cost advantage is, the more sustainable it is. For example, lowering costs by moving a call center to India will help a business, but most of its competitors can narrow this advantage by doing the same.

Economies of scale are a more structural kind of advantage. As a business with fixed costs grows, it is able to take advantage of lower per-unit costs. This way, it is able to charge lower prices for its products or services compared to competitors. This widens the competitive advantage and makes it more sustainable.

There are various ways for a business to create advantages based on economies of scale, including increasing efficiencies by consolidating a fragmented industry.

Obtaining a Cost Advantage through Industry Consolidation   In large, fragmented markets, especially those that have become commoditized, you can often see businesses with low-cost advantages building market share. The higher the market share, the more customer choice is limited, which gives the surviving dominant players an advantage.

For example, LabCorp and Quest each played large parts in the consolidation of the laboratory testing business. In the early 1990s, there were seven or eight national lab companies that all performed the same type of tests. As lab-test reimbursements increasingly fell to health-maintenance organizations (HMOs), the HMOs demanded lower prices. LabCorp and Quest acquired other businesses to achieve economies of scale, and they contracted with HMOs to offer lower pricing. Although end-customers could choose to use other labs, the scale already achieved by LabCorp and Quest made matching their pricing difficult for competitors. Other labs quickly found that their existing customers didn't want to pay higher co-pays for non-contract testing, and the competition folded.

Obtaining a Cost Advantage through a Good Location   Whenever a business has a geographic location that competitors are unable to easily duplicate, this can give a business a cost advantage. For example, cement plants in certain areas of the United States benefit when housing and public construction increase demand locally for cement. Because it is difficult to build new cement plants ("not in my backyard") and because it is generally inefficient to ship cement long distances because of its weight, those cement plants are able to undercut the prices of most competitors.

The Best Kind of Sustainable Competitive Advantage Is Structural

When customers have limited choices in the products or services they can use for extended periods of time the competitive advantage is likely structural. A structural competitive advantage can be a result of regulation, a prime location, or better distribution networks. For example, think about a prime piece of real estate in your community where there is easy access, visibility, and location. This location typically will be able to charge higher rents to retailers because it is in a good area where more customers are likely to shop.

The best way to identify a structural competitive advantage is to view it from the perspective of customer choice: Does the customer have limited products or services to choose from, or does the customer have many choices? For example, if you are buying infant formula you are limited to two main products: Enfamil manufactured by Mead Johnson and Similac manufactured by Abbott Nutrition. In contrast, when choosing a restaurant, you have a myriad of choices.

Structural advantages are typically the most sustainable advantages. For one thing, the more a competitive advantage is based on structural characteristics, the less the business depends on such factors as management execution. For example, bond ratings firms Moody's and Standard & Poor's both possess strong structural competitive advantages because the government limits the number of firms that can issue ratings through regulation, so they rely less on having good management. In contrast, a restaurant (and retail in general) depends a great deal on the quality of management, so they have far less of an advantage.

Why It's Hard to Find Businesses with Sustainable Competitive Advantages

For most businesses, a competitive advantage is not sustainable over an extended period of time. Competitive advantages expire. Even when a business appears most formidable and generates the strongest financial metrics, it can be on the verge of failure. If a business doesn't innovate successfully and defend itself, competitors will always be there to chip away at the business.

For example, Sony knows that when it creates a new product, it has between one and two years before other consumer-electronics manufacturers imitate that product. Therefore, when the management team sits down to decide how they are going to price their product, they price it at a level where they will be able to recover their investment in an 18- to 24-month period.

Most advantages are *temporary*, such as when a business launches a new product that is superior to the competition's product, and many advantages decline over time. For example, microchip manufacturer Intel used to make excess profits for long periods after introducing a new chip. The reason for this was that, in the past, there was less competition in chip making. Computer makers were willing to pay a premium to Intel to have the latest microprocessors in order to differentiate themselves. However, as more competitors have entered the industry, Intel now has a smaller window of time in which to earn a higher-than-average profit on a new chip.

It is increasingly difficult to find businesses with competitive advantages, for several reasons:

- Consumers are less loyal to products or brand names. Witness how private-label products continue to take market share from branded products.
- Increased global competition has lowered the bar for new entrants in most industries, such as manufacturing. For example, global competition has almost shut down manufacturing of shoes in the United States, where production fell from 121 million shoes in 1999 to only 31 million in 2007.[13]
- Technological advances have shortened the lifecycle of many competitive advantages. Let's take a closer look at this reason.

Competitive advantages are less sustainable when they are affected by changes in technology or if they are in rapidly emerging industries. Changes in technology threaten a competitive advantage when they expand customer choice, whether by offering the same product for less or by offering greater benefit for the same price or less. Here are just a few examples:

- Book retailer Barnes & Noble's historical ability to charge premium prices for books was diminished by online retailer Amazon.com, which is able to sell books at a lower price because it does not have the higher overhead in the form of store leases.
- The Internet has reduced the sustainability of many competitive advantages. For example, newspapers lost most of their classified advertisers and the large percentage of profits they represented to low-cost Internet sites.
- Other businesses are in terminal decline as their products and services are being replaced by new and improved offerings from competitors that exceed what they have to offer. For example, dial-up Internet service America Online (AOL) has been decimated by high-speed providers.

In all of these examples, customer choice improved due to changes in technology, whether because of lower costs or greater benefits.

Beware of Businesses that Were Simply at the Right Place at the Right Time

Too often, investors look at a business's past success as a result of a competitive advantage, when they should be asking *why* a business has a competitive advantage and if there are certain conditions that created it. Many businesses may simply have been in the right place at the right time.

For example, when the price of computers dropped and more consumers could afford personal computers, Dell was able to beat its competitors on price because it had the lowest cost structure of all computer manufacturers. In contrast, other computer manufacturers were locked into distribution agreements that increased the cost of a computer. Over time, however, Dell's advantage has eroded as competitors now manufacture computers at a lower or equal price. What many investors believed to be an enduring competitive advantage was not.

Most Investment Gains Are Made During the Development Phase, Not After

As you are learning about the source of a competitive advantage, it is important to remember that the greatest gains in a stock are usually made as a business is *developing* its competitive advantage rather than after it already has developed one. For example, we all know that Wal-Mart has a competitive advantage, but investors earned the biggest stock gains as Wal-Mart grew and developed this advantage.

Ideally, you want to identify those businesses that are in the early stages of building a competitive advantage. It can take years and sometimes decades for a business to develop its competitive advantage, and it is difficult to see a competitive advantage building, because in most instances, the business is losing money during that time. For example, online retailer Amazon.com lost money for eight years while using its capital to rapidly expand its customer base and develop its markets before committing to more efficient operations and profit. The best way to distinguish whether a business is building a competitive advantage or wasting money is to monitor the number of customers a business serves. The investments Amazon.com made increased the number of customers it served. In contrast, businesses that fail are those that continually spend money but do not increase the number of customers they serve.

Look for those businesses that continue to push product or service innovation by investing in research and development (R&D) or that are wisely spending marketing dollars to increase awareness of their products with superior value propositions or unique appeal. For example, Apple remained committed to its R&D program even after revenue dropped by 33 percent. Apple increased its R&D spending by 13 percent in 2001, which increased its R&D as a percentage of sales from 5 percent of sales in 2000 to 8 percent of sales in 2001, as stated in their 2001 10-K. During this time, many shareholders questioned why Apple would continue to increase its expenses, even though its revenues were declining. Yet because of these expenditures, when Apple introduced the iTunes music store in 2003 and the iPod in 2004, the stage was set for rapid growth.

Be cautious of those businesses that only imitate innovation. For example, Wal-Mart has always had cutting-edge information-technology (IT) systems for retail. It was one of the first retailers to invest in barcode scanners to increase efficiency. (It's hard to imagine, but barcode scanners were considered revolutionary at the time.) A couple of years later, Kmart added barcode scanners, which helped Kmart, but by then, Wal-Mart was already using the next generation of IT tools in the form of a private satellite network.

Table 4.1   Comparing Competitive Advantages in Education: Are They Easy or Difficult to Copy?

Competitive Advantages that Are Easy to Copy	Competitive Advantages that Are Difficult to Copy
Quick approval of student-loan applications	Accreditation
Ability of students to work on their own schedules	Quality Faculty
Study from home	Resources
Easy-to-navigate website	Quality of education

In IT and in other areas, Kmart's imitation of Wal-Mart wasn't as effective as Wal-Mart's innovation, and Kmart was left behind.

What Is Not a Sustainable Competitive Advantage?

It is important for you to distinguish a business's *competitive strength* from a *sustainable competitive advantage.* If a business has good customer service, a quality product, and knowledgeable workforces, those are all strengths, but those can often be duplicated. For example, a business that returns its phone calls within an hour is preferable to one that returns calls the next day, but a competitor can easily duplicate this enhanced customer service. Some strengths are more difficult to develop than others, such as having very knowledgeable employees, a strong employee culture, or an efficient production process.

For example, in the for-profit education industry, there are some advantages that are easy to copy and some that are difficult to copy, as shown in Table 4.1.

Therefore, *sustainable advantages* include factors that are difficult to copy, such as accreditation, whereas *competitive strengths* include such factors as an easy-to-navigate website.

☐ 16. Does the business possess the ability to raise prices without losing customers?

The best indicator of a competitive advantage is a business's ability to increase prices without losing customers. For example, the following companies (and others, of course) all have pricing power:

- Blood-testing equipment maker Immucor
- Luxury goods manufacturer Louis Vuitton

- Global financial information providers FactSet Research Systems and Bloomberg
- Salt producer Compass Minerals International
- Häagen-Dazs ice cream (owned by Nestlé S.A.)

Häagen-Dazs ice cream is able to sell its products at a large premium over its cost of production, therefore demonstrating pricing power. In contrast, commodity-type businesses, such as steel producers, do not have pricing power. In most cases, these types of businesses must *decrease* their prices to spur demand, and the price is typically set by the production cost rather than the value of the product to the purchaser.

Common Characteristics of Firms with Pricing Power

Businesses that have pricing power typically have a few characteristics in common:

- They usually have high customer-retention rates.
- Their customers spend only a small percentage of their budget on the business's product or service.
- Their customers have profitable business models.
- The quality of the product is more important than price.

Let's look at each of these individually.

High Customer-Retention Rates   A business with a high renewal rate on its services typically has pricing power. For example, financial-services information provider FactSet Research System's client-retention rate from 2002 to 2008 was greater than 90 percent. As a result of its high client-retention rate, FactSet is able to raise its prices when contracts renew. In contrast, a business that is always fighting for customers certainly is in no position to raise prices. It must typically decrease prices to attract new customers.

Low Price Sensitivity   To determine how price sensitive a customer is, find out how much of the customer's budget is spent on the product or service. The higher the percentage of the customer's budget spent on a product or service, the more likely it is that the customer will be price sensitive, which may impede the ability of a business to raise prices. For example, medical laboratory testing businesses have pricing power because their cost to the customer represents 3 percent of overall medical spending, yet they are pivotal to determining the great majority of treatments. This makes lab-test customers less price sensitive.

Customers Have Profitable Business Models   If customers have plenty of cash, or their businesses are highly profitable, they will be less sensitive to pricing. This is true as long as the product does not represent a large part of their overall budget. For example, Bloomberg's customers are mostly traders, who have highly profitable businesses. The cost of Bloomberg's financial terminals represents a small percentage of a customer's overall profits and therefore price is not the first consideration. If customers generate low profits, then they are likely to be under pressure to reduce purchasing costs, as in the case of a clothing manufacturer.

High-Quality Products or Services   Sometimes the quality of the product is more important to a purchaser than the price. For example, Precision Castparts is a leading manufacturer of high-quality castings, forgings, and fasteners. Jet aircraft engine manufacturers (such as Rolls-Royce) use Precision Castparts' parts to construct their engines. It is critical that these engines run smoothly and that components work flawlessly to ensure the engine does not malfunction while an airplane is in flight. Also, many of Precision Castparts' products last five times longer than competitors' products. This means that buyers are willing to pay a premium for Precision Castparts' products because the quality of the product matters more to the customer than price.

Similarly, Fastenal is an industrial parts supplier that makes sure it can supply a wide range of parts immediately to manufacturers. A simple bolt distributed by Fastenal represents a small percentage of a manufacturer's budget but can be critical to the operation. Speed and quality of service matter more to the customer than price in this case, because the cost of downtime is significantly higher than the price of the bolt to get the manufacturing plant moving again.

Are Pricing Advantages Sustainable Rather than Temporary?

Be certain that price increases are not just dependent on a temporary condition. For example, some commodity-type firms, such as disk drive manufacturers, are able to increase prices on their products when demand exceeds supply, but these price increases tend to be short lived because supply eventually catches up with demand. An example would be during the recession in 2008 when trucking capacity shrunk significantly due to many small carriers ceasing operations. Due to the limited capacity in the market, remaining carriers gained some pricing power over their shippers. The majority of the top 50 carriers increased rates by 3 to 9 percent in 2010, with the flat-bed carriers enjoying the higher end of that range.[14] This pricing power is temporary, however, because prices will drop as new carriers begin to enter the market again, expanding capacity.

Where to Find Pricing Power Information

Look for pricing power information in the following sources:

- The MD&A section of the 10-K
- Historical operating metrics
- Investor presentations, conference calls, and so on

Keep an eye out for important pricing power indicators such as:

- Multiple years of increases
- Increases that don't just offset costs (seen in operating profit per customer and operating income growth)
- Pricing that is higher than competitors

To determine if a business can raise prices, begin by looking at the Management Discussion and Analysis (MD&A) section found in the 10-K, and read management's explanations for changes in the gross profit margin. Read at least 5 to 10 years of this section of the 10-K.

For example, in its 2004 Form 10-K, salt producer Compass Minerals International states: "The increase in gross profit primarily reflects the impact of *improved prices* and volumes ($8 million and $15.3 million, respectively)."

Five years later, in the 2009 10-K, the company states: "The gross margin for the salt segment partially offset the decline in gross margin by contributing an increase of approximately $40 million due to *price improvements.*"

Compass can raise prices, and it specifies the additional revenues it receives by increasing its prices.

Next, determine if the price increases are lasting or not. Further reading of Compass' 10-K and other documents reveals that Compass' increases have been lasting, as they have been able to raise prices consistently over the last five years.

Finally, see if these price increases have translated into operating income growth, or if they have been used to offset increased expenses. To do this, compare the gross profit margin to operating-income margin over a one- to five-year period. If the operating-income margin is dropping as the gross margin is increasing, then expenses may be rising faster than price increases.

Another method to identify pricing power is to calculate historical operating profit metrics. For example, Western Union reports the total number of transactions and operating profit for its consumer division in the 10-K. You can divide consumer transactions by the operating profit for its consumer division to yield a single trending number representing operating profit per consumer transaction. In 2003, operating profit per consumer transaction was $9.44. By 2008, this decreased to $6.51. This downward trend in operating profit per consumer transaction indicates that pricing power is declining. In fact, Western Union disclosed in its 2009 10-K that it re-invests 1 to 3 percent of its revenues in price decreases to increase customer traffic.

Other useful sources for determining pricing power are company investor presentations, conference calls, or annual reports. These sources may provide other indicators of pricing power, such as whether a business is able to charge more than its competitors. For example, in historical annual reports, Four Seasons Hotels disclosed the daily room-rate premium (known as RevPAR premium) it achieved compared to its competitors. Historically, Four Seasons' pricing premium was 50 percent greater than its closest competitor, Ritz Carlton.[15]

In most cases, if a business has pricing power, it will disclose it. If the business does not disclose increasing prices, then it is highly probable the business does not have pricing power. Look for price increases in the context of other indicators of pricing power: trends in profit per customer, pricing that doesn't just offset increased costs, and price increases that can continue for multiple years.

Examine Whether Pricing Power Is Found Throughout the Overall Business or Only a Segment of the Business

Determine if the business's pricing power protects all of its revenues or just a percentage of them. Some businesses have pricing power in certain products or services, yet not in the majority of the products or services they offer. For example, airlines set their prices by how much competition they have on a certain route, rather than by distance. As a result, they have pricing power on certain routes rather than all routes. A plane fare from Austin, Texas, to Corpus Christi, Texas, (200 miles) may be more than a fare from New York to Los Angeles (3,000 miles) because there is more competition on the New York-to-Los Angeles route. If more of an airline's routes are similar to the New York-to-Los Angeles route, the airline has less overall pricing power than it would if more of its routes were like Austin-Corpus Christi.

Technology Creates Price Transparency

Technological changes have affected the ability of businesses to increase prices. The Internet in particular has helped create price transparency. In the past, some businesses were able to maintain higher pricing because it was more difficult for customers to compare pricing. For example, consider the changes in hotel room price transparency. In the past, customers relied on travel agents or had to call multiple hotels to compare pricing. In contrast, they now use online travel sites (such as Expedia and Travelocity) to do the same thing instantly. Customers can now easily see hotel pricing, and as a result, they have become more price sensitive. This greater visibility has lowered the room rates that hotels can charge.

☐ 17. Does the business operate in a good or bad industry?

Investing in the right industry is important because a large part of your potential rate of return is often attributable to the industry you are invested in, as opposed to a specific company you are invested in. As you evaluate an industry as a whole, ask how easy it is to make money in the industry. If it is easy, that's a good industry to be in, and your chances of making money in your investment are better.

To Begin, Calculate the Range of Industry Return on Invested Capital

To begin evaluating the industry, compare the distribution of returns on invested capital (ROIC, which question 26 discusses in more detail, including showing you how to calculate it). If it's easy to make money in an industry, you will find that most companies are doing well, and there will not be a wide range of distribution of ROIC. If there is a broad range of ROIC, with some companies doing well and some doing poorly, this is a tougher industry to be in.

For example, the pharmaceutical industry has a consistently high ROIC, with returns ranging from 13 to 21 percent over the last decade.[16] The best pharmaceutical businesses are not far from the worst in terms of ROIC. In contrast, ROIC for the major oil companies ranged from 3 to 15 percent over the last decade. This wider and lower range of ROIC indicates that it is harder to make money in this industry.[17]

To get a deeper understanding of whether an industry is good or bad, compare the best companies to the worst within the industry. By making comparisons between the extremes in an industry, you will identify the *reasons* why the industry is good or bad to be in. This information will also help you evaluate other companies if you decide to invest in the industry.

Another Method of Industry Analysis—from Imperial Capital's Steve Lister

To give you more in-depth methods of picking a good industry, I present a case study of the industry research methods of Steve Lister, co-founder of Toronto-based private equity firm Imperial Capital, who has been selecting companies from good industries for many years. Lister's case study illustrates several methods you can use to understand if the industry as a whole is a good one.

Lister's firm has a solid track record of identifying, evaluating, and investing in some of the most profitable industries, such as regional telephone-book publishers and refrigerated warehouses. Lister believes that finding the right industry is what counts most. Like many, Lister believes that your chances of picking a good investment are based more on the industry than on the individual company. He notes that if an industry is growing 5 percent to 8 percent a year, even if you do not identify the best individual company, your performance will still likely be good. Furthermore, Lister has discovered that over time, the profitability of a business will eventually trend toward the mean of the industry, as it is difficult for any business to outperform the industry for a long period of time.

Lister's firm has developed a scorecard system with 100 different items that helps him evaluate the economics of an industry. As Lister says:

> We score an industry on 100 items every time. There is a lot of judgment in terms of how to understand things such as the volatility of customer demand, profit margins, pricing power, and barriers to entry. We go through all of these items and rate them and create a sort of index. Maybe we are wrong on 5 percent to 10 percent of the items, but at the end of the day, it is the relative score that matters. If an industry scores positively on only 50 of the 100 items, we will pass on the industry, but if the industry scores anywhere from 60 to 75 of the 100 items, we will look for a business within that industry to invest in.

Some of the questions on Imperial Capital's scorecard include:

- What drives the industry?
- How do people compete within the industry?
- What is the larger macro picture?
- What are the industry trends?
- What is the average cash-conversion cycle for the industry?
- What is the industry's exposure to cyclical markets?
- Does the industry have the ability to pass on price increases?
- What is the volatility of demand from customers?

Once analysts at Imperial Capital narrow down the industries they will consider investing in, they then research the industry more closely to understand the trends in demand and what is driving demand. Lister identifies whether the trends are negative or positive, and whether they are temporary or structural. This allows him to understand whether the trends are sustainable.

For example, when Lister and his team evaluated the healthcare industry, they started by looking at more than 100 healthcare segments, or what he calls niches. They analyzed the growth rates, profitability, the number of businesses, and reimbursement risk for each of these niches. Then they developed a ranking of each of the different healthcare niches, based on this underlying research. Once they narrowed down the list to 12 niches with above-average profitability, they looked for healthcare practitioners who could help them answer the questions in their scorecard and further narrow down the industries that they could invest in. These healthcare practitioners were former or existing CEOs of businesses who had "lived, slept, and breathed the industry for a long time." As Lister says, "The only way you can know where the skeletons are buried in an industry is to partner with someone who knows where they are." To locate these CEO partners, Lister and his team go to industry conferences and use their established network of industry contacts.

One business that Lister's firm invested in because it met the majority of Imperial Capital's criteria (75 out of 100) was Associated Freezers Corporation, a refrigerated warehousing company. There were several factors that attracted Lister and his team to Associated Freezers, including these:

- Underlying demand was strong. As women entered the workforce, frozen foods made up a larger part of people's diets. Supermarkets showed evidence of this increased demand as they increased the number of frozen foods aisles.
- The quality of frozen foods improved. The old style TV dinner was replaced with more popular choices and higher-quality ingredients.
- Price was not the primary determinant. The customers (frozen-food manufacturers) chose warehouses based on service, real-time links to inventory, good temperature control, quality, and on-time delivery, not on price.
- There were barriers to entry. Industry regulation forced refrigerated warehouses to staff engineers because the extremely large refrigeration equipment is dangerous. Because of the expense and expertise required to build the refrigerated warehouses, entry was constrained by capital.
- The financial characteristics were strong. Earnings before interest, taxes, depreciation, and amortization (EBITDA) margins exceeded 36 percent once a refrigerated warehouse was built, and the maintenance capital expenditures were minimal. This allowed investors to earn excess free-cash flows.

- Finally, the average cash-conversion cycle was 120 days, so refrigerated warehouses could grow without using a lot of borrowed cash.

Lister and his investment partners were extremely successful in this investment because Lister and his firm had identified a good industry.

☐ 18. How has the industry evolved over time?

Understanding how an industry evolved will help you evaluate the business in the context of its competition, its operating environment, and the various other forces that shape it. When you study an industry, you will pick up on factors and forces that are not as obvious as when you study only one business. To understand the industry well, study its history over a long period (i.e., more than 10 years). Seeing change over time will help you pick up on factors and major forces that are not apparent in only one period.

For example, when I was interested in investing in a large advertising agency, I studied not only the individual agency, but the entire industry. I did not fully understand all the forces that affected the industry until I saw them unfold over time.

One of the main services of an ad agency, historically, has been ad placement. For decades, ad agencies charged on the basis of billings: In other words, the agency was paid a percentage of the amount their clients paid to television stations, newspapers, magazines, and so on, to run their ads, so if an ad campaign for a client cost $200 million, the ad agency's commission might be 10 percent of that, or $20 million. Obviously, this was very profitable for large agencies. In fact, the operating margins for the advertising industry used to exceed 20 percent.

As the industry consolidated, companies leveraged their balance sheets to acquire other agencies, assuming that those healthy margins would continue indefinitely. Two things happened that changed the margins within the advertising-agency industry. First, companies began to realize that paying a percentage of their total advertising bill to the advertising agencies wasn't a good value for them. They began to see that their sales results weren't tied to how much they paid, but instead depended on several other factors, including the quality of the ad, the research that went into it, and the number of potential customers it reached. Second, with the growth of Internet advertising, companies who wanted mass-market or national advertising campaigns were no longer stuck with major television networks and limited print media as the only avenues for reaching customers. Instead there were now hundreds of web sites where advertisements could reach a nationwide audience. Mass markets became fragmented and the brokering power of the large agencies diminished significantly. The large advertising agencies had to move to a lower pricing model, and operating margins began to decrease.

Interestingly, the large advertising agencies continued to acquire other advertising agencies. Curious about this, I asked managers what the benefit of size was for an agency during a time where markets were becoming more fragmented. The management teams of the large agencies explained that they were continuing to make acquisitions because customers would benefit from being able to use a single agency to run a global campaign: For example, Nike would be able to run a global campaign without having to hire 10 separate agencies. These managers claimed they had created synergies by combining agencies: With more distribution power under one roof, they believed they would enjoy the benefit of efficiencies on the cost side.

However, because I had studied the way that ad-agency industry consolidation had taken place in the past, I knew that consolidation didn't result in large cohesive agencies being able to offer seamless global advertising campaigns; I also knew that consolidation didn't result in efficiencies. In fact, as large agencies made acquisitions, the acquired agency was not absorbed; instead it often *competed* with other agencies in the same umbrella or conglomerate agency. Each agency within the conglomerate ran its own profit and loss statement and had few incentives to work with other agencies under the same roof. I followed up with additional research and found that the industry still operated in a similar fashion. So even though acquisitions resulted in increased revenue on paper, they weren't going to create cost efficiencies or synergies.

Studying the advertising industry over time allowed me to conclude that ad agency consolidation worked differently than consolidation in other industries. I concluded that margins would not grow in this new environment, and I passed on the investment. By knowing how the entire industry evolved, I was able to see the fallacy in management's claims of cost synergies and better customer service, and I sidestepped a poor investment opportunity.

A great source to help you understand how an industry has evolved is the collection of Standard & Poor's (S&P) *Industry Surveys*. S&P publishes surveys on many industries, including real estate investment trusts (REITs), chemicals, publishing, restaurants, and homebuilding, to name just a few. The reports are typically broken down into sections on how the industry operates, industry trends, key industry ratios and statistics, and a section titled "How to Analyze" a particular industry, such as a REIT. There is also a section on industry references, which can give you valuable leads for trade journals, industry associations, and other sources. There is a comparative-company analysis in the appendix, which will give you useful competitor information and a list of other companies in the industry. You can access these reports through a university or local library.

☐ 19. What is the competitive landscape, and how intense is the competition?

You can better understand what the competitive landscape is for a business by answering the following questions:

- Does the business have limited competition?
- Does the industry change often?
- How do the competitors compete within an industry, and how could that change?
- How fiercely do businesses compete?
- What risks does the business face from substitute products?
- Can competition from low-cost countries impact the business?
- Which competitor sets the industry standard?
- Why have competitors failed in an industry?

Let's take a closer look at each of these questions.

Does the Business Have Limited Competition?

Competition does not increase the value of a business. Generally, more competition means more customer choice and less profitability. In addition, a business with limited competition is easier to analyze than one that has lots of competitors.

For example, think about the competition in a supermarket aisle. There is limited shelf space on each aisle that name brands and private-label products compete for. If you are analyzing a name-brand food company, you can easily assess how a certain food brand is doing against a private-label brand or other brands by monitoring shelf space in various national supermarkets. In addition, there are many market-research organizations that can provide you with valuable information regarding market share, such as global information and measurement company A.C. Nielsen. In contrast, it is far more difficult to understand the competitive position of a business such as a check-cashing store, where there are thousands of direct and indirect competitors.

To begin your assessment, view the Competition section in the 10-K. If a business lists its competitors by name, the company has limited competition. For example, the 2009 10-K for bond-rating agency Moody's lists the following competitors:

- Standard & Poor's
- Fitch
- Dominion Bond Rating Service Ltd. of Canada
- A.M. Best Company Inc.
- Japan Credit Rating Agency Ltd.
- Rating and Investment Information Inc. of Japan
- Egan-Jones Ratings Company
- LACE Financial Corp.
- Realpoint LLC

In contrast, in such businesses as banking, homebuilding, or restaurants, the company will not list its competition but will simply disclose that it has many competitors. For example, the 10-K from June 30, 2010 for Dollar Financial (a check-cashing business and consumer loan provider) states:

In the United States, our industry is highly fragmented. According to Financial Service Centers of America, Inc., there are approximately 7,000 neighborhood check cashing stores and, according to published equity research estimates by Stephens Inc., there are approximately 22,000 short-term lending stores.

Does the Industry Change Often?

If the industry is one that is constantly changing, then it will be even more difficult to evaluate the competitive position of a business. For example, if you are evaluating competitors individually in the technology industry, by the time you have analyzed most of those companies, the technology may change, which of course opens the door to a new crop of competitors you never considered.

Therefore, to evaluate competitors in a fast-changing industry, view them from the customer perspective. You will need to locate and maintain close contact with customers to understand if they are switching to other products and services.

For example, when I first began analyzing the online travel industry, which was in its infancy at the time (in 2001), I attended several online travel-industry conferences (such as The PhoCusWright Conference) to look for potential investments. I knew that online travel was a growing industry, but I did not know which businesses to invest in. Most of the industry players—such as Expedia, Travelocity, and priceline.com (and many others that no longer exist)—were in their early stages of development. Because the industry was changing so quickly, I searched for customers and travel providers (i.e., hotels, airlines) who used these services. I wanted to find out which services they preferred and why.

When I first studied priceline.com, I personally did not like the business model because customers could only choose to bid on hotels with a certain star rating, and they could not choose the specific hotel where they would be staying. I thought this business model had limited potential, and many of its competitors agreed. However, the customers and travel providers kept telling me that because priceline.com was a differentiated service, it could represent a great investment. The travel providers and hotels liked this business model because they did not have to advertise discounted hotel rates, which could damage their pricing power.

The customers and travel providers ended up choosing the best investment in this industry: priceline.com has been one of the highest-returning stocks in the online travel industry, increasing from $8 per share toward the end of 2000 to more than $400 per share at the end of 2010.[18] Had I not viewed competitors from the customer perspective, I would have come to the wrong conclusion as to which business would be most successful.

How Do the Competitors Compete within an Industry, and How Could That Change?

Competition may be based on capital, service, or price. Determine whether the competitive dynamics can change, and then construct different downside scenarios for the business based on those dynamics. Let's look at each of these factors individually:

Competing on capital   If the businesses compete based on capital, then the advantage will always reside with the well-funded competitors. For example, BHP Billiton (a global resources and mining company) has an advantage over smaller mining operators because it has more capital that it can use to develop large mines. Competitors with less capital are limited in the types of mines they can develop.

Competing on service   If companies compete based on service, the company with a stronger, more ingrained customer service culture will have an advantage. Therefore, you should focus on understanding the reasons why one business has better customer service than another and whether that can change. For example, if a new management team takes over a company that has poor customer service and if they make improvements, they may be able to gain market share from a dominant competitor.

Competing on price   You need to determine if the competitors within an industry have to constantly match each other based on price. If so, the business may have a difficult time increasing its margins or earnings, as increases in margins will need to come from cost cuts which become more and more difficult to achieve.

Competing by copying   Be cautious investing in businesses whose management teams attempt to replicate the success of a competitor's breakthrough products or profitable business lines. Whenever competitors attempt to meet a competitor head on by entering the same business line where a competitor has an advantage, there is risk.

For example, Stanley O'Neal, former head of Merrill Lynch, was known to be obsessed with his competitors and made derivative trading a priority because it was generating so much profit for his competitors, including Goldman Sachs. O'Neal's goal was to increase profits through these exotic products; however, he did not understand the risks involved, which eventually destroyed Merrill Lynch.[19, 20]

In contrast, John McFarland, CEO of electric-motor manufacturer Baldor Electric Company, once told me he did not worry about his competitors, nor did he attempt to track them or copy them. Instead, he asked his customers which products they liked. He explained that if he spent his time tracking competitors, he might be tempted to incorporate some of their changes into his motor designs, and then later learn that the customers did not value these changes. It was better to let *customer* input drive his decision making, instead of competitor input.

How Fiercely Do Businesses Compete?

The degree of competition, or how fiercely competitors compete, can depend on such factors as whether the competitors are roughly equal in size or whether the industry is growing or mature. If competitors are numerous and roughly equal in size, then it will be an intensely competitive industry, such as the check-cashing industry. In these environments, there is typically no industry leader.

In contrast, for industries with only a few strong players controlling the market, these market leaders hold an advantage, simply because of their size. For example:

- Home Depot can offer lower prices on its products to customers because it often represents a large percentage of the sales for its suppliers.
- Philip Morris, maker of Marlboro cigarettes, is able to get more shelf space compared to its competitors.
- The Coca-Cola Company can invest more in advertising to increase brand awareness.
- Amazon.com has the resources to invest in more efficient distribution and Web page design.

In growing industries, competition is generally less fierce. When industry growth begins to slow, competitors fight for market share and, in some instances, will change the way they compete. There have been many instances in which two large, dominant competitors have entered into price wars.

For example, when Roger Enrico became PepsiCo's CEO in 1996, he started a price war with The Coca-Cola Company that lasted until 1998. As he tried to boost volume and increase market share, the price of a two-liter bottle of Coke or Pepsi sold for as little as 59 cents, compared to prices of $1 before the price war began.[21] Instead of competing based on marketing, Coke and Pepsi were competing based on price. When the price war ended, volumes at both businesses dropped because consumers, accustomed to the lower prices, decreased consumption.

Sometimes competitors become irrational in the way they compete with each other, even following strategies that lose money in order to gain market share. You need to determine if this is a temporary phenomenon or a long-lasting trend. If you identify a temporary change in the way businesses are competing, you can often profit.

For example, in 2007, Blockbuster launched its Total Access (TA) DVD-by-mail program to compete with its rival Netflix. Blockbuster decided to cut the price of its program by several dollars a month to undercut Netflix's pricing. Blockbuster quickly accumulated more than 2.2 million customers, and Netflix lost 50,000 of its subscribers. The stock price of Netflix dropped to under $17 per share, which was near its IPO price of $15 per share five years earlier, in 2002.

However, if you had spent some time reviewing Blockbuster's financial statement, you would have learned that it had a lot of debt and that it was losing money on its stores. The TA program was also losing money because it was designed to gain market share instead of generate profits. You would have learned that Blockbuster's strategy was not sustainable and that at some point, it would have to stop under-pricing Netflix. When Blockbuster was forced to raise its prices, it quickly lost the advantage it had over Netflix. Netflix's stock price increased to more than $175 per share at the end of 2010 (from $17 per share when the price war began), whereas Blockbuster's stock declined from over $6 per share in 2007 to $0.16 per share at the end of 2010.[22]

There are also financial metrics you can monitor to understand if an industry is becoming more competitive. This will alert you that future earnings may drop, decreasing the value of the business you are analyzing. Take total costs and divide by the number of customers, transactions, or another metric. Track the resulting ratio of operating cost per customer or operating cost per transaction. Is it decreasing or increasing for most of the competitors in the industry? As markets become more competitive, costs tend to increase.

For example, the customer-acquisition costs of wireless telecom businesses have gradually increased over the years as more competitors have entered the market and existing competitors try to increase their market share. As a result, many of these wireless telecom carriers have had to invest in customer support, marketing, and increased commissions to sign up new customers and retain existing customers. Therefore, if you had monitored the customer-acquisition costs for competitors in the wireless telecom industry, you would have seen that the wireless telephone business was becoming more competitive.

To get more insight into the reasons for differences in profitability, read articles about the industry. Search for articles using search terms such as "auto industry profitability" to locate articles that are written about how the profits of an industry or certain businesses are changing over time and, more important, the reasons for these changes.

What Risks Does the Business Face from Substitute Products?

Be careful not to define the competition too narrowly by considering only direct competitors. You must also consider the risks from substitute products. A substitute product or service performs the same function as the business's current product or service but by a different means. For example, plastic is a substitute for aluminum, and e-mail is a substitute for express mail. Sometimes, substitute products can be extremely different from the existing product or service. For example, for a Father's Day gift, power tools may serve as a substitute for a necktie. The threat of substitute products is high if they can offer the customer an attractive price or performance tradeoff to the current industry product or service. Here are a few examples:

- International calling cards suffered when low-cost Internet-based service Skype entered the market.
- Advancements in digital photography replaced the duopoly on traditional film that Kodak and Fuji had. Kodak and Fuji took too long to transition to the new digital medium and therefore lost significant market share.

There are certain types of businesses that are currently immune from the competitive threats of substitute products. For example, there are not any cost-effective substitute products for cement. You can build a house with steel, but this is not cost effective compared to using cement.

Some types of products and services are immune from substitute products for long periods of time and others for short periods of time. For example, the U.S. Postal Service dominated the transmission of mail for decades in the United States, but e-mail evolved to become a substitute product. Typically, the more asset-intensive a business is, the less threat it has from substitute products: For example, think of airplane manufacturer Boeing, chemical firm Dow Chemical, and cement producer CEMEX. Although substitutes may be developed in any industry, these businesses have longer periods of immunity.

Can Competition from Low-Cost Countries Impact the Business?

As economies become more interconnected, businesses face more competition from foreign competitors. You need to determine if a business is threatened by foreign competition. Generally, items that cannot be shipped long distances are not subject to foreign competition.

For example, plastic parts for automobiles can't be shipped long distances because they scratch easily, so there is less foreign competition. Rock quarries also face little or no competition from foreign businesses because it is extremely expensive to ship aggregates overseas. On the other hand, manufacturing firms where labor is a large component of the product cost face threats from foreign competition.

For instance, Pillowtex (a manufacturer of pillows, comforters, and towels) had $500 million in sales in 1995. In 1994, the United States began to phase out quotas on imports. Its competitors knew they would face extreme price competition from foreign markets, and they immediately began to outsource their manufacturing to developing countries. Pillowtex, however, acquired more businesses, hoping to capture a cost advantage through economies of scale; in fact, in its 1998 10-K, Pillowtex reported that it had spent $240 million on new machinery at its U.S. plants. By 2003, Pillowtex was liquidated as foreign competitors destroyed pricing within the industry.[23] Investors had eight years to exit their investment in Pillowtex before it went bankrupt. They should have seen that Pillowtex could not compete with countries with lower-cost labor.

Which Competitor Sets the Industry Standard?

Making comparisons is a valuable tool to help you understand the differences between competitors. Always try to locate the best business in the industry by finding the businesses with the highest operating margins, highest returns on capital, and lowest cash-conversion cycle. Create a spreadsheet comparing the financial and operating metrics of the various publicly traded competitors to help guide you. If a business is a subsidiary of another business, you might be able to get *only* the revenues and operating income information for that business in the Segments section of the 10-K. Also, you will not be able to get information from private competitors, but you can often turn to industry trade associations, which might compile a range of profit margins for an industry. Note the differences in the financial metrics between competitors. You can often learn more about the reasons for these differences in the Management, Discussion, and Analysis (MD&A) section found in the 10-K.

For example, Table 4.2 compares the net income margin of various freight forwarders.

As you can see, UTi Worldwide has historically earned an average net income margin of 2 percent since 2005.[24] By comparison, Expeditors International has earned net income margins between 4 and 5 percent since 2005.[25] By reading the MD&A section for both these competitors, you will learn that the main reason for the difference in margins is due to UTi's historical growth-through-acquisitions model, compared to Expeditor's more efficient practice of growing organically or building new offices from the

Table 4.2 Comparison of Net Income Margin for Several Freight-Forwarding Companies

	12/31/2005	12/31/2006	12/31/2007	12/31/2008	12/31/2009	12/31/2010
Expeditors International	4.90%	5.10%	5.10%	5.30%	5.90%	5.80%
C.H. Robinson Worldwide	3.57%	4.07%	4.43%	4.19%	4.76%	4.17%
Landstar System	4.59%	4.49%	4.40%	4.19%	3.50%	3.64%
UTi Worldwide*	1.93%	2.92%	2.26%	–0.10%	1.15%	1.54%

*January 31 year end Standard & Poor's Capital IQ

ground up. You can conclude that growing organically will create more value than acquiring competitors for growth within the freight-forwarding industry.

As you learn more about each competitor's strengths and weaknesses, you can begin to construct an ideal business using each competitor's strengths. You can then use this ideal business to make comparisons to help you understand the differences between the business you are analyzing and the ideal business. For example, when my firm was researching a refinery business, we identified three factors that combine to create the ideal refining business:

1. First, protected wholesale and retail markets are important because they ensure that demand for refined products will continue to exceed supply. In a high-demand/low-supply wholesale market, it is easier to pass along costs and protect margins. Generally speaking, in the United States, the east coast is highly competitive. By comparison, the west coast has more demand in relation to supply. One reason for this is that refineries in California are protected by stringent environmental policies that restrict new refineries being built. This means that gas prices will tend to be higher on the west coast compared to the east coast.

2. Second, the biggest cost component in producing gasoline or heating oil or refined products is the cost of crude oil. The ability to process multiple types of crude oil generally lowers costs. Compare the average price paid per barrel of crude oil across different refineries to identify those refineries with low crude costs.

3. Third, plant size is important because the larger the refining plant is, the more it can spread out its fixed costs. Labor is mostly a fixed cost in a refinery because it takes only a few employees to run the refinery, and generally speaking, you need the same number of employees whether the plant is large or small or running at minimal or optimal capacity. Therefore, the larger the refinery, the more profitable it will be.

Once you have constructed the ideal refinery, you can then compare the refinery you are evaluating to the ideal refinery and learn where its strengths and weaknesses lie. For example, it may highlight that the refinery you are interested in cannot process multiple types of crude oil, so you know that it is at a competitive disadvantage to refineries that can.

Why Have Competitors Failed in an Industry?

Search for articles written about why competitors have failed in the industry. You will gain great insights into flawed strategies or operational missteps.

For example, in 2005, a refinery owned by British Petroleum (BP) exploded, killing 15 workers and injuring more than 170 others. Cost cutting and a lax safety culture were to blame for the explosion at Texas City, according to a report issued by the Chemical Safety and Hazard Investigation Board, a federal agency. "I don't think I've ever seen anything that bad," said Carolyn Merritt, former chairwoman of the board. British Petroleum also had oil spills from BP's pipelines on Alaska's North Slope, which cost it billions of dollars in profits.[26]

Fast forward a few years later, and BP was once again involved in an accident, the largest marine oil spill in history at one of its offshore oil wells in the Gulf of Mexico. Because BP had continually cut costs and did not comply with environmental and safety regulations, it was only a matter of time until a new accident occurred. By studying oil-industry failures, you would have learned that one of the biggest risks to an oil and gas firm comes from having lax safety standards.

❑ 20. What type of relationship does the business have with its suppliers?

You need to determine the type of relationship a business has with its suppliers. Does the business have a hostile relationship, in which it is constantly finding ways to pay suppliers lower prices for their goods or services? Or does it have a good relationship, where it helps suppliers innovate new products and services for the benefit of the business's customers?

Investors often believe that a business needs to constantly negotiate lower prices from its suppliers in order to increase earnings. They fail to recognize that if these businesses continually take advantage of their suppliers, the suppliers will eventually go out of business. The business will then need to find new suppliers, disrupting its supply chain, and ultimately decreasing earnings. Instead, if there is trust between the suppliers and the business, then this is often a competitive strength, because good supplier relationships facilitate the flow of goods.

J.C. Penney thinks long term about its vendors and negotiates contract terms that are favorable to both itself and its suppliers. The *Wall Street Journal* quoted Darcie Brossart of J.C. Penney, "We don't view squeezing our vendors to protect our bottom line as a viable long-term strategy." In the same article, representatives from Macy's and Dillard's did not want to comment about their dealings with vendors.[27] It seems likely that if Macy's and Dillard's had good vendor relations, they would have communicated openly about that, in order to encourage more suppliers to work with them.

Similarly, dollar-store retailer 99 Cent Only Stores maintains good relations with its suppliers, because management believes this makes for good business. The retailer pays its suppliers quickly and has never cancelled a purchase order in the history of the company. It treats suppliers as if their roles were reversed, and 99 Cent Only Stores were the ones doing the delivering. By treating its suppliers fairly, the retailer is able to build a lot of goodwill with its suppliers. As a result, manufacturers of products prefer to sell their excess inventory to 99 Cent Only Stores, rather than to other retailers. This gives 99 Cent Only Stores a competitive advantage and allows it to sell products at lower prices.

The following questions should help you learn more about the suppliers of a business and whether a business has good supplier relationships.

- Does the business have reliable sources of supply?
- Does the business help the suppliers innovate by providing them with customer feedback?
- Is the business dependent on only a few suppliers?
- Is the business dependent on commodity resources, and to what degree?

Does the Business Have Reliable Sources of Supply?

If a business does not have reliable sources of supply, then it will generate more volatile earnings. You need to determine how a business is creating reliable sources of supply and the risks to those sources.

One of Nestlé S.A.'s fastest-growing divisions is Nespresso, which has grown 30 percent annually since 2000. The Nespresso system combines single-use coffee capsules with an espresso machine, which makes the specialty coffee easy to prepare. The biggest problem Nestlé S.A. encountered was in obtaining reliable sources of specialized coffees because most coffees are grown by small farmers in impoverished rural areas. To ensure a steady source of supply from what was an unreliable source, Nestlé S.A. worked with these small farmers, providing them with tools and advice (e.g., on farming practices, helping them obtain pesticides and fertilizers) to help them create more successful crops. As the production quality from these small farmers improved, this increased the reliable supply of specialized coffee beans for Nestlé.[28]

Supply Chain Management

Supply chain management is the process of matching demand for products with supply. This includes determining the amount of inventory to carry, handling product returns, and distributing products. If you are evaluating a business, such as a fashion or online retailer (e.g., Amazon.com), it is imperative that you learn how it manages its supply chain. You need to determine if the sources of supply are stable and if the quality is consistent. For example, in the late 2000s, there have been several prominent toy recalls related to the safety and quality of supplier products.

Ideally, you want to know how quickly a supply chain can adapt to changing business conditions. For example, what if a supplier runs out of product? What does the business do? You can often find articles written about the supply chain of a business or interviews written about supply chain managers in trade journals. For example, here are a few trade publications for operations and logistics management professionals:

- *DC Velocity*
- *Commercial Carrier Journal*
- *Supply & Demand Chain Executive*
- *Supply Chain Digest*
- *World Trade Logistics Journal*
- *Logistics Today*
- *Supply Chain Management Review*
- *Logistics Management*

There are many articles in these publications that have been written about Li & Fung, Toyota, Starbucks, Nike, and Wal-Mart— all of which have strong supply chains.

As you study a business's supply chain, consider how efficient it is. One way to do this is to calculate inventory turnover, which measures the number of times inventory is sold in a year. To calculate it, take cost of goods sold and divide it by average inventory for the year.

For example, from 1995 to 2010, Wal-Mart improved its inventory turns from 5.23 times to eight times. This meant it was able to turn its inventory over faster.[29] In contrast, the inventory turns for its competitor Sears Holdings went from 3.2 times in 1995 to 2.9 times in 2010,* indicating deterioration in their inventory-turnover and supply chain capabilities.

Does the Business Help the Suppliers Innovate by Providing Them with Customer Feedback?

In the 1990s, General Motors' warranty costs were higher than its profits. One of the reasons for this is that GM was more concerned with driving down its costs than with seeking improvements from its suppliers. In contrast, Chrysler provided customer feedback to its suppliers to help them develop new features that required fewer repairs and less frequent replacement. By seeking new innovations through its supply chain, Chrysler was able to take market share from GM.[30] You can find such information simply by searching for articles that are written about supplier relationships by combining search terms such as "supplier" and "[the company in which you are interested]."

Is the Business Dependent on Only a Few Suppliers?

You need to determine the potential risks for a business if it depends on only a few suppliers. If a supplier represents more than 10 percent of net sales for a business, that company will often disclose this risk in the 10-K.

For example, the 2010 PetSmart 10-K discloses that sales from its two largest vendors approximated 22.4 percent of net sales

---

*Note that in 2004, Sears merged with K-Mart; therefore, later years include K-Mart results.

for 2009. You would need to monitor these two vendors to learn whether they are vulnerable to supply disruptions. Read historical articles to learn more about these two vendors, and monitor articles written about these businesses to learn if they are having any difficulties. For example, one vendor sources most of its raw materials from China, so you would need to understand if there is a risk that it will not be able to obtain these materials. This will alert you to the potential risk that the sales of PetSmart may drop if it is having difficulty obtaining inventory.

Is the Business Dependent on Commodity Resources, and to What Degree?

If a business depends on certain commodities to manufacture its products, monitor those commodity prices. This will help you to understand whether rising commodity prices may force the business to increase prices, which can decrease profits if a business is not able to pass along price increases to customers. On the other hand, if the cost of supplies decreases, a business can either earn a higher profit margin or decrease prices to increase sales.

You need to follow the price of the underlying commodity closely so you can determine whether earnings will increase or decrease. For example, if you are analyzing apparel makers, then you must monitor cotton prices to understand if the costs will increase. If the apparel maker is not able to pass on these higher costs to its customers, then it will result in lower profits.

Those businesses that are highly dependent on commodity resources—such as oil, steel, or chemicals—are difficult to forecast because you must assume a certain price for the commodity in the future. This increases the risk that you will be wrong in your valuation of the business. You are essentially betting on one direction of the price of the commodity for your investment to work out. Some businesses will hedge their exposure to a commodity price, which can give you greater visibility, but often these hedges are short term.

For example, Southwest Airlines CEO Gary Kelly talked about how much commodity prices affected the airline industry saying, "Volatility in fuel prices is the industry's No. 1 challenge. All you have to do is look back at the last decade to see what kind of havoc it wreaks on our industry. It is the single biggest threat to aviation." When oil prices increased to $145 a barrel, airlines were forced to ground hundreds of planes, drop routes, and cut thousands of jobs.[31]

Key Points to Keep in Mind

Evaluate the Business's Competitive Advantages

- The more sustainable the competitive advantage, the more a business is worth because it can protect its profitability over a longer period of time.
- Competitive advantages add the most value to a business that has lots of reinvestment opportunities within that advantage.
- Competitive advantages expire. Even when a business appears most formidable and generates the strongest financial metrics, it can be on the verge of failure.
- Competitive advantages are less sustainable when they are affected by changes in technology or if they are in rapidly emerging industries. Changes in technology threaten a competitive advantage when they expand customer choice, whether by offering the same product for less or by offering greater benefits for the same price or less.
- The greatest gains in a stock are usually made as a business is *developing* its competitive advantage rather than after it already has developed one.
- Do not confuse a competitive strength or a business that is successful because it is in the right place at the right time with having a competitive advantage.

Assess the Business's Pricing Power

- Businesses that have pricing power typically have several characteristics in common such as high customer-retention rates; their customers spend a small percentage of their budget on the business's product or service; the customers generate high margins and lots of cash flow; or the quality of the product is more important to the customer than the price.
- One of the best methods for determining whether a business has pricing power is to monitor the reasons for increases or decreases in the gross margin.
- If the business does not disclose price increases, then it is highly probable the business does not have pricing power.
- Price increases add value to the business when they add to operating income, rather than just offsetting new expenses.

Consider the Health of the Industry as a Whole

- Investing in the right industry is important because a large part of your potential rate of return is often attributable to the industry you are invested in, as opposed to a specific company you are invested in.
- By making comparisons between the best and worst companies in an industry, you will identify the *reasons* why the industry is good or bad to be in.

(continued)

- The profitability of a business will eventually trend toward the mean of the industry as it is difficult for any business to outperform the industry for a long period of time.
- Understanding how an industry evolved will help you evaluate the business in the context of its competition, its operating environment, and various other forces that shape it.

Assess the Business's Competition
- Competition does not increase the value of a business. Generally, more competition means more customer choice and less profitability.
- In growing industries, competition is generally less fierce. When industry growth begins to slow, competitors fight for market share and, in some instances, will change the way they compete.
- If customer-acquisition costs are increasing then a business is facing more competition.
- A business is not threatened by foreign competition if its products cannot be shipped long distances, but if labor is a large component of the product cost, then the business will face threats from foreign competition.

Evaluate the Business's Relationship with Its Suppliers
- Good supplier relationships facilitate the flow of goods. If a business does not have reliable sources of supply, then it will generate more volatile earnings.
- If the inventory-turnover ratio is increasing over time, then this is an indicator that the business's supply chain is becoming more efficient.
- A business with a diversified supplier network has less risk than one dependent on only a few suppliers.
- Those businesses that are highly dependent on commodity resources—such as oil, steel, or chemicals—are difficult to forecast because you must assume a certain price for the commodity in the future.

5

Measuring the Operating and Financial Health of the Business

After you've assessed the environment, industry, and competitive framework (covered in Chapter 4) that a business is operating in, you want to focus on evaluating the company itself. Essentially, you want to understand whether the company is operationally and financially healthy. This chapter starts by showing you how to review a company's fundamentals and then how to measure its basic performance, using operating metrics. Operating metrics indicate improvement or deterioration of the business and allow you to compare the company to other companies. We'll look at detailed examples from a couple of industries and then walk through the process of figuring out which operating metrics matter most, and how to find, track, and analyze them.

As we move beyond basic operational performance, this chapter will explore the other factors that affect business function and health. As we look at risk, inflation, balance sheet issues, and debt, I'll focus on giving you tools to identify and evaluate the problems that are specific to the business you are considering investing in. For example, as we look at inflation, I'll show you characteristics of businesses that have less to worry about when inflation rises.

Finally, we will look at a general measure of business quality by seeing how well the business generates a return on the money invested in it (ROIC). I'll show you what ROIC is, how to calculate it, and where it matters most. Each of the sections in this chapter is designed to enhance your ability to recognize opportunities and avoid investment errors as you study individual companies.

☐ 21. What are the fundamentals of the business?

Fundamentals are the basic things a business must do in order to be successful: for example, an express delivery company has to deliver things on time; restaurants have to serve good food. Think of these as the blocking and tackling functions of the business.

Fundamentals also drive the value of the business. Said another way, the better a company executes its most important basic operations, the more valuable it is. For example, at a for-profit university, it is the quality of the academic faculty that creates employable students. In turn, employable students create demand for the for-profit university's services, which increases the overall value of the for-profit university. Here's another example: High employee productivity helps Southwest Airlines succeed, because that's how it keeps fares low, which increases the value of the airline.

Determine whether the management team understands what increases the value of the business and whether that shapes their actions. If management deviates from these, then it is likely that profits will decline. For example:

- Jeff Bezos, founder of online retailer Amazon.com, focuses on continually enhancing the customer experience by delivering orders in a timely manner and offering more products in order to enlarge the competitive advantage.
- Larry Page and Sergey Brin, founders of Internet search business Google, focus on "organizing the world's information and making it accessible."
- Christina Gold, former CEO of Western Union, focused on tying up the most desirable agents in the world in long-term contracts and then driving traffic to them. Agents are supermarkets, banks, or retail chains that offer Western Union's services.
- Robert Silberman, CEO of Strayer Education, focuses on academic quality, which drives good student outcomes.
- Michael Bloomberg, founder of Bloomberg, focused on giving his company's customers "the information they need—no matter what the information is—where and when they need it, in whatever form is most appropriate."

In each of these cases, there are specific outcomes you can identify and evaluate to understand if the company is successfully executing its fundamental operations. You can measure and track each of these: food quality or customer satisfaction, rate of on-time deliveries, employee productivity, graduate employment, or faculty quality. If a fundamental is deteriorating, then the value of the business will as well. If a fundamental is steady or improving, you can have more confidence in the business's underlying value.

Watch for those managers who chase too many ideas or have continually changing vision statements. This can distract them from focusing on fundamentals. Before company founder Howard Schultz returned to Starbucks in 2008, the company pursued too many new ideas that were not central to their success. From March 31, 2005, until the time Shultz returned, Starbuck's stock price declined from $26 per share to $19.86 per share.[1] When Schultz returned as CEO, he refocused the company on the most important projects, canceling the ones that were less relevant to the core business. Schultz took out sandwiches that interfered with the aroma of coffee, and pulled the plug on products like Mazagran, a soft drink the company made with Pepsi. He also took out some of the in-store products such as books and CDs.[2] Starbucks returned its focus to providing quality products in an inviting atmosphere, with exceptional customer service. The stock price increased from $19.86 per share when Schultz took over on January 8, 2008, to $32.48 per share on January 4, 2011.[3]

As an investor, identifying and tracking fundamentals puts you in position to more quickly evaluate a business. If you already understand the most critical measures of a company's operational health, you will be better equipped to evaluate unexpected changes in the business or the outside environment. Such changes often present buying opportunities if they affect the price investors are willing to pay for a business without affecting the fundamentals of the business. Being able to recognize deteriorating fundamentals is equally beneficial, as you can avoid investment mistakes. If a negative news announcement causes the stock price of one of your holdings to drop, always ask, "What impact does the announcement have on the fundamentals of the business?"

For example, in the past, I invested in money-management firm W.P. Stewart. The fundamentals of a money-management firm include acquiring and retaining accounts. Certain accounts, called *sticky* accounts, have more of a long-term relationship with a money manager and tend to stick with the firm even when the firm's funds are underperforming. Therefore, every time I listened to W.P. Stewart's conference calls or monitored news releases, I watched for any information that might indicate that their accounts were no longer sticky. On one conference call, W.P. Stewart's managers indicated that a large percentage of their accounts had shifted to consultant-related accounts. With these accounts, an intermediary determines whether to continue to invest in a money-management firm. These accounts are less sticky. I evaluated this deteriorating fundamental, and sold the stock. The stock dropped 80 percent over the next few quarters as the consultant-related accounts withdrew assets at an even faster pace. By recognizing which fundamentals were crucial to the value of the business and by closely monitoring them, I was able to avoid an investment mistake.

☐   22. What are the operating metrics of the business that you need to monitor?

The best way to monitor whether the fundamentals of a business are improving or deteriorating is to measure and evaluate the operating metrics of a business. Operating metrics are measures that help you gauge the true performance of the underlying business, similar to taking your blood pressure to monitor your own personal health. You can begin to use these metrics to learn about the business, and then as you gain in-depth knowledge, you can use them to continually monitor the health of that business, which will alert you to potential problems. You need to do the following:

- Identify the metrics for a particular industry.
- Research the sources of metrics.
- Monitor the metrics over time.
- Determine if changes in metrics are lasting or temporary.
- Compare the metrics of the business you are analyzing to those of competitors and identify the reasons for the differences.

The next sections cover each of these topics in depth.

Identify the Metrics for a Particular Industry

To determine which operating metrics are useful, first identify what you are trying to measure. The type of metric you use will depend on the industry or business you are analyzing. Below are a few of the most commonly used operating metrics in several industries:

- *Banks* use efficiency ratio, return on assets, and average cost of funds.
- *Real estate* uses occupancy rate, rent per square foot, and cost per square foot.
- *Airlines* use available seat miles, load factor, traffic, and capacity.
- *Retailers* use same-store sales, basket size, sales per square foot, and average ticket.
- *Internet firms* use conversion rate and traffic counts.
- *Subscription-type firms* use number of subscribers, average revenue per subscriber, average cost per subscriber, and customer churn.
- *Credit card firms* use net charge-offs, delinquencies, and payment rates.
- *Hotels* use occupancy, revenue per available room (RevPAR), and average daily rate (ADR).
- *Gaming businesses* use slot-win percentage, table-win percentage, and average daily win per table per day (WPT).

Following are more detailed examples of two of the metrics listed that you can use as models for examining metrics in many industries. Let's examine each to understand what the metric tells you, how it is calculated, and what its limitations are.

Efficiency Ratio (Used by Banks)   The efficiency ratio is defined as the ratio of noninterest expense to total revenues. It is used to indicate a bank's ability to control its expense levels. The lower the efficiency ratio, the better a bank is at controlling its expenses. Smaller banks tend to have higher efficiency ratios compared to larger banks, because larger banks can spread their expenses over more products, and larger banks tend to generate higher earnings from fees.

Monitoring this key banking ratio over an extended period can help you understand the industry in greater depth. In the early 1990s, for example, a ratio of 60 percent was considered a good target for banks. By the late 1990s, the most efficient banks had ratios in the low to mid 50 percent range.[4] The efficiency ratio reflects a fundamental industry change (increase in size and increase in fees) as banks continued to consolidate through the 1990s.

Same-Store Sales (Used in Retail)   If you are analyzing a retail business, same-store sales is one of the metrics you would look at to gauge the health of a retailer. Same-store sales are defined as the year-over-year sales changes for a store that has been open at least 12 to 18 months. It helps you understand if stores are maintaining their existing level of sales or if store sales are declining. If competitor sales are good, but the retailer you are studying has declining same-store sales, the retailer you are analyzing is losing market share.

Research the Sources of Metrics

Operating metrics are obtained from a variety of sources, including the Management, Discussion, and Analysis (MD&A) section found in the 10-K or 10-Q; industry primers and guides published for investors analyzing a certain industry; trade associations; company press releases; and articles written about the business. Let's look at each of these sources in a bit more detail.

10-K and 10-Q Reports   The 10-K and 10-Q reports are a great starting point for identifying the key operating metrics of a business. In the business description section, look for the following information:

- Number of transactions
- Number of customers
- Number of locations
- Number of employees
- Total square footage of operating locations

You can then take these operating numbers (such as the number of transactions) and divide by revenues and costs to calculate metrics such as these:

- Revenue per transaction
- Cost per transaction
- Transactions per location

Industry Primers   Useful sources for identifying the operating metrics typically used for an industry are industry primers, such as these:

- Reuters Operating Metrics
- Standard & Poor's Industry Surveys
- Fisher Investments guides

These are guides written for analysts who are researching specific industries. They are useful because they explain historical trends in operating metrics, and provide detail and additional information that helps you understand *why* a change in a metric took place.

Suppose you were researching telephone wireless carriers: Standard & Poor's *Industry Survey* explains that one of the most important operating metrics for these businesses is average revenue per user (ARPU).[5] The report goes on to describe historical changes in ARPU. For example, in an atmosphere of heavy competition for new customers, providers offered price cuts during the period from 1987 to 1998. This made ARPU decline. The report also explains why ARPU rose after that, citing data from the trade group CTIA—The Wireless Association. This data showed average local monthly bills rising from $39.88 in June 1998 to $49.57 in June 2009. The increase was driven by higher usage and data-related services. The report further notes that although rates went up after 1998, they've been flat since 2003, mainly because voice use decline has been offset by the increase in data use.

Internet Search and Books   A simple Internet search, using terms such as "industry metrics for [insert name of industry]" will help you begin to identify useful metrics. You can also search for metrics in accounting textbooks and other books written about an industry.

Trade Associations   Many trade associations and trade journals publish periodic statistics in the form of ratios. Often, the members of the trade association will send in confidential financial and operating reports to the trade association, which then compiles them in an industry study.

For example, the National American Retail Hardware Association published a 2007 report called the "*Cost of Doing Business Study,*" which outlines the average profit and the highest profit of hardware stores, home centers, and lumber/building material outlets. These types of surveys are useful when you are making comparisons because you can benchmark the business you are evaluating to the industry and also against the most profitable competitor. Many times, these reports will outline the reasons why a certain business within an industry has greater profitability.

Monitor Metrics over Time

Monitor metrics over an extended period of time, rather than drawing conclusions from a single year. Construct a simple spreadsheet to calculate operating metrics on a quarterly or annual basis so you can better understand trends. Then identify the reasons for changes in these metrics period by period by reading the MD&A section found in the 10-Q or 10-K reports.

For example, in the 2009 10-K report for restaurant business Cheesecake Factory, management describes why comparable sales decreased 2.3 percent from the prior fiscal year 2008:

> We realized effective menu price increases of approximately 1.2 percent and 0.8 percent in the first and third quarters of 2009, respectively. The decrease in comparable sales for fiscal 2009 was due to reduced traffic at our restaurants, which we believe was primarily driven by the macroeconomic factors affecting the restaurant industry in general.

Write down all of the reasons for the changes in a particular operating metric for at least a three- to five-year period. By studying the reasons behind the changes in the operating metrics, you will gain deeper insight into what factors have the greatest impact on the value of a business.

For example, if sales drop, identify *why* they are dropping, instead of focusing on *how much* they dropped. When you identify which factors have the most impact on a business, those are the operating metrics you want to track most closely. Suppose the changes in the cost of a particular raw material greatly affect costs, then you need to track a relevant metric for it, such as cost per ton.

Determine if Changes in Metrics Are Lasting or Temporary

Ultimately, you want to determine whether the changes in the metrics are lasting or temporary. For example, the most common reason for gains in same-store sales are increased customer traffic and higher pricing. If you discover a decrease in customer traffic, evaluate if this decrease is temporary or lasting. For example, extreme weather conditions generally cause a change in retail traffic. This is a temporary, rather than permanent, effect. In contrast, increased competition may be long lasting.

Comparing Metrics among Competitors

You need to determine the reason for the differences in metrics among competitors. When comparing operating metrics of one business to its competitors, make sure both businesses are using the same measurement and accounting standards. For example, when comparing same-store sales growth of two retailers, make sure the same time periods are used, such as 15 months versus 12 months.

If you are comparing two oil-exploration businesses, and they both use a metric such as finding costs per barrel of oil, make sure the accounting standards are the same. (*Finding costs* reflect the expenses of searching for new oil and gas reserves.) There are two very different methods for calculating finding costs under Generally Accepted Accounting Principles (GAAP). Check the footnotes of the 10-K to make sure the accounting methods used to calculate the metrics are comparable and adjust them if they are not.

☐ 23. What are the key risks the business faces?

Businesses face different types, frequencies, and levels of risk. As an investor, you need to evaluate how these risks may affect the business. The first place to start is the 10-K, in a section titled Risk Factors, where management discloses most of the known risks to the operations of the business. The risk factors section is broken up into two parts:

1. The first part highlights risks that relate to the *business or industry.*
2. The second part highlights risks that relate to the *stock price.*

The first set of risks is more useful because it outlines what can go wrong with the operations of the business, whereas the second set of risks tends to be standard legal language found in all 10-Ks: for example, "the stock price may fluctuate."

Most investors read through this section fairly quickly and do not take the time to understand the potential risks of the business. However, it is important for you to spend some time in this section and investigate whether the business has encountered the risks listed in the past and what the consequences were. This will help you understand how much impact each risk may have.

You may also want to review the risks section in the 10-K of direct competitors and look for risks that the business may not have covered. Trade associations will often outline common risks, and many articles are written on how to reduce them. This will help you build a comprehensive collection of risks the business may encounter.

Write down the operational risks you find in the 10-K or other sources in a report; these operational risks might include:

- Overcapacity
- Commoditization
- Deregulation
- Increased power among suppliers
- Shifts in technology
- Changes in laws and regulations
- Product obsolescence
- Patent expirations
- Development of new product lines where the business has limited expertise
- The emergence of competitors
- Brand erosion
- Overreliance on too few customers
- Limited geographic distribution
- Research and development failure
- Business-development failure
- Merger or acquisition failure
- A weak product pipeline
- And others

Spend time carefully reviewing each of these risks. As you learn about the different risks a business may encounter, use this information to construct downside scenarios for your valuation of the business. This helps you better understand the threats to the *value* of the business. Identify those risks that have the greatest impact on the value of the business.

For example, if five customers make up 70 percent of the revenues of the business, and if one customer who represents 20 percent of sales were to leave, what impact would this have on the financials of the business? If you discover that losing the customer might send the business into bankruptcy because the business has a high debt load, then you might want to avoid investing in that business.

You will learn that the majority of the risks the business will encounter are outlined in the risk factors section of the 10-K and the reasons a business will fail are also disclosed. For example, those investors who carefully read the risks section in global financial-services firm Lehman Brothers' 10-K avoided investing in the company's stock because they saw that those risks were being magnified as the financial crisis began to unfold. Some investors even made money by selling the stock short. The short sellers saw events transpiring such as counterparties refusing to trade with Lehman, which increased their conviction that Lehman could fail. The reasons that Lehman failed are disclosed below, which were also disclosed in the 10-K:

1. The company's capital position was severely weakened by excessive trading losses
2. Counterparties stopped dealing with Lehman as they remained defensive and shifted their activities to more stable competitors
3. Lehman's reputation was in trouble
4. Short-term secured creditors did not have any reason to continue to renew their loans to Lehman
5. Lehman was unable to sell complex instruments because they were difficult to value

By carefully studying the risks section, you will be in a better position to evaluate the downside in any potential investment and learn more about the potential impact of risks on the earnings of the business.

As you read articles about the business, look for examples where the business or its competitors have encountered a particular risk before. Learn what happened and what the financial implications were.

For example, when my firm invested in bond ratings firm Moody's at less than $20 per share, the stock price had just dropped from more than $30 per share because investors were worried about the many lawsuits that were being filed against Moody's. Most of these lawsuits were from state attorney general offices and institutional investors who claimed that Moody's caused them to lose money because they relied on their ratings to buy bonds. Many of these bonds that defaulted were rated AAA, which was Moody's highest rating. There were many newspaper articles written about these lawsuits, and every time the newspapers announced that a new lawsuit had been filed, the stock price dropped.

However, my firm was not as concerned as other investors, because there were many past examples of similar lawsuits filed against Moody's. In fact, some of the lawsuits even used the same legal language that was used in previous suits. In one such case, institutional investors unsuccessfully sued Moody's to recover money they lost investing in the municipal debt of Orange County, at that time the largest municipal bankruptcy in U.S. history. We used this evidence of past legal precedent to support our investment thesis that the threat from the lawsuits filed against Moody's was weaker than investors perceived.

When Evaluating Operational Risks, Adopt the Mentality of an Insurance Underwriter

When thinking through risks, adopt an insurance underwriter's mentality instead of relying on subjective measures. If you allow subjective measures to permeate your thinking, then such factors as prevalence in the news might lead you to believe that a risk is greater than another. Most of us are afraid of risks that are *new* rather than those we've lived with for awhile.

For example, when terrorists attacked the World Trade Center on September 11, the relative newness of domestic terrorism decreased the prices of many stocks. Investors believed that there would be many more terrorist attacks and that this was a risk that most businesses now faced. Thankfully, there were not any other major acts of terrorism that resulted in lost lives or damaged properties. Just because an event has occurred and the media constantly discusses it does not mean that the actual risk is greater. Therefore, how much people discuss something is a bad indicator of actual risk. In fact, the more people talk about a risk, the more likely that risk will be mitigated.

In contrast to popular thinking about risk, insurance underwriters think in terms of *frequency* (i.e., how often in the past has the risk happened?) and *severity* (i.e., what is the financial cost?). Therefore, when you are identifying operational risks, you should identify whether they are low, medium, or high for frequency and severity.

One valuable source to help you identify the frequency and severity of potential risks is insurance manuals written for insurance underwriters, such as *A.M. Best's Underwriting Guide*. The job of insurance underwriters is to identify all of the risks in a business so that they can properly price insurance coverage. This guide provides detailed descriptions and underwriter's checklists of all the key risks involved in running nearly 580 commercial and industrial classifications—from advertising agencies to beverage distributors, clothing manufacturers, e-tailers, furniture stores, crushed-stone-mining companies, money-lending businesses, wireless phone carriers, and hundreds of other types of businesses. The list of risks is thorough, and the main risks a business encounters are highlighted.

How Do You Measure Risk?

Risk does not just include the probability that something may happen; in addition, you have to consider how severe the outcome might be. The more severe the outcome, the higher the risk. For example, the threat of bankruptcy is much more severe than the threat of having to pay a fine for violating a law.

It is very difficult to measure risk because you never know what will happen for sure ahead of time. More than one outcome can occur.

To help you understand the potential financial implications of a certain risk, look for past evidence. Use appropriate historical data, instead of making subjective estimates. Look to other businesses that have encountered a similar risk. For example, in Chapter 1, we looked at Heartland Payment Systems, the credit-card transactions company that had a security breach. A hacker was able to obtain the credit card information of several merchants, and Heartland was responsible for paying the cost of replacing these stolen credit cards. A similar case had settled recently involving retailers TJ Maxx and Marshalls, whose computer systems were also hacked. These retailers settled with the issuing banks to replace the stolen cards for about 70 cents per card. Using this information as a reference point, you could make a better estimate of the potential cost of settling. If you do not have data on what the impact will be, then you might think about reducing the size of the investment or selling it.

Let's take a look at another example, in this case, why investment manager François Rochon did not invest in Canadian oil sands because he could not understand the potential financial implications of the risks involved.

Case Study: Investing in Canadian Oil Sands Deemed Too Risky

François Rochon, the founder of money manager Giverny Capital, outlined to his partners the risks of investing in businesses exploiting oil sands in Alberta, Canada, in his 2008 annual report. He explained why he felt these risks were too great for him because the business involved too many unknown variables:

> It is clear that oil sands in Alberta represent a source of fabulous wealth. The reserves are astronomical, and everything seems to be in place for a profitable exploitation. But this exploitation is not as simple as conventional fuel. There are extremely high capital requirements and a complex procedure to transform the oil sands into oil. To produce a barrel of petroleum from oil sands requires two to four water barrels, and the waste must be stored somewhere. This disposal of wastewater could become a major environmental problem. At the end of 2007, the American government passed the Energy Independence and Security Act. It stipulates that federal agencies cannot initial fuel procurement contracts anymore that are more polluting than conventional sources of oil. Experts estimate that emissions related to oil sands are approximately 20 percent to 25 percent higher than conventional petroleum sources. This political element is added to the increase of royalties ordered by the government of Alberta last fall. The growth prospects of this region are impressive, but there are numerous possible unexpected circumstances (including huge reliance on the price of crude oil). We are monitoring the major players of this industry, but for now, we just remain curious spectators.

If Rochon had past examples of the potential financial impact from these environmental liabilities or other data to support the oil sands investment thesis as safe from risk, he might have some basis on which to act. With no data, he decided to stay on the sidelines.

As you consider the risks as presented in the 10-K or other sources, think like an insurance underwriter, making sure that you understand both the risk's likelihood and potential financial cost. Learn more about these risks by reading articles and looking for examples where the business or competitors encountered a specific risk before. Attempt to understand the financial implications of these risks. Finally, base your evaluation on data and past examples, not noise. With limited or no data about a major potential risk, consider rejecting the investment.

☐ 24. How does inflation affect the business?

Inflation affects most businesses negatively. Most investors think about inflation as prices going up. It is not. It is *the value of money going down.* To evaluate the effect of inflation on your holdings or potential holdings, ask yourself if the business will be able to maintain its cash flows in real terms. In other words, in order to avoid inflation's value-destroying effects, cash flows must increase at the same rate as inflation. Inflation's biggest threat to the value of a business comes from the inability of a business to fully pass on cost increases to its customers without losing sales volume. If a business is unable to increase prices to offset the effects of inflation, then it will fail to maintain its cash flows in real terms. A business can offset the negative effects from inflation if it:

- Can pass on price increases to its customers (pricing power)
- Has the ability to reduce its costs
- Has low capital-expenditure requirements and minimal levels of debt on its balance sheet

Let's look at each of these factors in a bit more detail.

The Ability to Pass Along Price Increases

Price increases allow the business to offset the effects of inflation because the business can pass along the increase in costs. If the business can maintain sales volume, its cash flows will be maintained in real dollars.

The Ability to Reduce Costs

If a business can reduce its cost structure, it can offset the increased cost of labor and materials during an inflationary period. A business that has a high fixed-cost structure or one that needs to constantly reinvest capital in its assets (for example, a refinery) will have a difficult time decreasing costs to offset the negative effects of inflation. Those businesses with variable cost structures (for example, money-transfer business Western Union, where variable costs represent more than 75 percent of the business's total costs) can more easily adjust their costs.

Low Capital-Expenditure Requirements

For businesses with large capital expenditures, inflation increases the cost of replacing existing assets. For example, businesses that are growing, such as a retailer, may suffer from inflationary effects because the cost to build new stores increases. On the other hand, businesses that have invested capital at a lower cost might benefit in an inflationary environment as the value of older assets increases. For example, an investor who built a building 10 years ago in a growing area benefits when new buildings in the area are constructed at a higher cost. This causes the value of the older building to rise as rental rates increase in the area.

Long-Term Debt Maturities

The common view is that businesses with a lot of debt benefit from inflationary periods as the value of the debt declines. This is true if the business does not have to refinance its debt in the near term, because inflation generally causes borrowing to become more expensive, not less expensive. Lenders, in fact, avoid making long-term contracts and are more demanding on covenants during inflationary periods. Businesses that have long-term debt maturities or limited debt on their balance sheets are therefore in a better position, as they can avoid both increased interest expenses and more restrictive loan covenants.

Inflation Risks

There are various types of inflationary risks—such as increasing costs (including wage inflation) and rising interest rates—and you need to develop an understanding of how each of these inflation risks will affect each of your investment holdings. This will prepare you to make investment decisions in an inflationary environment. Let's take a closer look at each of these risks.

Wage Inflation   Businesses with a large number of employees, such as a grocery store, will be affected by wage inflation. Wage inflation can come from a variety of sources, such as an increase in the minimum-wage rate in a particular state, increases in the costs of benefit packages, or high employee-retention rates. Whatever the source, rising labor costs significantly reduce free-cash flow.

Rising Interest Rates   Most stocks are negatively affected by rising interest rates. In a rising interest-rate environment, the price-to-earnings ratios of stocks typically drop. This is why stocks have always tended to perform badly during periods when inflation is rising and corporate earnings are declining. Businesses that invest in real estate would be negatively affected, as capitalization rates in a rising interest rate scenario increase which would then decrease overall asset values. If a business has large amounts of variable debt (versus fixed-rate debt), then rising interest rates will also increase interest expense.

To evaluate the effects of inflation on potential or current holdings, determine how well the business will be able to maintain cash flows in real terms in scenarios where material costs, wages, or interest rates are rising.

❐ 25. Is the business's balance sheet strong or weak?

A strong or weak balance sheet may be the difference between your investment facing insolvency or simply a bump in the road. A strong balance sheet will provide management with the financial flexibility it needs to take advantage of opportunities during all economic periods. Your primary goal should be to figure out if the cash-flow stream the business generates is predictable enough to assure that debt payments, both on and off the balance sheet, can be made. You need a sufficient margin of safety to pay the debt over time should cash flows decline.

Let's start by looking at a business's motivation for taking on debt.

Identifying a Business's Motivation for Debt

It is often useful to determine the motivation behind a business's debt on the balance sheet. Did it take on debt to fund losses, make acquisitions, pay special dividends, or enter new product lines?

For example, during the credit boom in 2005 to 2007, many businesses were taken private by private-equity firms and subsequently taken public again. In order to recover more of their equity investments in these businesses they had just taken public, the private-equity firms forced the businesses to issue debt and pay large one-time dividends. Dominos Pizza, for example, issued a special one-time $13.50-per-share dividend to shareholders. CEO David Brandon could provide little justification for this action, stating only, "We believe this new capital structure is the appropriate corporate finance decision for our company." This and similar scenarios saddle many businesses with high amounts of debt. Management often attempts to justify its actions by stating that the balance sheet needs a better capital structure and needs leverage to maximize the value of the business. When you discover a business in this situation, realize that you are considering partnering with a management team and board that may have compromised the financial strength of the company.[6]

Considering the Advantages of Low Debt

There are several advantages to businesses with limited amounts of debt. Think of limited debt as, say, debt that can be paid back in less than three years out of existing cash flows. First, the business has less risk of entering bankruptcy, allowing you, as an investor, to sleep better at night. Second, a strong balance sheet allows the business to be opportunistic. Businesses that have strong balance sheets are often able to gain competitive ground, because they are able to invest in their business in ways that their leveraged competitors cannot. For example, during the credit downturn that began in 2008, those businesses that were beholden to the credit markets were scrambling for cash to pay off debt, while those in a stronger position were able to be opportunistic and buy back stock, make acquisitions, or grow.

Case Study of a Company that Uses Debt Conservatively: Brookfield Asset Management

Global asset manager Brookfield Asset Management is a great example of a firm that uses debt conservatively. Brookfield strives to finance its business on a conservative basis by financing its operations primarily using long-term, investment-grade, non-recourse debt. Most debt is secured by specific assets, which ensures that the weak performance of one asset or business unit will not hurt the rest of the company. To further protect itself, Brookfield will only borrow the amount that it would typically be able to pay back in one business cycle.

Brookfield also staggers the maturity of its debt repayments so that they don't all come due at the same time, thus decreasing refinancing risk. Brookfield will typically finance assets that generate predictable long-term cash flows with long-term fixed-rate debt, instead of variable-rate debt, in order to provide stability in cash flows and protect returns in the event of changes in interest rates. It also maintains access to a broad range of financing markets, such as equity and debt markets, so that it can facilitate access to capital throughout the business cycle. This way, it is not dependent on any particular segment of the capital markets to finance its operations.[7]

Determining How Much a Business Can Borrow

You need to determine how much a business can borrow. The capacity to borrow depends on several factors, such as profitability, stability, relative size, asset composition, and the industry position of a business. It also depends on external factors, such as credit-market conditions and trends. During difficult credit environments, banks and other financial institutions are less likely to lend money and typically impose more restrictions, such as lower debt-to-income ratios. During easy-credit environments, financial institutions have looser requirements, such as higher debt-to-income ratios, as they try to expand the pool of credit applicants.

The amount of total debt a business can put on its balance sheet depends on the amount and distribution of cash flows a business generates as well as the value of the assets securing the debt. The more stable the cash flows are for a business, the more debt it can take on.

For example, think about a utility business, where the cash flows are steady. This business can easily handle high amounts of debt on its balance sheet. By comparison, a business with a more cyclical cash flow pattern, such as a homebuilder, cannot handle high amounts of debt. This is because it will have a more difficult time paying back its debt when its cash flows contract with the business cycle.

Factoring in Off-Balance Sheet Debt

To calculate the total debt of a business, you must factor in any off-balance sheet debt obligations. Any time there is a contractual obligation that does not show up on the balance sheet, you are dealing with off-balance sheet debt. These include:

- Lease obligations
- Warranties
- Purchase contracts
- Unfunded pension liabilities
- Any other contractual obligations

These are typically disclosed in the footnotes to the financial statements under the section titled Commitment and Contingencies. Retailers, ship operators, airlines, and many other types of businesses have large contractual obligations that are off-balance sheet.

For example, many businesses rent buildings and equipment using long-term lease contracts. If these lease obligations are classified as *operating* leases rather than *capital* leases, they are not required to be reported on the balance sheet and are instead placed in the footnotes. However, these required rental payments are contractual obligations similar to debt. A good rule of thumb for estimating a business's total lease obligation (and a method that is often used by credit-rating agencies) is to multiply one year's rental expense by seven. Otherwise, you will have to discount the future rental payments to the present using a discount rate.

Another example of an off-balance sheet liability is when a utility is required to purchase a certain amount of coal per year at a fixed price per ton, or when there is a lawsuit that is pending and the business has estimated potential liabilities in the form of damages it will be required to pay in the future.

Using Ratios to Determine a Company's Ability to Pay Its Debts

There are two types of ratios you can use to find out how easily a company can pay its debts. One is coverage ratios, and the other is static ratios. Let's look at each individually.

Coverage Ratios   Coverage ratios measure the ability of a business to meet fixed obligations. A coverage ratio takes the income available for paying the total fixed obligations for a given year and divides that by the annual interest expense and fixed charges. There are various types of coverage ratios:

- Earnings before interest, taxes, depreciation and amortization (EBITDA) to interest expense
- Earnings before interest and taxes (EBIT) to interest expense
- Cash flow from operations to interest expense

For example, if a company generates $200 million in pre-tax income and pays $50 million in interest expense, then its interest coverage ratio is four times. This is the number of times a business can cover its interest expense out of pre-tax income. A more conservative calculation uses EBIT, which does not add back depreciation charges. Many times, depreciation charges equal the amount needed to maintain a business's assets, which is a real cost to the business. By not adding back depreciation, you are effectively accounting for those maintenance costs.

When calculating coverage ratios, it is preferable to use cash flow for the numerator because liabilities must be paid in cash. Earnings are a softer accounting measure and can be manipulated, so using cash flow provides a more consistent, dependable measure.

To interpret coverage ratios, you must consider the distribution and predictability of cash flows. You cannot use one coverage ratio, such as five times EBITDA to interest expense, for all businesses, and assume it is conservative. The more cyclical the cash flows, the higher the coverage you will need. Healthcare and pharmaceutical companies typically have a more narrow distribution of cash flows than, say, oil and gas companies. For example, a conservative coverage ratio for a healthcare company might be EBITDA/interest expense of eight times, but it might be 10 times for an oil and gas business.[8]

Static Ratios   The next most useful ratios are static ratios, which measure the ability of a business to repay its debt obligations at one point in time. These include:

- Current assets to current liabilities
- Debt to equity
- Debt to total assets

Using Rating Agencies

One simple and straightforward way to understand the degree of leverage on a business's balance sheet is to examine the ratings from firms such as Moody's, Standard & Poor's (S&P), and Fitch. You should not rely on these ratings, but you should instead use them as a starting point. These are publicly available, and they will help you to gain a quick insight into a business's balance sheet. Rating agencies focus on examining a debt-issuing company's assets, financial resources, earning power, management, and the specific provisions of the debt security.

Below are sample coverage and static ratios that Moody's uses to rate debt:

Table 5.1   EBITDA/Interest Expense Ratios

Company Rating	EBITDA/Interest Expense Ranges
Aaa to A	17× to 8.2×
Baa to B	5.1× to 1.5×
Caa to C	0.3×

Table 5.2   Debt to EBITDA Ratios

Company Rating	Debt to EBITDA Ratio
Aaa to A	0.9× to 1.7×
Baa to B	2.4× to 5×
Caa to C	6.3×

J. Tennant, "Moody's Financial Metrics Key Ratios by Rating and Industry for Global Non-Financial Corporations," *Moody's Special Comment*, December 2007.

The downside to using these ratios is that they only give you a snapshot of the business at a certain point in time. A business can change dramatically from quarter to quarter, so static ratios can be misleading when not analyzed over a longer time frame. For example, if you are analyzing a retailer, the ratios will fluctuate depending on the quarter. In the first and second quarters, the retailer is stocking up on inventory and may have greater debt, more assets, and generate less earnings. In the fourth quarter, the same retailer may have less debt and assets but generate higher earnings because of holiday sales.

Assessing the Short-Term Financial Strength of a Business

You want to get an understanding of how *liquid* the balance sheet is, which tells you the amount of time the business would normally require to convert assets into cash. This will help you assess the ability of a business to pay its short-term liabilities. Short-term liquidity is extremely important to lenders because it is the inability to pay short-term liabilities that causes most businesses to enter bankruptcy.

The assets on a balance sheet are organized in order of their liquidity. The current assets are things such as cash, accounts receivable, and inventories. Long-term assets include property, plant, and equipment.

To determine a business's short-term liquidity needs, evaluate how quickly the current assets on the balance sheet can be liquidated. First, start with cash.

Cash   Sometimes cash is not as liquid as you may think, so you will need to make adjustments. Many businesses earn their revenues in foreign jurisdictions and keep cash balances in the country where they earned the revenues, in order to avoid paying taxes in the United States. If such a business were to repatriate this cash to invest in the United States, then you would need to discount the cash for the taxes the business would have to pay. For example, in 2009, computer manufacturer Dell had the majority of its cash domiciled in foreign jurisdictions. If Dell wanted to use this cash to buy back its stock in the United States, it would have had to pay taxes in the United States at rates as high as 30 percent. Therefore, the cash balance needs to be adjusted for these potential taxes.

You may also need to make adjustments to the cash balance for the amount needed to fund operations. For example, children's retailer Build-A-Bear Workshop had $60 million of cash on its balance sheet as of the fourth quarter of 2009. However, by the end of the second quarter of 2010, Build-A-Bear's cash balance had declined to $31 million. This was due to Build-A-Bear's need to build inventory during this period in advance of the busier holiday season. An investor who assumed that $60 million in cash was available to pay short-term obligations would have been making a mistake, due to the fact that Build-A-Bear's cash balance fluctuates due to seasonal working-capital needs. Investors should normalize cash amounts to account for these patterns.

Accounts Receivable   Next, you need to understand the quality and liquidity of a company's accounts receivable. This is especially important for those businesses that sell on credit. You need to calculate receivables turnover in order to understand how quickly a business is able to collect on its accounts receivable. This is the time needed to translate receivables into cash. The receivables turnover is calculated by dividing net sales by average total accounts receivable. You can convert this to the number of days it takes to turn accounts receivable into cash by dividing the turnover figure by 365. For example, if it takes 120 days for a business to convert its receivables into cash, and it had only 30 days to pay down short-term debts, then a business might potentially face a short-term liquidity crunch. In other words, the bills are coming in before the money is there to pay them!

Inventory   Understanding how long it takes to convert inventory to cash will also help you understand how quickly a business can pay back its short-term liabilities. You can calculate this by dividing the cost of goods sold by average inventory. Convert this to the number of days it takes to turn inventory into cash by dividing this turnover figure by 365.

Inventory is an important asset and inventory turnover represents one of the main ways that a business generates revenue. A business needs to have sufficient inventory because if it runs out of products it will lose sales. Having too much inventory for long periods, however, is not good either. In addition to failing to produce revenue, a business would have to pay to store it, and it can go bad or become obsolete.

Assessing the Long-Term Liquidity Needs of a Business

Short-term liquidity is far easier to evaluate compared to long-term liquidity because it is easier to make a reasonable projection in the short run than the long run. If you are unable to make long-term projections (which is often the case with cyclical businesses), then you will more than likely be unable to understand the long-term financial strength of a business. As a result, the measures used to evaluate the long-term liquidity needs of a business are less specific. The liquidity will depend on whether the business has permanent equity capital or uses short-term funds, which are temporary and thus a more risky source of capital.

One business that uses permanent equity capital instead of short-term funds to finance its business is global asset manager Brookfield Asset Management. In 2010, Brookfield was funded by $30 billion of permanent equity capital. CEO Bruce Flatt explained why, "This is capital that does not come due, has no margin calls and whether it trades for less in the market due to external factors has very little effect on the capital base."[9] Over the years, Brookfield has been strengthening its permanent equity capital in order to strengthen its balance sheet. For example, in 2001 when Brookfield converted debentures, which are mid- to long-term debt, into common shares, this added permanent equity to Brookfield's capital base. It also strengthened the balance sheet and eliminated the interest cost and risk of these debentures.

Determining Whether the Debt Interest Rate Is Fixed or Variable

Determine if the interest rate on the debt is fixed or based on variable rates, such as LIBOR plus 5 percent (LIBOR is the London Interbank Offered Rate). You will find this information in the financial statement footnotes under the note titled Debt. If the interest rates are fixed, then you will be better able to assess the impact of debt financing. If interest rates are variable, you must allow for the possibility that interest rates may increase or decrease, adding uncertainty to your projections.

Determining the Debt-Maturity Schedule

Refinancing debt represents risk for a business. It is important for you to determine when debt is coming due. You can find the dates when debt is due in the notes to the financial statements under the Debt footnote. For example, a business may have issued debt when interest rates were low. If interest rates rose during that period, and the business intends to refinance the debt instead of pay it off, it will have to pay a higher interest rate which will decrease the earnings of the business.

Other constraints can also limit the availability of credit. Many businesses in 2008 were unable to refinance their debt because the credit markets dried up.

Evaluating Loan Covenants

To understand if a business is financially strained, evaluate its loan covenants and determine if the business is nearing the limits of the loan covenants set by its lenders. Loan covenants are the terms of the loan that the lender requires, and they serve to protect the lender. Loan covenants define default limits and legal remedies available, which give a lender an early start before bankruptcy so that the lender still has time to negotiate a solution. Most bond indentures and credit agreements restrict corporate actions that would impair liquidity in any way by setting minimum ratios that a business may not exceed. For example the covenant might state that the current ratio (which is current assets divided by current liabilities) cannot be below 1.1.

You can usually find information on loan covenants in the 10-K report or other financial filings. If the business is nearing the limits of its loan covenants, this is an indicator that it is financially strained. However, being in good shape with respect to loan covenants is no guarantee of solvency; management is sometimes able to stretch the definition of covenants to present a better financial picture than really exists.

Determining Whether the Business Has Recourse or Non-Recourse Debt

The most benign form of debt is *non-recourse debt*, which is debt that is secured by a particular asset and not by the overall business. In a non-recourse situation, if the business defaults on a loan backed by a certain property, then it has the right to turn over the property to the lender, without further losses, in exchange for the forgiveness of the loan.

For example, real estate firm Vornado Realty Trust (among the largest U.S. commercial landlords), was able to simply turn over its ownership of some very large properties when it was unwilling to continue to make debt payments on an unprofitable venture. It turned over its ownership of the second-largest furniture showroom owner and operator in the United States to the special servicer overseeing the mortgage. Vornado had $217.8 million in non-recourse debt associated with the purchases of many properties in North Carolina, such as the Market Square complex, where tens of thousands of buyers come to buy from home furnishings manufacturers and wholesalers. Vornado was able to walk away from the debt because it was non-recourse debt, or debt that is secured only by the individual property.[10]

☐ 26. What is the return on invested capital for the business?

Return on invested capital (ROIC) is the profit a business generates relative to the amount of money invested in the business. It shows you how well a business is using its assets. The more profit that comes out relative to the amount of investment required, the better the business. It is calculated by taking income and dividing by the investment used to generate that income. Here are two rules of thumb regarding ROIC:

1. A business with a ROIC below 5 percent is typically considered a *low-quality* business, unless it is developing a competitive advantage.
2. In contrast, a business that generates a ROIC in excess of 10 percent is a *high-quality* business.

The average ROIC varies from industry to industry and ranges from negative to more than 50 percent; here are some examples of high-end, mid-range, and low-end ROIC industries:

- At the high end, with ROIC typically greater than 20 percent, are industries such as software firms, soft drinks, pharmaceuticals, distilled spirits, luxury products, and medical instruments.
- Industries with ROIC of 10 to 20 percent include hotels, packaged foods, grocery stores, drug stores, and book publishing.
- On the low end, with ROIC from negative to 5 percent, are industries such as airlines.[11]

Why It's Important for You to Calculate ROIC

Suppose you are analyzing two different businesses. The first one earns $100,000 in net income from $10 million in sales, and the second earns $500,000 in net income from $5 million in sales. The first business generates a 1 percent net profit margin, while the second business generates a 10 percent net profit margin. At first glance, which one would you prefer to invest in? Based on this information alone, most investors would prefer the business that earns a higher net profit margin.

However, to better answer this question, you must take one more step. You need to determine what level of investment or assets were required to generate these earnings.

Let's say in the first business, it takes $1 million in capital to earn $100,000, and in the second business, it takes $10 million in capital to earn $500,000. The return on capital of the first business is 10 percent ($100,000/$1,000,000), while the second business is 5 percent ($500,000/$10,000,000). After considering ROIC, you can see that *the first business is a higher-quality business* because it requires less capital to generate the same level of profits.

The reason for this is that the higher the ROIC, the more a business is able to earn. Say you buy a business that has $100 in capital and it earns a 5 percent ROIC. What are the earnings of the business? $5 is the correct answer. Now say the business can earn an 80 percent ROIC. What are the earnings of this business? $80 is the correct answer. A business with a high ROIC will deliver more wealth to its shareholders over the long term from higher earnings. Ideally, you want to own a business that over an extended period of time can reinvest excess earnings at high ROIC.

For example, at oil and gas business EOG Resources, Inc., the ROIC has been 20 percent on average since 2000 under the stewardship of CEO Mark Papa. As a result, the book value per share increased from $4.12 per share on December 31, 1999, to $40 per share at December 31, 2009. This caused the stock price to increase from $7.75 per share at January 1, 2000, to $97.77 per share at December 31, 2009, a 1,161 percent increase, not including dividends that would further enhance returns. Furthermore, the stock price increase was not a result of EOG's stock simply being bid up under pricey market conditions; the price in this case was driven up by earnings, as EOG essentially maintained the same P/E multiple during this entire period.[12]

It is important for you to calculate ROIC because ultimately the value of a business is based on the returns a business is able to achieve on its invested capital. ROIC also turns out to be a fairly good predictor of stock return over the long haul. In other words, if you pay fair value for the stock and hold it five years, odds are that if ROIC is 5 percent, then your return will be similar.

You must place ROIC for a business in context with the price you pay for the stock, as the price you pay determines your rate of return. If you pay too high a price for a stock such as a high multiple of book value, then a high ROIC will not help you earn a satisfactory return on your investment. You must remember that ROIC calculations are the return earned by the business, instead of the return realized on your stock cost basis. Since your return is based on what you pay for the stock, make sure you can benefit from high ROIC by paying a low price for a stock.

Methods of Calculating ROIC

The basic method for calculating ROIC is to take income and divide by the investment used to generate that income. There are a number of different ways to calculate ROIC, and no one method is universally accepted. You can calculate ROIC with goodwill, without goodwill, using gross assets, or net assets. You need to adapt the calculation to the type of business you are analyzing. The pros and cons of each method are highlighted below.

The Basic Equation   Let's first start with the basic equation for ROIC:

Return on invested capital = earnings before interest and
taxes/invested capital

Invested capital =
total assets
− excess cash
+/− accumulated amortization and depreciation
+/− goodwill or other intangible assets
+ off-balance sheet items
− non-interest bearing current liabilities

Calculate the Numerator   First, isolate the earnings from the operations of the business by removing interest income, taxes, and interest expense:

- Remove *interest income* from cash balances because it is not generated by the core operations of the business.
- Exclude *taxes* because you need to isolate the effects of differences in tax rates, tax loss carry-forwards, or any other forms of tax management.
- Exclude *interest expense* to remove the effects of financing decisions, which vary across businesses and industries.

- Also consider subtracting non-recurring items, such as restructuring and impairment charges and amortization charges of intangibles from pre-tax earnings.

Calculate the Denominator Next, you need to determine which assets should be included, what liabilities should be deducted, and how the assets should be valued when determining the investment base. Ideally, you want to determine how much investment is needed to operate the business day to day. You will have to make several adjustments before calculating the investment base, such as removing excess cash, deciding whether to use gross or net assets, including or excluding goodwill, removing current liabilities, and including off-balance sheet assets and liabilities such as accounts receivable that have been securitized, pension liabilities, and capitalized operating leases.

Be sure to use average amounts for the investment base instead of relying on one specific quarter. For example, if you are evaluating a retail business and you use the end of first quarter numbers, these will be unusually low as the retailer typically has sold off most of its inventory. As a result, the ROIC figures you calculate would be unusually high and misleading.

Let's now review the pros and cons of adjusting each line item for the investment base:

Remove Excess Cash You need to remove excess cash that is not needed in the operation of the business so you can better understand the ROIC the core business is generating. Excess cash is any cash that is not needed to operate the day-to-day activities of the business.

For example, at discount retailer 99 Cent Only Stores, ROIC averaged 20 percent from 1995 to 1999, but then it began to drop as the cash balance increased. Many analysts were concerned about the drop and believed it was due to deteriorating business conditions, when in fact, it was dropping because of the excess cash on the balance sheet. By removing excess cash, you will understand the ROIC being generated by the operations of the business. This is often referred to as the return on operational capital. In the case of 99 Cent Only Stores, the ROIC excluding cash was much higher than the ROIC including cash, as shown in Table 5.3.

Table 5.3   99 Cent Only Stores Return on Invested Capital (ROIC)

99 Cent Only Stores	1995	1996	1997	1998	1999
ROIC with Cash	24.3%	21.9%	20.4%	19%	18.5%
ROIC excluding Cash	26.7%	43.4%	28.7%	28.6%	37.3%

Source: Time Value of Money, LP internal research and Standard & Poor's Capital IQ.

Include Property, Plant, and Equipment Costs   You must include the purchase of fixed assets necessary to operate the business, such as real estate, plant, and equipment. You need to determine whether to use the gross book value of these assets or the depreciated, net book value of these assets:

- *Gross book value* takes the historical or acquisition cost of assets without deducting accumulated depreciation or amortization.
- *Net book value* is the value if you remove accumulated depreciation. Because the net book value of an asset is less each year, this causes ROIC to increase each year. This results in a lower rate of return during the early stages of an investment and higher rates of return in later stages, as the asset base decreases.

Let's look at an example. If a business is depreciating its asset base and earning the same amount of income, then ROIC will naturally increase because the denominator is decreasing. Take an asset with a book value of $200,000 and assume that for the next five years, the business depreciates it by $30,000 each year. If the business generates $10,000 in earnings for the next five years, the ROIC would increase from 6 percent at the end of the first year ($10,000 divided by $200,000 minus $30,000) to 20 percent ($10,000 divided by $200,000 minus $150,000) by the end of the fifth year. Therefore, the same asset generates an increasing ROIC as it gets older. Table 5.4 is a chart showing these amounts (in thousands).

To counteract this effect, you might want to consider using gross assets by adding back accumulated depreciation. This way, the investment base is not affected by depreciation or write-downs of assets.

Most investors do end up using net book value. The argument for using net assets rather than gross assets is that depreciating

Table 5.4   Effect of Depreciation on ROIC

	Y0	Y1	Y2	Y3	Y4	Y5
Book Value Depreciation	$200	$170	$140	$110	$80	$50
Earnings	$10	$10	$10	$10	$10	$10
ROIC	5%	5.9%	7.1%	9.1%	12.5%	20%

assets are offset by maintenance and repair costs, which rise as equipment gets older, thus tending to offset the reduction, if any, in the asset base.

Include or Exclude Intangibles or Goodwill   When calculating the investment base, you may want to remove goodwill or other intangibles, which are not assets that the business must continue to replenish. By removing goodwill, you can more easily see improvements in tangible returns. On the other hand, realize that if you exclude goodwill from your calculations, it may mask the fact that management has overpaid for acquisitions, making the return on capital seem higher than it really is.

There are a few situations where it might be prudent to include goodwill or intangibles, such as when you are analyzing a media business that must buy television rights. These television rights are reflected on the balance sheet as intangibles but are a necessary investment for the business to operate.

Include Off-Balance-Sheet Liabilities   You should add off-balance sheet liabilities to the investment base when calculating ROIC because these are contractual obligations that are similar to debt. These liabilities include operating leases, underfunded pension plans, or securitized accounts receivable.

Operating Leases   An operating lease is the rent a business contractually owes, and it's not included on the balance sheet, whereas a capital lease is shown as an asset and liability on the balance sheet. You can find operating leases in the notes to the financial statements, and you can either discount the future operating lease obligations using a discount rate or multiply one year's rent by a multiplier rule of thumb, such as seven.

For example, at CVS Caremark, a pharmacy services company, the Notes section of the 2009 10-K summarizes significant contractual obligations. The total obligation for operating leases are $26.9 billion which is significantly higher than the long-term debt on the balance sheet which totals $8.8 billion at the end of 2009. Thus, off-balance sheet obligations represent a large percentage of total liabilities. If you use off-balance sheet items, such as converting operating leases to capitalized leases, make sure you make the proper adjustments to the numerator. For example, if you are adding off-balance sheet operating leases, you must add rent expense to the numerator (to income) so you avoid double counting.

Underfunded Pension Plans   An underfunded pension plan is a liability because the business must use its cash to make up for the funding shortfall. For example, at Raytheon, a defense technology business, the funded status of the pension plan for 2009, which is shown under the heading of "Net amount recognized on the balance sheets" was a deficit of $4.6 billion. You must include this deficit when calculating the total contractual obligations of a business.

Accounts Receivable   Accounts receivable that are removed from the balance sheet when they are securitized and sold to other investors at a discount should also be added back.

Remove Non-Interest-Bearing Current Liabilities   Remove short-term liabilities, such as accounts payable, compensation and benefits, other accrued items, advance payments, unearned income, and noncurrent deferred income taxes from the investment base. A payable is effectively an interest-free loan where the business does not have to lay out any money and therefore should be removed from the investment base.

Evaluating a Company's Ability to Reinvest Excess Earnings

Avoid jumping to the conclusion that one business is better than another business just because it has a higher ROIC. What counts is the ability of a business to reinvest its excess earnings at a high ROIC, which is what creates future value. You need to determine the percentage of excess cash flows that the business can reinvest and whether the ROIC on new investments will be the same.

For example, lubricant manufacturer WD-40 generates a high amount of free-cash flows, which it is unable to reinvest in the business. The reason it can't reinvest very much capital back into the business is because WD-40 does not have many growth opportunities. Therefore, the company pays out the majority of its free-cash flows as a dividend. If it were able to instead reinvest these excess free-cash flows at its ROIC of 15 percent, then the value of the business would increase significantly due to the effects of compounding.

Contrast this to global asset manager Brookfield Asset Management, which is able to reinvest the majority of its excess cash flows back into its business, at ROIC of 10 to 15 percent. This allows Brookfield Asset Management to create more value.

How to Improve ROIC

To better understand ROIC, it is necessary for you to understand how a business can improve its ROIC. ROIC can be improved by:

1. Using capital more efficiently, such as managing inventory better or managing receivables better, or
2. Increasing profit margins, instead of through one-time, non-operating boosts to cash earnings.

A supermarket chain is content earning a low net profit margin, typically 1 percent, because it turns over its inventory very quickly. It has a relatively low investment in assets because most of its assets are leased. On the other hand, a capital-intensive business such as a steel manufacturer has a heavy investment in assets. This heavy investment contributes to lower asset-turnover rates. The steel manufacturer must achieve a high net profit margin in order to offer investors a reasonable return on capital. In another example, Goodyear also has a low asset turnover rate. Although its net profit margins are comparable with Whirlpool (both a bit over 5 percent), Goodyear's ROIC is much lower than Whirlpool's, mainly because it has lower asset turnover. The ROIC at Whirlpool is 17 percent whereas the ROIC at Goodyear is 9.6 percent. Here are some other examples:

- A business can be more productive with its long-term fixed assets. If a business can generate more sales for each dollar of property, plant, and equipment it owns then it will be able to generate a higher ROIC. For example, a restaurant that wants to increase its ROIC might think about opening for lunch as well as dinner. This allows the restaurant to generate more sales per dollar invested in restaurant assets.

- A business can use online sales channels to improve efficiencies in inventory and sales costs, while also reaching additional markets. Williams-Sonoma (an upscale housewares and furniture retailer) began as a catalog retailer. By 2010, e-commerce represented 77 percent of direct-to-consumer revenues and was significantly more profitable than either retail stores or catalog sales. Relative to the retail and catalog business, the e-commerce site for Williams-Sonoma has a lower fixed-asset base, higher inventory turns, and a higher operating income margin which causes it to earn a higher ROIC.[13]

- A business can improve its ROIC through higher inventory turns (cost of goods sold/average inventory) because operating with higher inventory turns requires less capital to finance the business. The more inventory turns, the faster a business gets back the money it has spent on inventory. In effect, a business has its money invested in inventory for a shorter period of time.

- A business can collect its accounts receivable from customers faster. For example, wine distributor Constellation Brands reported, "Last year, we really focused on receivables in the United States. We were actually able to bring the number of days that sales are outstanding (DSO) down by four days. That's worth about $9 million a day. We think that's a permanent improvement."[14] By collecting accounts more quickly, Constellation Brands has less capital invested overall, increasing its ROIC.

- A retailer can be more selective in the product lines it carries, focusing on those that sell quickly and removing those that sell slowly. Wal-Mart opened smaller stores in 2010, compared to the mid-1990s when it opened 200,000-square-foot stores. This change helped to minimize inventory levels, and reduce capital investment. Because the smaller stores were stocked with faster-selling items, rather than a wide assortment of items, the change also improved inventory turnover. This has helped Wal-Mart increase its ROIC.[15]

- A manufacturing firm can use lean manufacturing to cut the inventories it needs to stock, or it can make its suppliers responsible for stocking inventories.

When ROIC Is Less Useful

There are certain instances when calculating ROIC is less useful, such as when the investment base does not add to the earnings of a business. This is typically the case in knowledge-based businesses such as in money management, information services businesses, or other non-capital-intensive businesses.

For example, if mutual fund manager T. Rowe Price increases the number of desks and computers at its office, this investment will not add to the returns of the business. Therefore, calculating the ROIC of a firm like T. Rowe Price is less useful than calculating the ROIC of a firm that has a higher amount of invested capital, such as Praxair, a producer and distributor of industrial gases, which builds new manufacturing plants every year to meet the demands of its steel mill, glass furnace, or chemical plant customers.

Do Not Rely on Historical ROIC When Making Forecasts

One common mistake investors make is they rely too much on the historical ROIC and project it indefinitely into the future without considering that returns typically decline over time or that a business is limited in the amount of capital it can redeploy in the business. There have been very few businesses that are able to maintain high ROIC over a long period of time, and those that do often have limited growth prospects. When forecasting ROIC for a business make sure you are not extrapolating past returns without understanding how those returns were earned.

Some examples of things you need to look out for (adjustments you would need to make) before extrapolating future ROIC include the following:

- A business may have a new product that has limited competition that allows it to earn high ROIC in the early years. If competition enters the market, you may need to reduce your forecast of ROIC.
- A retailer may have saturated its growth in the best locations and is now beginning to locate new retail sites in secondary

locations, which may not generate the same returns as the older locations. In this case, you would reduce your forecast of future ROIC.

- Increased regulatory requirements may force a business to reinvest capital in the business that does not earn a return, such as when the Environmental Protection Agency (EPA) introduces new regulations. In 2002, the EPA required big rig trucks to emit fewer pollutants. The trucking industry estimated that the cost to meet the EPA requirements added $3,000 to $5,000 to the cost of an engine, which typically cost $15,000.[16] This will decrease the ROIC a trucking firm can earn.

Limitations of Making Comparisons

When you are making ROIC comparisons between businesses in the same industry, you often need to make several adjustments to make meaningful comparisons. For example, if you are comparing the ROIC of two refineries (one that is older compared to a newer one), the depreciated cost of the old refinery will generate a higher ROIC than the one with the new refinery. The newer refinery may be more efficient and operate at a lower cost, but you would have to adjust the asset value of the old refinery for inflation to make a meaningful comparison between the two firms.

Differences in accounting methods also complicate the ability to make comparisons. If you are comparing two firms within the same industry, you have to adjust the accounting statements of both businesses to make sure their accounting methods are consistent. For example, you would want to make sure both businesses are using the same inventory-accounting method, such as first-in-first-out (FIFO) inventory methods.

When comparing a faster-growing business to one that is not growing, you might find that the ROIC is higher for the business that is not growing. The reason is that in a faster-growing business, investments are more heavily weighted to the more recent investment projects (such as recent equipment purchases or new store openings), leading to higher book-value denominators, thus pulling down ROIC.

Businesses that constantly reinvest in their business to build an advantage—such as maintaining their property, plant, and equipment or investing in product development and marketing—will show lower ROIC than those that do not. This can have the unfortunate effect of producing lower ROIC in cases where managers are making prudent investment decisions and higher ROIC where managers have minimized crucial investments just to make short-term earnings look good.

Key Points to Keep in Mind

Assess the Business's Fundamentals
- Managers should understand and have a laser focus on what is creating value at the business. Watch out for managers with continually changing vision statements or managers who chase too many ideas.
- If a fundamental is deteriorating, then the value of the business will as well. If a fundamental is steady or improving, you can have more confidence in the business's underlying value.

Understand the Company's Operating Metrics
- Operating metrics will help you gauge the true performance of the underlying business. By monitoring them, they will alert you to potential problems at the business.

Identify the Key Risks Facing the Business
- When evaluating risks it helps to think like an insurance underwriter. Think in terms of *frequency* (i.e., how often in the past has the risk happened?) and *severity* (i.e., what is the financial cost?)
- With limited or no data about a major potential risk, consider rejecting the investment.

Understand How Inflation Affects the Business You're Evaluating
- Most investors think about inflation as simply prices increasing. That is not accurate. Inflation is the value of money *decreasing*.
- To avoid inflation's value-destroying effects, cash flows must increase at the same rate as inflation. To do this, a business must be able to pass on price increases to its customers, be able to reduce its costs, have low capital-expenditure requirements, or have long-term debt maturities.
- Most stocks are negatively affected by rising interest rates. In a rising interest-rate environment, the price-to-earnings ratios of stocks typically drop.

Pay Attention to a Business's Debt
- Businesses with limited amounts of debt, or those that can pay back total debt obligations in less than three years out of existing cash flows, make safer investments.

(continued)

- A strong balance sheet provides management with the financial flexibility it needs to take advantage of opportunities regardless of economic conditions.
- A business that finances its balance sheet conservatively uses long-term, fixed-rate, investment-grade, and non-recourse debt.
- The amount of total debt a business can put on its balance sheet depends on the amount and distribution of the cash flows a business generates as well as the value of the assets securing the debt. The more stable the cash flows are for a business, the more debt it can take on.

Evaluate a Business's Return on Invested Capital (ROIC)

- Ultimately the value of a business is based on the returns a business is able to achieve on its invested capital.
- A business with an ROIC greater than 10 percent is considered a *high-quality business*, whereas one with less than 5 percent ROIC is a *low-quality business*. The reason for this is that the higher the ROIC, the more a business is able to earn.
- What creates the most value is the ability of a business to reinvest its excess earnings in the business at a high ROIC.
- ROIC can be improved by utilizing capital more efficiently (such as managing inventory and receivables more efficiently) or by increasing profit margins.
- ROIC is less useful when the investment base does not add to the earnings of a business.
- There have been very few businesses that are able to maintain high ROIC over a long period of time, and those that do often have limited growth prospects.

CHAPTER 6

Evaluating the Distribution
of Earnings (Cash Flows)

The future is inherently unknowable. No one can say with certainty that a business will generate a given amount of earnings two or three years from now, but we can estimate with some certainty what the *range* of earnings might be. The range (or distribution) of future earnings of a particular business is a key factor in how much investors should be willing to pay to invest in that business. The wider the distribution of future earnings is for a business, the more difficult it is to value that business and therefore to know at what price the business represents an attractive investment. Businesses with recurring revenue streams or those selling consumer staples have a much narrower distribution of future earnings.

For example, at Procter & Gamble, the range of outcomes for the future earnings is very narrow: You will not see a 50 percent drop in the use of Tide detergent in one quarter. When the distribution of earnings is narrow, you can use single-point-estimate valuation methods, such as earnings yield, free cash-flow yield, and price-to-earnings ratios. In contrast, if the distribution of earnings is wide, as in a cyclical business, you need to use other valuation methods, such as scenario analysis.

This chapter explores various factors that will help you determine whether the distribution of future earnings and cash flows is most likely to be wide or narrow. To start, you must first understand whether the earnings that were calculated under Generally Accepted Accounting Principles (GAAP) represent the true earnings of a business. To do this, you must determine if management uses liberal or conservative accounting standards. So let's begin with that.

☐ 27. Are the accounting standards that management uses conservative or liberal?

Your ultimate goal in determining whether management uses liberal or conservative accounting methods is to help you determine the true operating earnings of that business. In most cases, you will need to make adjustments to the accounting numbers to understand how much a business actually earns. The reason for this is that there are many ways to calculate financial numbers under GAAP standards.

As this book is being written, there are many changes occurring to accounting standards with the adoption of International Financial Reporting Standards (IFRS), such as disallowing the use of last-in-first-out (LIFO). Even though there are many changes occurring, the methods management can use to manipulate earnings will unfortunately remain.

Here are several ways to determine whether management is using liberal or conservative accounting standards.

Read the Income-Tax Footnote

A good place to begin learning if a business's reported earnings approximate its actual earnings is to read the income-tax footnote found in the company's 10-K report. A business keeps two sets of books. The first one is based on GAAP accounting and the other is used to calculate the amount of taxes a business owes to the IRS. The IRS books tend to be a conservative benchmark, because in most cases firms seek to minimize their tax-return income. On the other hand, management can select from various accounting methods to calculate GAAP income. If there is a large difference between earnings for these two sets of books, it will be captured in the income-tax footnote. The footnote reconciles the difference between GAAP taxes on earnings (known as the *income tax provision*) and the amount of tax paid to the IRS (known as *current taxes*).

In the income tax footnote, compare the differences between the *Income Tax Provision* and *Current Taxes* for at least 5 to 10 years. Calculate how much book earnings are overstated or understated compared to current taxes. If you discover a business is reporting earnings yet is not paying taxes, this should set off some alarm bells, as businesses rarely cheat the IRS.

For example, one business reported $189 million in after tax earnings, but it paid the IRS and foreign tax authorities only $5 million! That suggests a *huge* difference in profits reported to shareholders versus profits reported to the IRS.

In comparison, National Presto Industries, a company that makes housewares such as pressure cookers, waffle makers, and frying pans, reported that its current taxes (both federal and state) totaled $70.9 million from 2007 to 2009 compared to a total tax provision (i.e., book taxes) of $74.8 million over this same time period. This means that its GAAP earnings approximate actual cash earnings, indicating that you would not need to make adjustments to the financial statements in order to understand what the real earnings of the business are.

Compare Cash Flow from Operations to Net Income

Management has less flexibility in manipulating cash flow from operations than it does net income because net income contains a large number of highly subjective estimates.

Note the differences between net income and cash flow from operations over the last one to five years. If net income closely approximates cash flow from operations, then there is less likelihood that it is being manipulated. However, if net income is consistently higher (more than 30 percent) than cash flow from operations, this may be a sign that management is managing earnings.

Evaluating Whether Management Manipulates Earnings

One objective way to gain insight into the integrity and character of a business's management team is to learn whether they employ conservative or liberal accounting practices. A company's accounting books are written by its managers, and the accounting practices they employ are, to a degree, a reflection of the kind of people they are. If the accounting is too complicated to understand, this may be a signal that management does not really want you to understand how the business makes money or how well they are running the company.

Management can manipulate earnings in several ways. The degree of manipulation varies from minor changes to outright fraudulent transactions. Earnings are most often manipulated to cover up deteriorating earnings within the core business. Other times, management wants to meet the quarterly expectations of Wall Street analysts by shifting earnings from good years to bad years or by shifting future earnings to the present.

There are several ways that management manipulates earnings despite being within the technical bounds of what GAAP accounting standards consider acceptable. Look for any (or all!) of the following:

- Improperly inflating sales
- Under- or over-stating expenses
- Manipulating discretionary costs
- Changing accounting methods
- Using restructuring charges to increase future earnings
- Creating reserves by manipulating estimates

Let's take a look at each of these manipulations.

Inflating Sales Management can book a sale before revenue is actually earned by incentivizing customers to take more product than they need. This is most likely to happen when the business sells its products through distributors or resellers, when it has a few large customers, or when a sales representative needs to hit a quarterly sales number.

For example, Telecom equipment company Riverstone Networks inflated its sales numbers in 2006 by improperly recognizing revenues. In this case, Riverstone had side agreements with its customers saying payments to Riverstone were contingent upon resale of Riverstone's products, but Riverstone booked them as sales even though they didn't actually receive payment. The Securities and Exchange Commission's (SEC) complaint against Riverstone cited almost $30 million in fraudulent revenues over several quarters, with overstatements ranging from 14 percent to more than 20 percent of revenue during each quarter.[1]

You can identify methods used to accelerate revenues by looking for large increases in accounts receivable growth compared to sales growth. When accounts receivable are growing faster than sales consider it a warning sign. Growth rates in sales and in accounts receivable should be roughly equal. If sales grow by 10 percent, then accounts receivable should grow by 10 percent.

For example, the sales of contact-lens manufacturer Bausch and Lomb grew 12 percent in 1992 and 10 percent in 1993, while receivables grew 35 percent and 39 percent in those same years. The reason for the difference was that Bausch and Lomb changed the way it accounted for revenues. It previously recognized sales when made to end customers, but it changed to recognizing sales when made to distributors. A sale to a distributor is not the same as selling to an end customer, because selling to distributors doesn't guarantee that the end customer will actually buy the product, and the distributor can return any unsold goods.

By the end of 1994, the SEC began a formal investigation into Bausch and Lomb's accounting practices. The SEC investigators concluded that during 1993, executives artificially boosted the company's earnings by wrongly recognizing revenue from the sale of contact lenses. This accounting scandal led to an earnings restatement and the departure of executives.[2]

There may be legitimate reasons for differences in accounts receivable and sales growth, although any discrepancies should be carefully investigated. For example, sometimes receivables growth *exceeds* sales growth, and this may happen for several reasons:

- First, the disparity in growth rates might reflect a deliberate change in sales terms designed to attract new customers. For example, instead of requiring payment within 30 days of shipment, a business might allow customers to pay in 45 days.
- Second, it can be due to deteriorating creditworthiness among existing customers, which would represent another problem.
- Third, a business could have changed its financial-reporting procedures, which determine when sales are recognized.

Under- or Over-Stating Expenses   Management sometimes shifts current expenses to later periods in order to boost short-term earnings. Management can do this by capitalizing an expense item over several periods. This way, it can deduct the expense over many years, instead of all at once when it is incurred. Capitalized costs end up on the balance sheet as assets, which are then amortized over future periods.

Common types of expenses that are capitalized and later depreciated include:

- Start-up costs
- Research and development (R&D) expenses

- Software development
- Maintenance costs
- Marketing
- Customer-acquisition costs

You can find out if a business routinely capitalizes its costs by reading the footnotes to the financial statements.

For example, Internet service provider America Online (AOL) disclosed in its footnotes to the 1994 10-K that it was classifying marketing costs as balance sheet assets rather than operating expenses, naming them Deferred Subscriber Acquisition Costs. By capitalizing these expenses, AOL was able to overstate its earnings for several years.

Beginning in 2001 and continuing through May 2002, telecom company WorldCom capitalized more than $9 billion of ordinary expenses in order to mask its deteriorating financial condition and increase the price of WorldCom's stock. On July 21, 2002, WorldCom filed for Chapter 11 bankruptcy protection and on March 15, 2005, CEO Bernard Ebbers was convicted of fraud and sentenced to 25 years in prison.[3]

Manipulating Discretionary Costs Discretionary costs include advertising, R&D expenses, and maintenance costs. These costs can also be manipulated in order to smooth earnings. Management can curtail spending in any of these areas to meet an earnings goal. This reduction in expenses may compromise the long-term viability of the business. You should monitor these expenses on a quarterly basis and look for any irregular patterns. If you discover that in the fourth quarter, R&D expenses dropped by a material amount compared to the same quarter a year ago, this may indicate that management is attempting to smooth earnings.

Manipulating discretionary expenses is quite common. Professors Campbell Harvey and John Graham at Duke University and Shiva Rajgopal at the University of Washington surveyed 401 financial executives at U.S. companies in 2003 asking them what actions they might take to smooth earnings and meet analyst estimates. Close to 80 percent of the financial executives surveyed responded that in order to meet an earnings goal, they would reduce spending on discretionary items like maintenance, research, and advertising.[4]

Changing Accounting Methods   Look for changes in the accounting methods the company uses. A business must always disclose in a footnote if it changes accounting methods, and it must disclose any impact on earnings.

One of the more popular methods used to defer expenses is to extend the useful life of assets in order to reduce depreciation expenses. A business must disclose in the footnotes to the financial statements whether it has extended the useful life of an asset or changed depreciation methods. Also, when the book value of the asset is more than the present value of projected cash flows from the asset, some companies simply write down the value of the asset. Management may be tempted to write down the value of assets substantially during years when earnings are lean. The effect of writing down the asset is that depreciation and amortization expenses are also reduced for all periods in the future, causing earnings to automatically increase during future periods.

For example, Waste Management artificially boosted earnings by extending the useful life of assets and using high residual values. The alleged fraud unraveled in 1997 when new interim CEO Robert Miller ordered a review of Waste Management's past accounting practices. Waste Management issued a restatement of $1.7 billion, which was the largest in corporate history at that time. Stockholders lost more than $6 billion in market value when, after the restatement, the price of the stock fell by 33 percent.[5] In its 1997 annual report, the company described how it changed to more conservative accounting:

> Effective October 1, 1997, the Board of Directors approved a management recommendation to revise the company's North American collection fleet management policy. Front-end loaders will be replaced after 8 years, and rear-end loaders and rolloff trucks after 10 years. The previous policy was not to replace front-end loaders before they were a minimum of 10 years old and other heavy collection vehicles before they were a minimum of 12 years old. Also effective October 1, 1997, the company reduced depreciable lives on containers from between 15 and 20 years to 12 years, and ceased assigning salvage value in computing depreciation on North American collection vehicles or containers.

Restructuring Charges or One-Time Expenses   If the business is reporting a large restructuring loss, management may add extra expenses in that restructuring charge in order to decrease future expenses. Later, management can reverse these restructuring charges to increase future earnings.

You can find these reversals in the footnotes to the financial statements by looking for *liability reserves*. Typically, a liability reserve is set up by writing off the expected cost of the restructuring as an expense and crediting a restructuring reserve or other accrued liabilities and payables account that is recorded as a liability on the balance sheet. Later, as the costs of the restructuring are paid in cash, the restructuring reserve liability is reduced. If management initially overestimates the amount of the restructuring expense, it can reverse the liability and add the amount to earnings.

For example, when Albert Dunlap became CEO of Sunbeam in July 1996, he took several restructuring charges that reduced net income from $50 million in 1995 to a loss of $228 million in 1996. By recording such unusually high restructuring costs, Sunbeam was able to move future-year expenses into its 1996 results. As a result, by 1997, net income jumped to $109 million, more than two times the amount of net income Sunbeam reported only two years earlier in 1995.

It was later discovered that Dunlap was manipulating earnings by taking large restructuring charges and then reversing these charges in later years. In 2001, the SEC sued Dunlap for many instances of fraud and barred him from serving as a public company executive.[6]

Using Reserves   Reserves are often called the cookie jar of accounting manipulation because they require a large degree of judgment to estimate. The term *cookie jar* refers to the ability to artificially store earnings in the balance sheet, so that dishonest management can draw on them in unprofitable future years and lessen the impact of the negative times on its financial statements. This is not a desirable occurrence, and the result can be financial statements that are intentionally misleading. Management can overestimate the size of a reserve account, which it can then later draw on to increase future earnings. Reserves can be booked for:

- Bad debts
- Sales returns
- Inventory obsolescence

- Warranties
- Product liability
- Litigation
- Environmental contingencies

To create reserves, management can take a charge against current earnings for one of the above-listed reasons. Sometimes management can use unrealistic assumptions when they estimate reserve charges. They can over-reserve in good times, then cut back on or even reverse charges in bad times. This is what makes the reserve (the cookie jar) such a convenient income-smoothing mechanism for management. Look in the footnotes at the allowance for doubtful accounts and then compare the provision for doubtful accounts to actual charge-offs. If the provision account estimates increase or decrease by a material amount over a three-year period while charge-offs remain constant, this may be a sign that management is using reserves to manipulate earnings.

For example, food distributor Sysco uses a conservative method for its allowance for doubtful accounts. In 2009, the company charged $74 million to costs and expenses (provision for bad-debt expense). In 2009, it wrote off $72 million in customer accounts (charge-offs), net of recoveries.[7] Therefore, it correctly matched its provision for doubtful accounts to actual charge offs. You can therefore assume that Sysco conservatively estimates the charge-offs. Table 6.1 illustrates.

On the other hand, Krispy Kreme Doughnuts manipulated earnings by failing to book adequate reserves for doubtful accounts.

Table 6.1   Sysco: Allowance for Doubtful Accounts

	2010	2009	2008
	(In thousands)		
Balance at beginning of period	$36,078	$31,730	$31,841
Charged to costs and expenses	34,931	74,638	32,184
Allowance accounts resulting from acquisitions and other adjustments	(139)	1,587	72
Customer accounts written off, net of recoveries	(34,297)	(71,877)	(32,367)
Balance at end of period	$36,573	$36,078	$31,730

Source: 2010 Sysco 10-K.

Table 6.2   Krispy Kreme: Allowance for Doubtful Accounts Related to Trade Receivables

	2007	2006	2005
	(In thousands)		
Balance at beginning of year	$13,656	$11,379	$1,265
Provision for doubtful accounts	1,836	3,978	12,696
Reserves associated with acquired businesses	—	41	—
Effects of deconsolidation of subsidiaries	(115)	(132)	—
Chargeoffs	(12,632)	(1,610)	(2,582)
Balance at end of year	$2,745	$13,656	$11,379

Source: 2007 Krispy Kreme 10-K.

The provision for doubtful accounts and the actual charge-offs are shown in Table 6.2.

As you can see in Table 6.2, the provision for doubtful accounts was $12.7 million in 2005, which management overstated because actual charge-offs were $2.6 million in 2005. By over-estimating the provision in 2005 and under-estimating the provision in 2006 and 2007, the management of Krispy Kreme was able to increase earnings in 2006 and 2007.

☐ 28. Does the business generate revenues that are recurring or from one-off transactions?

Businesses that earn their revenues from recurring sources are easier to value when compared to those that generate revenue from one-off transactions. Businesses that have recurring revenue include:

- Subscription-based businesses, such as a cable television business.
- Razor/razorblade-type business models, such as Immucor, which sells blood-bank equipment and consumable reagents to be used with the equipment.
- Franchisors such as Choice Hotels, which earns license fees on hotel brands such as Comfort Inn, Rodeway Inn, and Sleep Inn.
- Service businesses, such as Fiserv, which provides integrated data processing and information-management systems to financial-services providers and earns more than 95 percent of its revenue from recurring service contracts.

It is easier to forecast the future revenues for these types of businesses because a recurring revenue business's starting base isn't zero, but a certain percentage of last year's level of sales. Suppose a business earns $1.00 per share in revenue and $0.90 is from recurring revenue, then you know that $0.10 is at risk. Recurring revenue allows new sales to add to the revenue base, rather than simply replace lost revenues. For example, Praxair provides hydrogen and other gases to industrial clients under 15-year contracts, which produces an extremely predictable revenue stream. Every new customer Praxair is able to add then provides additional revenue.

Other advantages of businesses that earn recurring revenues include:

- *Less dependence on new products.* A business does not have to continually come up with new products or services to replace the prior year's revenues. On the opposite side of the spectrum from recurring-revenue businesses are those that generate revenues from one-off transactions or those that depend on continually selling the same number of products to maintain their sales from the prior year. These types of businesses range from consumer-products businesses, such as navigation-equipment maker Garmin, to equipment manufacturers that secure large individual contracts, such as Caterpillar. These types of businesses depend on orders that come in one at a time, with no guarantee or predictability in the revenue stream, and are therefore more difficult to value.
- *Greater predictability.* If there is a lack of visibility into a business, it is difficult for management to know how much to invest or how much to budget for expenses, which increases the odds of making mistakes. For example, if management makes a mistake in its sales forecast for the year and budgets its expenses to that level of sales, the business will likely generate a loss. Therefore, recurring revenues help put a limit on the downside earnings of the business.

You can typically find information on recurring revenues in the 10-K under the Management, Discussion and Analysis (MD&A) section. For example, the 2010 10-K for hotel franchisor Choice Hotels states, "Our company generates revenues, income, and cash flows primarily from initial, relicensing, and continuing royalty fees attributable to our franchise agreements (20-year agreements on average)." This indicates that Choice Hotels generates the majority of its revenue from recurring sources.

☐ 29. To what degree is the business cyclical, countercyclical, or recession-resistant?

As the economy speeds up or slows down, industries and individual businesses may either go along with the economic cycle, go in the opposite direction, or not be affected at all. There is tremendous variation in how businesses react to economic cycles. In general, if a business's earnings decline during an economic downturn, the business is classified as cyclical. If earnings increase during an economic contraction, we call it countercyclical. It is important to determine the degree to which a business is cyclical or countercyclical when forecasting earnings. Earnings that fluctuate up and down with the business cycle are more difficult to forecast than earnings that display greater stability over the economic cycle.

For example, it is difficult to know what the future economics will be for a homebuilder. Demand for homes is driven by many macro-economic factors such as interest rates, the cost of materials, the employment situation (people don't buy houses if they are worried about losing their jobs), and the general health of the economy. It is difficult, if not impossible to forecast how these multiple macroeconomic factors will change and what the cumulative effect on homebuilders will be.

To determine the degree to which a business is cyclical or countercyclical, you must first ask which types of economic conditions make it easier for a business to attract customers. If a business does well during an expanding economy yet does not prosper when the economy is shrinking, it is *cyclical*. For example, the following businesses are cyclical:

- Household furniture
- Apparel
- Appliances
- Vacation travel
- Automobiles
- Homebuilding

- Big-ticket luxury manufacturers
- Residential construction

These are products that consumers can defer purchasing in tough economic times. The longer a consumer can defer purchasing these items, the more cyclical a business will be.

Some products and services are *less cyclical.* Customers buy less, but do not completely defer the purchase—for example, businesses in these industries:

- Advertising
- Medical equipment
- Drugs
- Periodicals
- Insurance carriers
- Dairy products
- Legal services
- Accounting services
- Bakery products

Countercyclical businesses do well when the economy is contracting; for example:

- Discount retailers
- Private-label products (store brands versus nationally branded products)
- Medical care

While rare, certain industries operate independently of the economic cycle. In this case the product or service may be more of a necessity; for example:

- Tobacco companies, where customers are addicted to the product
- Pipelines carrying oil and gas
- Student-housing REITs
- Funeral services

The following sections take a closer look at industries that are recession resistant. If a business is recession resistant then its earnings will not be impacted as the economy enters a recession, thereby making it easier to value.

Recession-Resistant Businesses

A recession-resistant business, which is rare, is one where the earnings of the business are less affected by a contraction in the general economy. For example, consider the economic contraction that began in 2007. To understand if a business is recession resistant or resilient, study how it responded to that economic slowdown. Start by reading the MD&A section found in the 10-K. Read about the reasons for changes in the financial statement line items, such as sales, so you can gauge the effect of recessions. Read articles written about the business during the recession as well as historical conference calls. It is highly likely that analysts and journalists will be asking company management how their business is responding to the recession, and management's answers will yield many insights.

For example, specialty gas distributor Airgas sells the majority of its products to non-cyclical and counter-cyclical businesses. Many of its products are used for maintenance and represent a small portion of a customer's total costs. If you look back at previous recessions, Airgas generated relatively flat revenues and earnings before interest, taxes, depreciation, and amortization (EBITDA), indicating that Airgas is a *recession-resistant* business. In a fourth quarter 2009 conference call, COO Micheal Molinini said:

> 25 percent of our sales are the customers impacted by the more traditional cyclicality of industrial manufacturing, while 30 percent of our sales are the customers whose growth profiles tend to outperform GDP. Another quarter of our sales are the customers who use our products primarily for repair and maintenance, and the volumes in that business tend to stay more stable than manufacturing. In today's economy, the diversity of our customer base has helped soften the impact of the rapid decline in U.S. manufacturing.

Therefore, by reading a conference call transcript, you would have learned that at least 55 percent of Airgas's revenues are recession resistant.

Degree of Recession Resistance

The degree to which an industry or business is affected by recessions depends on several factors:

- The amount of recurring revenues a business generates (more recurring revenue means less volatility in earnings and more resistance).
- The percentage of the customer's budget that is spent on that business's product or service (if a small percentage of the customer's budget is spent on that business's product or service, the customer is less likely to drop the product or service).
- The percentage of its customers that are exposed to business cycles and how sensitive they are to these cycles (if a business sells to homebuilders, that business will be greatly affected by cycles in residential construction).

Past Recessions

Many industries and businesses are labeled as recession resistant because they were able to survive a previous recession without a large drop in revenues. Be cautious when you see an industry labeled as "recession resistant" because not all recessions are created equal, and each recession impacts businesses in different ways. Be sure to understand if there were complicating factors, such as supply/demand imbalances in previous recessions. Such factors can mask the true effects of a downturn.

For example, Las Vegas casinos were considered to be recession resistant during the 1980s and 1990s because they had fared better than other businesses during previous recessions. The real reason they did so well was because Las Vegas casino demand was growing and supply was limited during those years. During the recession in 2007, however, there was an oversupply of casinos in the Las Vegas market, which caused Las Vegas casinos to experience their worst operating results ever.

Be certain to consider location and context as you evaluate supply and demand. Regional casinos, for example, were much less affected by the recession in 2007, mainly because of limited supply. In regional markets, the numbers of slot machines and table games are strictly limited by local gaming regulation. As a result, these markets have less chance of being oversupplied. For example, regional gaming company Penn National Gaming found that even though customers were spending less on their visits, they continued to visit the casinos at the same frequency. By comparison, in Las Vegas, there was both a drop in trip frequencies and in how much customers spent during each visit.

The veterinary industry has also been labeled a recession-resistant industry because spending on pet health did not drop during the recession that began in 2007. According to an annual industry survey, veterinary spending increased 3 percent in 2009 against a 2.4 percent drop in GDP. There is evidence that veterinary spending is becoming less discretionary, with people more likely to demand higher-quality vet care and less likely to defer spending during downturns. However, increased demand has also been fueled by changes in pet testing. In the past, most vets diagnosed an animal through touch and direct observation; however, new vets are increasingly taught to use tests as a tool for diagnosis. Before drawing the conclusion that veterinary spending as a whole is recession resistant, consider that recent resistance may have been due to increased testing. This underlying trend may not fuel demand during the next recession so the veterinary industry may not be as recession resistant as investors believe it to be.

☐   **30. To what degree does operating leverage impact the earnings of the business?**

Operating leverage measures the impact of changes in sales on earnings. The higher the operating leverage a business possesses, the more difficult it is to forecast the earnings of the business. For example, a relatively small error in forecasting sales can be magnified into large errors in earnings projections. If sales decrease by 10 percent, then earnings may decrease by 30 percent. This means that businesses that have *high* fixed costs typically report erratic earnings, which makes them more difficult to value. In contrast, businesses that have *low* fixed costs and high variable costs present lower volatility in earnings and are simpler to value. For example, a 10 percent growth rate in sales for a variable-cost firm could translate into 10 percent growth in earnings. The earnings are therefore not as volatile as a business with high amounts of operating leverage.

Types of Businesses with High Operating Leverage

The following businesses typically have high operating leverage:

- Businesses that have a high labor component
- Businesses with high capital-expenditure requirements
- Manufacturers with high material and production costs
- Businesses that are required to invest a lot of money in inventory

These types of businesses include:

- Airlines
- Aluminum manufacturers
- Auto manufacturers
- Bond rating firms
- Chemical manufacturers
- Gaming businesses
- Hotels
- Mining companies
- REITs
- Retailers
- Steel makers
- Supermarkets
- Theme parks
- Universities

Calculating the Degree of Operating Leverage

Businesses have varying degrees of operating leverage. Some businesses have low amounts of operating leverage, such as hotel franchisor Choice Hotels, and some have high amounts of operating leverage, such as a theme park.

To calculate the degree of operating leverage (i.e., how much earnings are influenced by changes in sales), divide the percentage change in operating income by the percentage change in sales. The higher the degree of operating leverage, the more volatile the operating-income figure will be relative to a given change in sales. For example, let's look at two companies, Boeing and Choice Hotels:

- Boeing has a high degree of operating leverage: For the year ended 2008, Boeing reported in its 10-K that revenues decreased 8.3 percent and operating income decreased 33.9 percent.

- By comparison, also in 2008, hotel franchisor Choice Hotels in its 10-K reported revenue increased 4.3 percent, with a corresponding 1.5 percent increase in operating income, which means it has a lower degree of operating leverage compared to Boeing.

Let's examine one business in more detail to understand why it has high operating leverage.

Case Study: Why Theme Parks Have High Operating Leverage

A theme park has very high fixed costs and low variable costs. A theme park requires significant capital investment in terms of land and equipment. Each year, a park has to make significant investments in new attractions in order to attract more customers. Fixed costs do not change with the number of customers and a lot of these costs are still incurred even when the theme park is closed. After reaching a certain level of attendance, where a theme park achieves its break-even point, every new customer's ticket revenue drops straight to the bottom line which contributes to high marginal profit. Therefore, it is in the interest of a theme park to increase attendance.

Table 6.3 compares the revenue growth and earnings before interest and taxes (EBIT) growth for theme park Six Flags.

This shows how sensitive earnings are in relation to revenue. High operating leverage can make a company vulnerable on two fronts:

- If the business faces any risk of say, reduced revenue, as in the case of Six Flags, it has the additional, amplified earnings risk that accompanies it.
- If the business has high amounts of debt, this combination can be disastrous.

Table 6.3   Revenue Growth Compared to EBIT Growth for Six Flags Theme Parks

	2005	2006	2007	2008	2009
Revenue growth	8.8%	−1.5%	3%	5.2%	−10.6%
EBIT growth	15.4%	−42.9%	−16.5%	108.9%	−58%

Data source: "Six Flags Emerges from Bankruptcy," *HedgeWorld News* via Reuters, May 3, 2010, and Standard & Poor's Capital IQ.

Be careful if you invest in businesses that have high operating leverage and large amounts of debt. They can go bankrupt quickly, because small declines in revenue are amplified into larger declines in earnings, bringing about an inability to make interest payments.

To calculate the actual amount of the degree of operating leverage at a business, you need to understand what the break-even sales are for the business. This way, you can determine how a corresponding increase or decrease in revenue will impact the operating income of a business.

Calculating Break-Even Sales

Ideally, you would want to understand at what level of sales a business would generate break-even earnings. This way, you would be in a better position to understand at what level of sales operating leverage will start to work against the earnings of the business or in its favor.

Here's a method used to calculate break-even sales: If a business generates $1 million of sales and has a 30 percent gross profit margin (GPM) and incurs $200,000 in fixed costs, it will earn $100,000. Therefore, break-even sales would be $666,667 (Sales × 30 percent = $200,000), assuming everything else stays equal. Unfortunately, in the real world, everything else does not stay equal, which makes it difficult to calculate at what level of sales a business will break even.

Further complicating things, it is difficult to calculate the exact amounts of fixed and variable costs: Even management has difficulty calculating exact amounts. The reason for this is that most fixed costs are more flexible than they appear because equipment can be sold, a labor force can be resized, leases can be renegotiated, or certain production lines can be shut down. For example, hotels over the last decade have been able to change their break-even cost for occupancy. For example, break-even occupancy for hotels declined steadily between 1986 and 2000.[8] In 1986, a hotel had to have an average occupancy of 66.4 percent to break even. By 2000, this amount changed to only 47.4 percent. Why the drop? Because hotels shifted their revenue mix to focus on high-margin room revenues. They cut costs related to accounting, telephones, and other back-of-the-house staffing, and they lowered debt levels. These changes enabled them to break even if a hotel was only half full.

Instead of calculating an exact amount for break-even level, you can calculate rough estimates for the businesses you're considering investing in: After all, a rough approximation is better than no approximation. Let's start by examining how to identify fixed and variable costs using the 10-K report so you can estimate break-even sales.

Identifying Fixed Costs   A fixed cost is a cost that does not change with the number of outputs. For example, with a stainless steel manufacturer, certain machinery needs to be kept running even if it is not making anything. Heaters must be constantly kept running even if the plant isn't making steel because if they were turned off, the equipment would disintegrate. Also, fans that handle pollutants must always be kept on because turning the motors on and off can damage them. These costs remain the same whether the steel mill makes one batch of steel or 10 batches. If demand for steel drops, these plants must continue to operate, and when sales drop, that contributes to a large decrease in earnings.

Identifying Variable Costs   Variable costs are costs that change in direct proportion to changes in revenue. If a business sells more items, costs increase, and if sales decrease, then costs will decrease. The types of businesses with the highest variable costs are franchisors.

An example would be real estate brokerage firm Coldwell Banker, which sells franchise rights to use its brand. When Coldwell Banker's franchised brokers sell properties, the company receives a fee from the sale proceeds. Coldwell Banker then pays for national advertising and marketing from the proceeds of sales, and so tends to incur costs only in relationship to transactions.

To begin learning more about how to identify fixed and variable expenses and how to calculate them, two examples are presented below. The first is Southwest Airlines, which has a high fixed-cost structure and low variable costs; the second is Choice Hotels, (a franchisor of hotel brands such as Comfort Inn, Comfort Suites, and Clarion), which has high variable costs and low fixed costs. Both examples illustrate how you can use the balance sheet and income statement to help you identify the fixed and variable expenses. Let's start by reviewing the balance sheet.

Reviewing the Balance Sheet

Start by looking at the fixed assets as a percentage of total assets of the business. A business that has a large percentage of long-term assets compared to total assets typically has a high fixed-cost structure.

At Choice Hotels, total assets are $340 million as of December 31, 2009. The total long-term assets are $64 million, of which $43 million are net property, plant, and equipment, and $21 million are long-term investments. Total long-term assets are 19 percent of total assets, which implies that Choice Hotels has a *low* level of fixed costs.

In contrast, as of the end of 2009, Southwest Airlines had total assets of $14.27 billion. Its total long-term assets are $10.39 billion, made up of net property, plant, and equipment. Total long-term assets are 73 percent of total assets, which implies that Southwest Airlines has a *high* level of fixed costs.

Reviewing the Income Statement of Southwest Airlines to Identify Fixed and Variable Costs

Next, review the income statement and begin with the total selling, general, and administrative expenses (SG&A). The SG&A section is where the majority of fixed costs are typically found. To walk you through this process, let's use the 2009 income statement of Southwest Airlines as an example. The breakdown (in millions) is shown in Table 6.4.

Next, use the MD&A of the 10-K to classify whether expenses are fixed or variable. The examples shown below (in quotation marks) are from the 2009 Southwest Airlines 10-K:

- **Salaries, wages, and benefits—Fixed Costs**: "Salaries, wages, and benefits expense per ASM (Available Seat Miles) was

Table 6.4   2009 Operating Expenses of Southwest Airlines

Total Operating Expense Breakdown	Amount (in millions)
Salaries, wages, and benefits	$ 3,468
Fuel and oil	$ 3,044
Maintenance materials and repairs	$ 719
Aircraft rentals	$ 186
Landing fees and other rentals	$ 718
Depreciation and amortization	$ 616
Other operating expenses	$ 1,337
Total operating expenses	$10,088

9.6 percent higher than 2008, primarily due to the fact that the Company's unionized workforce, who make up the majority of its Employees, had pay scale increases as a result of increased seniority, while the Company's ASM capacity declined 5.1 percent compared to 2008." In addition, the notes section of the 10-K states, "Approximately 82 percent of the Company's Employees are unionized and are covered by collective bargaining agreements." You can therefore conclude that most of the salaries, wages, and benefits are fixed.

- **Fuel and oil—Fixed Costs in Short-Term and Variable Costs in Long-Term**: Southwest states that fuel and oil expense decreased 18 percent as the available seat miles decreased by 13.6 percent. Most of this decrease was due to a decrease in the prices of jet fuel. The majority of fuel and oil expenses are fixed in the short term and variable in the long term. They are fixed in the short term because it would take time for Southwest to adjust its flights to a decrease in demand.

- **Maintenance materials and repairs—Mainly Variable Costs**: "The majority of the increase in engine costs related to the Company's 737–700 aircraft, which for the second half of 2008 and all of 2009 were accounted for under an agreement with GE Engines Services, Inc. (GE Engines) that provides for engine repairs to be done on a rate per flight hour basis. Under this engine agreement, which is similar to the 'power-by-the-hour' agreement with GE Engines the Company has in place for its 737–300 and 737–500 fleet, payments are primarily based on a rate per flight hour basis." In other words, Southwest Airlines has outsourced its maintenance materials and repairs to General Electric, and Southwest pays General Electric based on the number of air miles flown: Therefore, this is a variable expense.

- **Aircraft rentals—Fixed Costs**: "Aircraft rentals expense per ASM increased 26.7 percent and, on a dollar basis, increased $32 million." Furthermore, in the Notes to the financial statements, you'll see that total rental expense for operating leases, both aircraft and other, charged to operations in 2009, 2008, and 2007 was $596 million, $527 million, and $469 million, respectively. In other words, aircraft rentals are fixed expenses because they represent multi-year contractual obligations.

- **Landing fees—Fixed Costs**: "Landing fees and other rentals increased $56 million on a dollar basis and increased 14.1 percent on a per-ASM basis, compared to 2008. The majority of both the dollar increase and per-ASM increase was due to higher space rentals in airports as a result of higher rates charged by those airports for gate and terminal space." Landing fees can be thought of as an operating lease. Southwest will pay the same fee for the gate whether the plane is full or not. Assuming a stable flight schedule, these costs can be considered fixed.
- **Other operating expenses—Fixed Costs**: Other operating expenses include interest expense, capitalized interest, interest income, and other gains and losses. Most of these are long-term contractual expenses and therefore are fixed.

Conclusion: Southwest Airlines Has High Operating Leverage   To summarize, here are the fixed expenses for Southwest Airlines (in millions):

- Salaries, wages, and benefits where 82 percent of the workforce is unionized and has a contract ($3,468).
- Aircraft rentals as well as landing fees and other gate leases ($718 + $186).
- Other operating expenses mainly representing contractual obligations ($1,337).
- Depreciation and amortization ($616).
- Total fixed expenses are approximately $6,325.

Here are the *variable expenses* for Southwest Airlines (in millions):

- Fuel and oil are mainly variable expenses ($3,044).
- Maintenance, materials, and repair are variable expenses which vary by the number of miles flown ($719).
- Total variable expenses are $3,763.

Therefore the percentage of fixed expenses is 63 percent, and variable expenses approximate 37 percent. Many of these variable expenses are fixed in the short run because Southwest Airlines would need to adjust its flights to meet lower demand. Therefore, approximately two thirds of Southwest Airlines' costs are fixed and one third are variable, which means if sales were to drop, this would have a disproportionate effect on the earnings of the business compared to a business that has largely variable costs. In other words, if sales dropped 10 percent, then earnings could easily drop by more than 40 percent. You would need to pay a lower price for this business because its earnings are less stable. Now let's take a look at Choice Hotels' income statement and see how that compares to Southwest Airlines.

Reviewing the Income Statement of Choice Hotels to Identify Fixed and Variable Costs

Choice Hotels is a franchisor that licenses hotel brand names such as Comfort Inn, Comfort Suites, Econo Lodge, and Clarion. As of December 31, 2009, the Company had franchise agreements representing 6,021 open hotels and 843 hotels under construction. Table 6.5 shows a breakdown of the total operating expenses (in thousands) found in the fiscal year 2009 Choice Hotels 10-K, with excerpts below (again in quotation marks).

- **Selling, general and administrative—Mainly Fixed Costs**: "The cost to operate the franchising business is reflected in SG&A expenses on the consolidated statements of income. SG&A expenses were $99.2 million for 2009, a decrease of $19.8 million from the 2008 total of $119.0 million. The decline in adjusted SG&A costs for the year ended December 31, 2009, was primarily due to cost containment initiatives as well as lower variable franchise sales compensation." Also, in the Notes to the financial statements, there is a section titled Contractual obligations, which breaks out the debt and lease expenses of the business: Operating lease obligations total $14 million. Advertising expense was $81.3 million in 2009 representing

Table 6.5   2009 Operating Expenses of Choice Hotels

Total Operating Expense Breakdown	Amount (in thousands)
Selling, general, and administrative	$99,237
Depreciation and amortization	$8,336
Marketing and reservation	$305,379
Hotel operations	$3,153
Total operating expenses	$416,105

82 percent of SG&A. Advertising is a variable cost but you should probably consider it to be a fixed cost as advertising is necessary to maintain high brand awareness. Leases are $6 million in 2009, which are a fixed cost because they are contractual obligations. Although Choice Hotels' SG&A has some variable components, you can conclude that the majority of expenses are fixed costs.

- **Marketing and reservation—No income or loss from these expenses, so they break even**: "The Company's franchise agreements require the payment of franchise fees, which include marketing and reservation system fees. The fees, which are based on a percentage of the franchisees' gross room revenues, are used exclusively by the Company for expenses associated with providing franchise services such as central reservation systems, national marketing, and media advertising. The Company is contractually obligated to expend the marketing and reservation fees it collects from franchisees in accordance with the franchise agreements; as such, no income or loss to the Company is generated." These marketing and reservation expenses are passed on to the franchisees. These break-even expenses (meaning Choice Hotels does not make a profit or a loss on them) should be considered neither fixed nor variable.

Conclusion: Choice Hotels Has Low Operating Leverage   Fixed costs are close to $108 million, out of a total of $416 million, but $305 million of those expenses represent areas where Choice does not earn a profit or breaks even. Therefore, the business needs to generate revenue in excess of $108 million in order to break even. In 2009, excluding the $305 million in revenue it earned from marketing and reservations, Choice Hotels generated close to $250 million in revenue, which can easily cover these fixed expenses. If revenues were to drop by 55 percent in one year, Choice Hotels would break even. Because Choice Hotels has a low level of operating leverage, an investor takes less risk that the earnings will fluctuate widely when revenues decline.

As a result, investing in businesses with low operating leverage results in less risk than investing in one with high operating leverage. The reason for this is that businesses that have a large percentage of variable expenses are able to decrease their expenses quickly if sales change. Those that have a high fixed-cost structure are unable to react quickly to a drop in sales. Therefore the earnings of a business with high operating leverage can change quickly, which makes it difficult to forecast earnings. You should always pay a lower price for a business that has high operating leverage to give yourself a sufficient margin of safety to account for these large fluctuations in earnings.

☐ 31. How does working capital impact the cash flows of the business?

Working capital is the cash a business uses to fund its day-to-day operations. For example, a business uses cash in order to buy inventory, which it needs to operate. A business then gets paid by customers after it sells this inventory and then uses that money to pay its suppliers. By understanding working capital, you will be able to assess whether a business can grow by using its own capital, rather than having to depend on its customers and suppliers to finance the business. The faster a business can turn its inventory and collect its receivables and the longer it can stretch out its payables, the higher the operating cash flow.

If it is difficult for you to understand the working-capital needs of a business, then it will be difficult for you to forecast the cash flows of a business. To account for this risk, you must pay a lower price for the stock.

Calculating Net Working Capital

Working capital is calculated by subtracting current assets from current liabilities. Current assets are balance-sheet items such as accounts receivable and inventory. These are assets that can be turned into cash in less than one year. Current liabilities are balance-sheet items such as accounts payable and short-term debt. These are liabilities that are due within one year.

Increases in working capital are considered a cash outflow even though the capital does not leave the business. For example, an increase in inventory consumes cash, even though the business still holds the inventory. The business does not have access to the cash it has invested in the inventory until it sells that inventory. As a result, the business cannot use the cash for other investments. You can think of working capital in terms of opportunity cost where the business foregoes the ability to use cash whenever it has to hold inventory or if customers delay payment. By better managing working capital, doing such things as selling inventory more quickly, a business is able to free up cash that would otherwise be tied up in inventory.

Amount of Working Capital Needed by a Business

The amount of working capital a business needs depends on the capital intensity and the speed at which a business can turn its inventory into cash. The shorter the commitment or cycle, the less cash is tied up and the more a business can use the cash for other internal purposes.

For example, most restaurants need to retain very little cash on hand because their inventories are turned into cash very quickly. Service businesses typically require little or no inventory and are paid in cash by customers before providing the service. On the other hand, airplane manufacturer Boeing takes much longer to turn a pile of sheet steel and a bunch of electronics into an airplane; therefore, Boeing needs a lot of cash on hand to cover necessary cash disbursements.

Calculating a Company's Ability to Generate Working Capital: Using the Cash Conversion Cycle (CCC)

The primary tool you can use to measure how quickly a business is able to convert its inventory and receivables into cash and pay its short-term obligations is the Cash Conversion Cycle (CCC). The CCC calculates the number of days that cash is invested in inventory and accounts receivable, and the extent to which the cash outflow is covered by accounts payable. The faster a business can turn over its inventory and collect its receivables and the longer it can stretch out its payables, the higher the operating cash flow. Here's the formula:

Cash Conversion Cycle = Inventory conversion period (Days)
+ Receivables conversion period (Days)
− Payables conversion period (Days)

- Inventory conversion period (Days Inventory Outstanding): Average Inventory/(Total Cost of Goods Sold/365)
- Receivables conversion period (Days Sales Outstanding): Average Accounts Receivable/(Total Revenue/365)
- Payables conversion period (Days Payables Outstanding): Average Accounts Payable/(Cost of Goods Sold/365)

If you add DIO (days to sell inventory) to DSO (days to collect receivables), that will tell you the total conversion period of inventories. Let's say it takes 50 days to sell inventory and 30 days to collect receivables. Therefore, you can conclude that it would normally take 80 days (50 + 30) to sell inventory on credit and to collect the receivables.

Then, you would subtract the time that it takes to pay back suppliers. For example, if the days payables outstanding (DPO) is 20 days, you would subtract this from 80 days to arrive at the total time it takes to convert inventories into cash, or 60 days.

A business can improve its CCC in several ways:

- By selling its products as fast as possible (high inventory turns)
- By collecting payments from customers as fast as possible (high receivables turns)
- By paying suppliers as slowly as possible (low payable turns)

Table 6.6 lists some examples of businesses with different cash-conversion cycles. They range from negative CCC (which means that suppliers are funding the business) to high CCC, such as homebuilder Toll Brothers, which is required to keep a lot of land in inventory in order to operate.

Calculate the CCC for at least a five-year period for the business you are analyzing. You want to understand why the CCC is changing over time. You can do this by examining each of the components that makes up the CCC—that is, the DIO, DPO, and DSO.

Table 6.6   Cash Conversion Cycle of Different Businesses FY2009

Company	No. of Days
Apple	−48 days
Southwest Airlines	−15.4 days
Whole Foods Market	14 days
Verizon Communications	25 days
Energizer Holdings	151 days
Amgen	340 days
Tiffany	437 days
Toll Brothers	847 days

Source: Standard & Poor's Capital IQ.

For example, Hughes Communications (a broadband satellite business) improved its cash conversion cycle from 62 days in 2008 to 39 days in 2009. It did this by encouraging customers to use credit cards to pay their bills, which speeded up its collection of receivables. This had the effect of reducing DSO from 70 days to 65 days. In addition, Hughes also increased the time it paid its suppliers from 48 days in 2008 to 67 days in 2009, which further helped Hughes free up more cash flow. During 2008, the stock price of Hughes dropped from more than $50 per share, to as low as $9 per share at the beginning of 2009. As Hughes's management improved cash flows, this helped the stock price recover to $26 per share on December 31, 2009.[9]

Determine Whether Changes in Working Capital Are Sustainable

Next, you want to determine if the improvements or deterioration in the CCC are sustainable or temporary. For example, during the recession that began in 2007, many businesses improved their working capital because they were forced to find additional cash to finance their operations. In the past, they were less disciplined in managing their working capital because they did not face financial constraints. However, many of these improvements are temporary rather than sustainable.

If the improvements in working capital are sustainable, then every dollar of freed-up working capital will boost cash flows. However, if improvements are temporary, you need to adjust cash flows in order to normalize them for these temporary improvements. For example, most businesses can get away with delaying payments to suppliers. If the company has increased its DPO (days payable outstanding) from 40 days to 45 days, and you believe that improvement isn't sustainable, then you should use 40 days when calculating that company's CCC. At some point, suppliers may demand stricter payment terms, so the delay may be only temporary.

Negative Working Capital

When a business has more current liabilities than current assets, it has negative working capital. This means the customers and suppliers are financing the business, which is a less expensive way of funding growth. For example, let's say you own a retail business and you invest $1 million in inventory, and it costs $1 million to build a store. Now let's say you can finance 50 percent of your inventory by paying suppliers 90 days later. The upfront capital investment would then be $1.5 million instead of $2 million. Your suppliers are allowing you to delay payments for your investments and giving you a ready supply of cash.

A common attribute of businesses that benefit from negative working capital is that cash flow from operations exceeds net income. Here are two examples, from 2009:

- At online retailer Amazon.com, cash flow from operations exceeded net income by $2.4 billion.
- At online travel website Expedia, cash flow from operations exceeded net income by $377 million.

This means these businesses were able to generate more cash flow from operations than net income. Many times the excess free-cash flows are invested in short-term investments, such as cash, which generate interest income that drops straight to the bottom line. These businesses thus generate a safer cash-flow stream.

Negative Working Capital Only Works in Your Favor When Sales Are Growing

You cannot rely on negative working capital being a consistent, meaningful source of cash flow, especially if growth isn't strong. If the business experiences a significant downturn, either due to a secular decline, demand shocks, or market-share losses, then the business may face a liquidity strain. When the business stops growing, it is unable to push out liabilities further into the future, and the positive effects of negative working capital will reverse and decrease the cash flows of the business. Instead of continuing to pay suppliers out of growing cash flow, if growth slows down, the business will have to pay the suppliers out of its existing cash balance.

For instance, in the third quarter of 2008, Dell generated negative cash flow from operations, which it has done only two times since 1993.[10] At the beginning of the third quarter, demand for products was stable and Dell was ordering supplies on a normal basis, when midway through the quarter, customers stopped placing orders due to the financial crisis that was taking place. This meant Dell could no longer keep pushing out its accounts payable balance, and it had to use more of its cash to pay its payables. In the fourth quarter of 2008, this situation reversed itself as demand stabilized and Dell's customers returned to a more consistent ordering pattern. Luckily, Dell had a sizable amount of cash on its balance sheet so it was able to fund the shortfall. If a negative working capital business does not have enough cash on the balance sheet, then the business will run into short-term liquidity problems and potentially face bankruptcy. If you foresee that happening, that company is obviously not a good investment at that time!

☐ 32. Does the business have high or low capital-expenditure requirements?

Determining the capital-expenditure requirements of a business will help you understand how much free-cash flow the business is able to generate. If the capital-expenditure requirements are high, then the cash flows of the business need to be continually reinvested in the business just to maintain existing assets. High capital expenditures reduce cash flow, which is what the value of a business is based on.

For example, a paper manufacturer often loses money due to the cyclical nature of the business. When the paper manufacturer finally generates excess cash flow, management must spend the excess cash flow upgrading its manufacturing plants. Therefore, the cash flows are continually recycled into the business, which causes the value of the business to be stagnant. On the other hand, a business with low capital-expenditure requirements (one that requires less capital to maintain its assets) carries less risk, especially in inflationary environments. Because a business does not need to continually recycle its excess cash flow to maintain its assets, this allows it to reinvest excess cash flow to create more value or distribute these excess cash flows to shareholders.

A capital-intensive business is a business that requires a large amount of capital or assets for every dollar of sales. Here are some examples of capital-intensive businesses:

- Semiconductors
- Telecom
- Retail
- Chemicals

- Cement
- Steel
- Pulp and paper
- Materials
- Mining
- Oil and gas
- Theme parks
- Airlines
- Traditional manufacturing companies
- Distribution companies

The ratio of capital expenditures to sales of most of these businesses is more than $0.20 of capital for every $1 in revenue. Telecom businesses are some of the most capital-intensive businesses because they require, on average, $1 of capital for every $1 in revenue.

In contrast, businesses that are not capital intensive include:

- Franchisors
- Intermediaries that earn commissions for connecting buyers and sellers
- Software businesses

These businesses are not capital intensive because they do not require major investments in new facilities to grow or maintain their business. These types of businesses add employees, instead of physical plants, to grow the business.

Calculate Maintenance Capital Expenditures

It is important for you to calculate the amount of maintenance capital expenditures a company needs to maintain its business in order to calculate the distributable free-cash flows of a business. Maintenance capital expenditures are the amount of investment necessary to keep the company in a steady state: For example, replacing or upgrading administrative or support facilities such as buildings or parking lots. These expenditures typically do not earn an excess return on the capital expended. They generally help maintain current cash flows, but they do not increase cash flows.

Many businesses require large amounts of maintenance capital expenditures to keep their equipment operational. For example, an oil refinery must constantly reinvest capital to maintain its business. These types of businesses need to spend a lot of their capital updating their plants to meet government regulations or environmental standards, such as Occupational Safety and Health Administration (OSHA) or U.S. Environmental Protection Agency (EPA) regulatory standards. This capital does not earn a return, although in a few instances, it can make a facility more productive. You need to determine what percentage of capital needs to be reinvested to meet these regulatory standards or other non-discretionary required investments. By doing this, you will understand the amount of excess cash flows a business generates, which will help you value the business.

Some businesses continually defer capital expenditures to maintain property and equipment, but that can increase risk because those assets may lose value or require extremely heavy expenditures at a later point in time. For example, if a refinery does not maintain its assets, then the refinery will suffer prolonged periods of downtime when the assets need to be repaired or replaced. This will result in lower cash flows from the business because the refinery will have to shut down parts of its plant to fix the assets that were neglected.

You can find the capital expenditures of a business by reading the company's cash-flow statement, and you can find further explanation of the breakdown in the MD&A section. Some businesses will differentiate between capital expenditures needed for growth and capital expenditures needed to maintain a business.

For example, Whole Foods Market reported in its 10-K that for fiscal year 2010 (which ended on September 26, 2010) that its capital expenditures amounted to $256.8 million, of which approximately $171.4 million was used for new store development and approximately $85.4 million was spent on remodels and other property and equipment expenditures. However, this is unusual: Most businesses do not separate out the amount of capital expenditures used for growth and those to maintain the business.

Whenever you are unable to calculate the maintenance capital expenditures, you can use depreciation as a rough approximation. It is easier to use depreciation if the business has a low or well-defined growth pattern or steady state. In other cases you will have to adjust the depreciation upward or downward depending on the types of assets a business must maintain.

For example, at book retailer Barnes & Noble, the depreciation of the shelves in the bookstore is higher than the reinvestment needed to maintain them, therefore using depreciation to calculate maintenance capital expenditures would not be appropriate. In contrast, the children's entertainment restaurant Chuck E. Cheese constantly has to invest more than its depreciation charges to refresh its store base. Those high maintenance expenses decrease the distributable free-cash flows of the business.

For any business you're considering investing in, you will need to determine how long the assets will last before they need to be replaced. Read the notes to the financial statements in the section where management discloses the breakdown of property, plant, and equipment into categories such as information technology, property, machinery, equipment, buildings, or land. You can then focus on those assets that need to be maintained or replaced (such as machinery) and exclude those that don't (such as land) when estimating depreciation.

Suppose you're considering investing in an airline, you should know that planes are replaced every 10 to 20 years. The time to replace an asset depends on the asset and the age of that asset: For example, a plane that is utilized more than another will have to be replaced sooner. As assets age, maintenance capital expenditures typically increase. In order to get a rough estimate of the average age of assets, calculate the ratio of *net* property, plant, and equipment (PP&E) to *gross* property, plant, and equipment (note: If a business uses accelerated depreciation, adjust it to straight-line depreciation).

For instance, in 2009, the ratio of net assets to gross assets at cement maker CEMEX was 61 percent, which means that the assets are getting close to their half life. This means that CEMEX potentially faces higher maintenance capital expenditures in the future to upgrade many of its older plants. You would therefore adjust your estimate of future cash flows downward to account for these potential future capital outlays. The closer the ratio of net assets to gross assets is to one, the more this means that a business will not face higher maintenance capital-expenditure requirements to replace its existing assets in the future.

Key Points to Keep in Mind

What You Need to Know about Earnings

- The range or distribution of future earnings (cash flow) is a key factor in determining how much investors should be willing to pay for that business.
- The wider the potential distribution of future earnings is, the more difficult the business is to value.

For Businesses that Use Conservative Accounting Methods:

- The difference between current taxes (taxes paid to IRS) and the income-tax provision is less than 10 percent.
- Cash flows from operations closely approximate net income.
- Revenue is recognized when it is earned instead of front-loaded.
- Items are expensed quickly rather than capitalized.
- Discretionary costs are not manipulated by cutting advertising, research and development (R&D), or maintenance expenses in order to smooth earnings.
- Depreciation expenses are not artificially reduced by extending the useful life of assets.
- Restructuring charges are not inflated to lower future expenses.
- Reserve accounts are neither overstated nor understated.
- Provisions for doubtful accounts are correctly matched to charge-offs.

For Businesses that Use Liberal Accounting Methods:

- Revenue may be overstated and expenses understated.
- Deteriorating fundamentals may be masked.
- Low-quality earnings may be derived from unsustainable sources such as:
  - Gains and losses from debt retirement
  - Asset writeoffs from corporate restructurings
  - Temporary reductions in discretionary expenditures for advertising, R&D, or maintenance expenses

Evaluate a Business's Recurring Revenues

- It is easier to forecast the future revenues for a business with recurring revenues because the starting base is a certain percentage of last year's level of sales, rather than zero.
- A business with recurring revenue does not have to continually come up with new products or services to replace the prior year's revenues, and management is able to more easily budget its expenses.

(continued)

Identify Whether a Business Is Cyclical, Countercyclical, or Recession Resistant

- Earnings that display greater stability over the business cycle are easier to forecast. These businesses are also easier to value.
- If customers can defer purchases for a long time, the business will be more cyclical than if customers can only defer purchases for a short time.
- The degree to which an industry or business is affected by recessions depends on the amount of recurring revenues a business generates, the percentage of the customer's budget that is spent on that business's product or service, and the percentage of the business's customers that are exposed to the economic cycle.
- When a business is labeled as *recession resistant*, make sure it did not benefit from supply/demand imbalances in previous recessions.

Assess a Business's Operating Leverage

- The more operating leverage a business possesses, the more difficult it is to forecast the earnings of the business because small changes in revenue will cause large swings in earnings.
- Those businesses that have high operating leverage typically have a high labor component, high capital-expenditure requirements, high material and production costs, or are required to invest a lot of money in inventory.
- Businesses that have high operating leverage and large amounts of debt have a higher probability of going bankrupt.

Identify How Much Working Capital the Business Has

- The amount of working capital a business needs depends on the capital intensity and the speed at which a business can turn its inventory into cash.
- Businesses that manage working capital inefficiently have less cash flow to put to work.
- If improvements in working capital are sustainable, then every dollar of freed-up working capital will boost cash flows.

Know How the Business Handles Its Maintenance Capital Expenditures

- A business with high maintenance capital expenditures has to continually reinvest cash flow just to maintain existing assets, typically without making an excess return on that investment.
- Whenever you are unable to calculate the maintenance capital expenditures, use depreciation as a rough approximation.

7

Assessing the Quality of Management—Background and Classification: Who Are They?

Most investors overlook the human aspect of operating a business, yet, in most cases, the future success of a business is directly tied to the quality of its people. Instead of focusing on management, many investors spend their time determining whether a business has a competitive advantage or if it is trading at a low valuation, because they believe that products or operational strengths are what set the most successful organizations apart, such as Microsoft's ubiquitous Windows operating system. The truth is that, over time, these advantages can be imitated, and if the talented managers who created these advantages leave the business, then the business will struggle to continue to innovate and create value.

In fact, Microsoft did lose many talented people who either called in rich or joined new businesses, such as Google. This is one reason that Microsoft has created fewer innovative products. Microsoft's stock price peaked during the tech boom at $60 per share on December 29, 1999, dropping to $22 per share only a year later. Since then, it has appreciated to $28 per share as of December 31, 2010—not exactly a great rate of return over a 10-year period.

As an outside investor, you cannot know every detail of what's going on inside a business. There are too many variables that impact the future valuation of a business. You must trust management to make the right decisions. More important, you must know that management can recover quickly from setbacks. In order to trust managers, you need to gain insight into their character and their ability to execute. This will help you improve your forecasts for the business going forward.

Think about how many great businesses of the past have faced ruin due to mismanagement—for example, energy business Enron. Early on, Enron held many high-quality assets, including pipelines. Over time, management transitioned the business into a trading firm, and Enron spun off or sold these high-quality assets. While Enron went bankrupt, many of these spin-offs, such as pipeline business Kinder Morgan Energy Partners (operated by highly capable chief executive officer Richard Kinder), went on to become extremely successful.

To appreciate how essential sound management is to the long-term success of a business, consider that top managers typically:

- Are responsible for designing the business.
- Determine the future growth rate of a business.
- Are in charge of choosing the right people and providing the right environment for these people to perform at their highest potential.
- Determine how to allocate the firm's capital.

Knowing the type of management team you are partnering with will help you forecast the future of the business, because the most logical predictor for the future success of a business is its management. A business does not need to have every manager be an allstar, but at the very least, the managers in key positions need to be allstars. Give yourself plenty of time to understand the quality of the management team running a business. This topic is so important that I've devoted three chapters to it: Chapters 7, 8, and 9.

It is best to evaluate a management team over time. By not rushing into investment decisions and by taking the time to understand a management team, you can reduce your risk of misjudging them. Most errors in assessing managers are made when you try to judge their character quickly or when you see only what you want to see and ignore flaws or warning signs. The more familiar you are with how managers act under different types of circumstances, the better you are able to predict their future actions. Ideally, you want to understand how managers have operated in both difficult and favorable business environments.

Your overall strategy should be to develop a working picture of a manager and the management team. You can start learning about management by gathering all of the historical and current articles written about each manager. These articles serve as a trail of evidence as to the past accomplishments of the management team, the type of people they are, and how they have dealt with different types of situations. You can answer a great number of questions in this book just by reading articles. You can use aggregated news archives, such as *Dow Jones Factiva* or *LexisNexis*, which archive historical articles as far back as the 1980s from publications including the *Wall Street Journal,* the *Financial Times,* the *New York Times,* and various trade journals. Look for articles that reveal how the top managers run the business and the type of people they are. Interviews are especially useful, because managers tell you a great deal about their business philosophy or how they operate the business. Use interview sources such as the *Wall Street Transcript* or the *Charlie Rose* show, which often feature roundtable discussion or lengthy interviews. Pay particular attention to what motivates the managers and why they are where they are professionally.

Some of the best sources of information are trade journals and local newspapers where a business is headquartered. Subjects often reveal more information to industry journalists than they will to a national publication such as the *Wall Street Journal.* Local journalists also have experience in covering the company and may ask questions that reveal deeper insights. The articles also tend to be longer because the local company is important to the community where it is based.

As you read articles, look for evidence in four basic areas: passion, honesty, transparency, and competence. Look for the ability of a manager to recognize and learn from mistakes and also try to see how quickly they are able to recover from mistakes. Look for articles that talk about how a manager helps employees become engaged in the business or keeps customers happy. If there are not many articles written, you either have to rely more on other sources or simply admit that you do not have enough information to assess a manager.

The questions in Chapters 7, 8, and 9 will help guide you in collecting the evidence you need to determine whether a management team is competent and proven.

- The first set of questions, in Chapter 7, helps you learn about the background of the managers and how to classify them.
- The questions in Chapter 8 help you understand how the CEO and other managers manage their business, which will help you determine if they are competent.
- The questions in Chapter 9 help you understand the personality and character of the manager.

Let's begin by exploring the background of the management team and how they are compensated.

☐   33. What type of manager is leading the company?

It is important to classify the type of manager you are partnering with at a business. This way, you will be in a better position to gauge potential execution risk. If you are investing in a manager who has a long track record (i.e., more than 10 years) of successfully managing a business, the odds that he or she will continue to manage the business successfully are in your favor. On the other hand, if you are investing in a new management team that has limited experience serving the customer base of the business, the odds are not in your favor. Here is a simple classification system you can use:

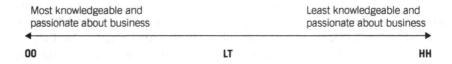

This is a continuum, from left to right; here's a quick overview of what each means, followed by a more detailed description:

- OO is an *owner-operator*, typically the founder of a business.
- LT is a *long-tenured manager* or one who has worked in the industry for at least 3 to 10 years.
- HH is a *hired hand*, a manager who has limited experience serving the customer base of the business and has worked at the business for less than three years.

For example, on the far left side are owner-operators such as the late Sam Walton, founder of Wal-Mart. On the far right-hand side are hired hands who did not have any prior experience at the business before joining as CEO, such as Robert Nardelli, who joined Home Depot in December 2000 from General Electric. Most managers of publicly traded businesses fall into the long-tenured or hired-hand category, and these are the most difficult managers to evaluate. Let's take a closer look at each type, which is further broken down into sub-categories shown below.

Owner-Operator 1 (OO1)   These are the ideal managers to partner with in a business. An owner-operator is a manager who has genuine passion for their particular business and is typically the founder of that business, for example:

- Sam Walton, founder of Wal-Mart
- Dave and Sherry Gold, co-founders of 99 Cent Only Stores
- Joe Mansueto, founder of Morningstar
- John Mackey, co-founder of Whole Foods Market
- Warren Buffett, CEO of Berkshire Hathaway
- Founders of most family-controlled businesses

These passionate leaders run the business for key stakeholders such as customers, employees, and shareholders alike, instead of emphasizing one constituency over the other. They typically are paid modestly and have high ownership interests in the business. For example, according to the Berkshire Hathaway 2010 proxy statement, Warren Buffett earns $100,000 in salary and directly owns 37.1 percent of the stock. These managers take a long-term perspective when making business decisions and identify their personal success with the survival and growth of their businesses. Much like a parent who will do anything to save a critically ill child, these CEOs will go to great lengths to ensure the survival of their businesses.

Owner-Operator 2 (OO2)   This is an owner-operator who is passionate about running the business but is in between the two extremes of being completely stakeholder oriented and operating the business for his or her own personal benefit. These managers typically receive higher compensation packages than OO1 managers. For example, Leslie Wexner, founder of the Limited Brands (owner of Victoria's Secret), earned more than $10 million in total cash compensation in 2009, and he owns 17.7 percent of the business.

Owner-Operator 3 (OO3)   OO3 managers are owner-operators who are passionate about the business but primarily run the business for their own benefit. They do not take shareholder interests into consideration and will often siphon off profits to themselves through egregiously large compensation packages. You can usually identify these types of managers by viewing the Related-Party-Transaction section found in the company's proxy statement, where you might find such items as personal use of company aircraft, estate planning, personal or home security, and real estate that is owned by the CEO and then leased to the business.

For example, in one business, the company's founder received a loan from the business that bore an interest rate of 1 percent over prime to buy a personal aircraft. Another CEO was reimbursed more than $2.6 million a year for security expenses. Both CEOs of these firms could easily afford to pay for these luxuries out of their own pockets, but they used the company to pay for them. You should be careful investing in companies with these types of CEOs because they typically fail to create a lot of value for shareholders over long periods.

Long-Tenured 1 (LT1)   LT1 managers are those who have a long tenure at the existing business. These are managers who have been promoted from within the business and who have worked there for at least three years. The biggest risk with these types of managers is that sometimes they are the wrong manager for the position. Perhaps they were a great chief financial officer (CFO) or chief operating officer (COO), but once promoted to CEO, they fail to execute.

For example, when Kevin Rollins took the management reigns from company founder Michael Dell and became CEO of Dell computers in 2004, most investors believed that this would be a smooth transition, because Rollins had been Dell's COO since 2001. Yet Michael Dell took back the CEO role in 2007 after Rollins mismanaged the business and inflated Dell's cost structure. In April of 2008, Michael Dell spoke to analysts in Texas and explained how the company was going to regroup. He outlined the challenges he saw[1]:

- Declining market share. They had missed being in the fastest growing parts of the industry.
- The wrong cost structure, both in COGS (cost of goods sold) and OpEx (operating expenses).
- Eroded profitability. The result of the combination of the wrong cost structure, inefficiencies in the system, and missed execution.
- Too many priorities. The list of things to do was too long and the company needed focus.
- Incomplete product coverage. They were "trying to do too much with too limited a product line."

How could this have happened? Rollins had made enormous contributions at Dell, including implementing the negative working capital business model that Dell is so well known for today. Simply put, Rollins made a great lieutenant to Michael Dell, but he was not equipped to be CEO of Dell. He was the wrong manager for the position.

Long-Tenured 2 (LT2)   LT2 stands for a long-tenured manager who joined from outside the business but who has worked in the same industry. The manager may have been recruited from a competitor or a business that serves a similar customer set.

An example of this type of manager is Frank J. Williams, CEO of healthcare research business The Advisory Board Company. He joined Advisory Board in September 2000 as an executive vice president (EVP) and has been CEO and a director since June 2001. Before joining the business, he was President of MedAmerica OnCall, a consultancy for physician organizations, hospitals, and managed-care entities. In both businesses, he was in charge of advising healthcare businesses on how to run their practices, which means he had prior experience serving the same customer base.

Hired Hand 1 (HH1)   An HH1 is a manager who joined the business from a related industry. Hired hands tend to jump from job to job. These managers typically make short-term decisions because they are not accountable over the long term. Most of these managers are cost cutters rather than revenue builders.

Hired Hand 2 (HH2)   An HH2 is a manager who joined the business from a completely unrelated industry and typically has no experience with the customer base. HH2s have steep learning curves in the new business. Think of CEOs such as Robert Nardelli, who was CEO of Home Depot from December 2000 to January 2007: Prior to joining Home Depot, Nardelli worked at General Electric, an industrial conglomerate.

The Importance of Managers' Tenure in Operating the Business

As you move down the continuum from OO to HH, the less information you will have on how a manager will choose to operate the business. For example, if you invest in an HH with a limited track record operating the business, this increases your potential downside risk because when a new management team enters a business, the company's past results provide less insight into its future prospects. You will take less risk partnering with managers who have a proven track record of running a business because you can give more weight to the historical track record. These established management teams understand the intricacies of running the business day to day and most important of all, they understand the customer base. Outsiders typically do not have this depth of knowledge.

It is difficult to find CEOs who have operated their businesses for a long period. For example, consider these two statistics according to an analysis conducted by recruiting company Spencer Stuart for the *Wall Street Journal*:

- Out of the 500 businesses in the S&P 500, *only 28* have CEOs who have held office for more than 15 years.
- The typical CEO has held the title for *only 6.6 years*.

As confirmation that tenure improves stockholder returns, consider this: Of the 28 long-term CEOs above, 25 of them had total shareholders returns during their tenures that beat the S&P 500 index (with total shareholder return calculated as stock price change plus reinvested dividends).[2]

☐ 34. What are the effects on the business of bringing in outside management?

Many investors will bid up the stock price of a business when an outside manager or CEO enters the business. These investors believe that management skills are transferable and react positively when a new management team enters a business, especially one that has been mismanaged. These investors think outside managers can instill changes and improve underperforming companies, because the outside managers are objective and not married to the culture. If this person was a great manager at The Coca-Cola Company, the thinking goes, then he or she will be great at operating any other business. This is similar to saying that a great value investor would make a great trader because both are in the investment business. Obviously, these two styles of investment require different types of expertise and experience to execute properly.

Investors also often make the mistake of underestimating the importance of the support networks these managers had at their prior company that helped make them successful in the first place. When these managers then enter a new business, they often run into problems because they don't have that support network, and many fail to perform.

In addition, most of these managers are great cost cutters but fail when it comes to growing the business. There are very few cases where a manager is good at both cutting costs and building the business such as Steve Jobs, founder of Apple. When he returned to Apple in 1997, Apple was on the brink of bankruptcy. Jobs was able to cut costs to keep Apple out of bankruptcy and then rebuilt its entire product line and organization.

When you learn that an outsider has joined to lead the business, respond with extreme caution. RHR International, a Chicago-headquartered management consultant, states that 40 percent to 60 percent of high-level corporate executives brought in from outside the company will leave within two years. Many have problems and leave in just a few months.[3]

A manager with a lot of organization-specific knowledge is critical to generating long-term growth at a business, whereas an outsider needs a significant amount of time to learn the business. Jeffrey Immelt, CEO of General Electric, said, "You see that the most successful parts of GE are places where leaders have stayed in place a long time. Think of Brian Rowe's long tenure in aircraft engines. Four or five big decisions he made—relying on his deep knowledge of that business—won us maybe as many as 50 years of industry leadership. . . the places where we've churned people, like reinsurance, are where you will find we've failed."[4]

In addition, relative to managers who have been at the business for long periods of time, outside managers have a more limited understanding of a business's resources and constraints. The risk you take as an investor is that instead of *building on* an existing business's capabilities, they *deviate* from them. Therefore, a new management team creates unpredictability.

There are some industries where specialized knowledge of the business is especially critical: for example, pharmaceuticals, chemicals, and insurance. It is difficult for an outsider to successfully manage these types of businesses, and you should probably avoid investing in them if an outsider does become CEO.

For example, it is critical for the CEO of an insurance firm to have spent a lot of time in the insurance industry because there is a long learning curve in this industry. An insurance firm is insuring against risks that may occur in the future, and managers who have been in the industry for a long time have lived with the fallout of their mistakes. This helps them understand how to properly underwrite insurance. Without this experience, managers are likely to make many more mistakes, which *you*, as a shareholder, will pay for.

There are a few cases where outside managers tend to be good hires: For example, when a business needs to break from past strategies or needs to cut costs quickly. If the industry changes very quickly, this will also improve the odds that an outside manager will succeed, but if the industry is stable, then industry knowledge is more important. Most of these new managers tend to do well early on in their tenure as they cut costs, but later they start to do badly when it comes time to build the business. In other words, they are good at doing the rapid cost-cutting and divestment, but when it comes to building and sustaining long-term growth, they fail.

For example, Al "Chainsaw" Dunlap created a lot of value for his investors by quickly turning around and selling such companies as American Can, Lily-Tulip, Crown-Zellerbach, Diamond International, Consolidated Press Holdings, and Scott Paper. Dunlap's strategy was slash-for-cash, where he would take a floundering business and make it profitable within a year. He did this at Scott Paper, which had just lost $227 million in 1993: During his 20 months at Scott, Dunlap increased the company's market value by 155 percent, from $2.9 billion to $7.4 billion. He accomplished this turnaround by firing 11,200 employees (which consisted of 70 percent of its head-office staff, 50 percent of its management, and 20 percent of its blue-collar workers) and by cutting the research and development (R&D) budget in half, suspending corporate philanthropy, and deferring plant maintenance. He succeeded with this strategy for a few years and was lauded as a legendary turnaround artist and a role model for many managers.

So when he became CEO of appliance maker Sunbeam in 1996, the stock price promptly rose 60 percent, as investors anticipated that Dunlap would quickly turn around the fortunes of the business. At that time, this was the greatest jump due to a CEO change that had ever occurred in the history of the NYSE. Unfortunately, the techniques he used to turn around other businesses in the past—such as slashing expenses—worked against him at Sunbeam, and the company declared bankruptcy in 2001, two years after Dunlap was dismissed as CEO. In fact, after all the dust settled, Dunlap had to accept a lifetime ban from serving as an officer or director of any public company because the SEC alleged that Dunlap engineered a massive accounting fraud.[5]

When an outside manager enters the business, closely monitor his or her actions. The best types of outside managers are those who don't make changes quickly and make an effort to understand the business and its customer base as well as solicit the opinions of employees before they implement major changes. This way, they gain the support of the employees whom they will need to execute their plans; just as important, they avoid the problem of under- or over-estimating the capabilities of the employees. If instead, the manager joins the business and starts to make changes immediately, without getting buy-in from the employees or understanding their limitations, it is likely he or she will fail, and you should avoid investing in this company.

☐ 35. Is the manager a lion or a hyena?

Another simple way to categorize management is to classify management teams as either *lions* or *hyenas*. This idea was created by Seng Hock Tan, CEO of Aegis Group of Companies, a Singapore-based investment management organization, who came up with this classification while watching a Discovery channel program about lions and hyenas. As he learned about how lions and hyenas interact in the wild, he felt that their behavior was very similar to that displayed by managers.[6]

As he watched the program, he learned both are super predators and are often in direct competition with one another. However, here's the difference between the two. Lions typically hunt together in a group (called a pride), so that they can go after bigger game, which means more food for everybody. Instead of having a single dominant leader, as is commonly believed, males have equal status, as do females. In contrast, hyenas group together only when hunting is easy: After an easy kill, they disband. On their own again, they go back to scavenging carcasses. Status is extremely important to hyenas, with a higher rank netting more respect within the troop. They do not build a team under them except when it immediately benefits them, and loyalty is weak. If a hyena becomes wounded or weak, the troop abandons that hyena. Interestingly, the hyena recognizes the lion's status: As the hyena's only natural predator, the lion commands the hyena's respect.

Tan applied these differences in the animal world to management styles. Table 7.1 summarizes the contrasts.

Tan goes on further to explain that a lion manager is able to build the infrastructure for a 100-story skyscraper, whereas a hyena manager can construct only a five-story building because it can be done in less time: Investing and building a long-term infrastructure taxes the nature of the hyena. For example, investing in a team and sustainable infrastructure takes a lot of time, which a hyena manager does not have the patience to do. The hyena continually enriches himself by repeating the short cycle of building and selling five-story buildings. Hyena managers never build the more valuable 100-story building that lasts longer than a five-story building.

Table 7.1   Contrasting the Management Style of Lions and Hyenas

Lion Manager	Hyena Manager
Committed to ethical and moral values	Has little interest in ethics and morals
Thinks long term and maintains a long-term focus	Thinks short term
Does not take shortcuts	Just wants to win the game
Thirsty for knowledge and learning	Has little interest in knowledge and learning
Supports partners and alliances	A survivor and an opportunist; works mostly alone
Treats employees as partners	Treats employees as expenses
Admires perseverance	Admires tactics, resourcefulness, and guile

Source: Interview with Seng Hock Tan October 2010.

As Tan says, "The hyena manager is therefore an opportunistic trader, not an all-season builder of a lasting structure."

Although, the skyscraper will generate huge returns for its investors over long periods of time, the flipped five-story building, although profitable to the lone hyena, will generate more limited returns for outside investors.

Tan explains further: "How did Apple catapult from $5 billion in market capitalization in early 2003 to a market cap of $220 billion?" Tan contrasts Apple with Palm, which brought out the pioneering Palm Pilot product. Why was Palm, with a $90 billion market cap at its peak, bought out in 2010 by Hewlett-Packard, as Seng Hock asks, "for a mere $1.2 billion?" The difference was that Apple was run by a Lion manager: Steve Jobs.

Most competent early-stage companies do not cross the chasm to an established business because they lack the lion manager's infrastructure—the teamwork, the know-how, the necessary institutional structures, and the culture. This is the groundwork needed to survive and grow sustainably, and it is why companies run by lion managers become multi-bagger investments.

As you look at the manager on a personal level, also note characteristics that indicate how likely they are to be able to build and lead an effective team. Look for their lion characteristics. Does the manager value people more highly because of power, influence, or what they can do for them? Or do the managers consider themselves to be better than those around them? Perhaps they are extremely nice to you and your friends, but when they deal with a waiter, for instance, they are rude. In other words, they are nice to people they consider to be important, but disrespectful to others whom they consider beneath them. If you are engaged in a conversation with someone and a higher-status person walks into the room, does your conversation end as they quickly leave to join the higher-status person? This is a hyena characteristic.

For example, I remember attending Berkshire Hathaway annual meetings and speaking with many of the CEOs who run subsidiaries of Berkshire Hathaway. Often, someone else would walk up to them and tell them that someone important, such as another CEO, wanted to speak with them. Even though they did not know me, they continued to answer my questions and didn't cut me off. In contrast, most of the money managers I knew well would immediately walk away mid-sentence if someone passed by whom they thought was more important. Look for managers that display the lion characteristic of showing respect for people, regardless of status. It is a strong predictor of their ability to command the respect of others, and an important leadership characteristic.

The hyena/lion metaphor is a powerful tool for evaluating managers. When Tan and his team interview managers, one of the first questions they ask themselves is whether the manager is a lion or a hyena. This is an easy-to-use and highly effective tool, and the mental imagery may be extremely useful for quickly summarizing the character of a manager.

☐ 36. How did the manager rise to lead the business?

To understand the management team's background, start by constructing a chronology of the careers of the top five managers, using the biography section found in the company's proxy statement. The goal is to get the details of a manager's career so you can map out the manager's professional life. You need to use historical proxy statements, going back at least five to 10 years, because in more recent proxy statements, earlier jobs are not emphasized. You can then fill in the gaps of the manager's career by reading articles written about the CEO and the other top four managers over a 10-year period.

For example, by using a combination of historical proxy statements and articles, my firm compiled the career of Larry Young, CEO of Dr. Pepper Snapple Group, shown here:

2008:	Remains CEO when Dr. Pepper Snapple Group spins from Cadbury
2007:	CEO/President of Dr. Pepper Snapple Group (Cadbury)
2006:	President and COO of Cadbury Schweppes Bottling Group (Cadbury acquires Dr. Pepper/Seven Up Bottling)
2005:	Joins as President/CEO of Dr. Pepper/Seven Up Bottling Group in Dallas
2005:	Leaves PepsiAmericas
2002:	EVP of Corporate Affairs for PepsiAmericas
2000:	President/COO combined company for PepsiAmericas/Whitman
1999:	COO of Pepsi General Bottling (operating company of Whitman)
1998:	EVP and COO of Whitman and Pepsi General Bottling
1997:	President, Pepsi General Bottlers—East European Division
1996:	President, International, Pepsi General Bottling
1995:	Vice President of Sales and Marketing—International, Pepsi General Bottling

1994:   Director of Sales and Marketing—International, Pepsi General Bottling

1989:   Director, On Premise Sales & Marketing for Springfield Pepsi General Bottling

1969:   Begins his career with a Pepsi franchise (Pepsi General Bottling) as a route salesman in Springfield, Missouri.

This is a very detailed biography; in contrast, if we had used only the 2009 proxy biography for Larry Young, we would have a more limited view of his career, as shown below:

> Larry D. Young, President and Chief Executive Officer and Director, age 55, has served as our director since October 2007. Mr. Young has served as our President and Chief Executive Officer (our "CEO") since October 2007. Mr. Young joined Cadbury Schweppes Americas Beverages as President and Chief Operating Officer of the Bottling Group segment and Head of Supply Chain in 2006 after our acquisition of Dr Pepper/Seven Up Bottling Group, Inc. ("DPSUBG"), where he had been President and Chief Executive Officer since May 2005. From 1997 to 2005, Mr. Young served as President and Chief Operating Officer of Pepsi-Cola General Bottlers, Inc. and Executive Vice President of Corporate Affairs at PepsiAmericas, Inc.

By building a chronology of the career of a manager, you will understand how the manager came up through the ranks of the companies he or she worked for, and you can better determine whether the manager has a history of making deals, financial engineering, marketing, or creating new products. For example, if they worked for businesses owned by private equity firms for most of their careers, then the managers are likely to have a short-term mentality and may emphasize cutting costs over other initiatives.

Ask questions such as:

- Does the manager have a background in operations, marketing, or finance?
- Did the manager jump from job to job, or does he/she have a long tenure in the industry?
- Why are there gaps in his or her employment history?

Pay particular attention to how much interaction the manager has had with both customers and employees. For example, determine whether the manager has a lot of experience in operating the business or if the manager's career has been limited to the corporate suite. If the manager has been a controller, treasurer, or CFO, and was then promoted to CEO, then most of that manager's time has been spent in the corporate suite. In contrast, if the background of the manager is VP of Sales, VP of Marketing, COO, and then CEO, that manager has had more interaction with the operations and customer base of a business.

Be Aware of the Risks of a Manager with a Non-Operating Background

A related risk you may be exposed to is that managers who have risen from inside the corporate suite of the business often do not make good operators. This is because they have less experience with the day-to-day operations of the business. If the managers have spent most of their careers in the corporate executive office, then how will they know how to operate the business at the customer level? These managers have a narrow view of the business due to the fact that they have only viewed the business from one particular angle. This traps many managers into a constricted way of thinking about the business. Their past interaction with the employees of the business will have been more limited, as well.

For example, there is no doubt that new drug development has suffered in the pharmaceutical industry as more of the CEOs who lead these companies are promoted from within the corporate suite (such as managers who have been CFOs or General Counsels), or from outside, unrelated businesses instead of CEOs with science backgrounds. As a result, most pharmaceutical firms have not had many blockbuster drugs from 2000 to 2010 and many currently face their patents expiring, without any drugs in the pipeline to replace them.[7]

Merck's greatest stock market returns came during the time it was managed by Roy Vagelos, who was a scientist (both chemist and doctor) and worked as head of Merck's research department and then CEO, from 1978 to 1994. Vagelos changed the way Merck did research by emphasizing scientific discovery. Under his tenure, he brought in hundreds of new scientists and modernized Merck's labs. He also focused on new product categories like cardiovascular treatment. He sought and found what he termed "really better people who wanted to work in drug development." When Vagelos led the research department, he increased R&D spending by an average of 17.2 percent a year. Merck focused R&D on cures that were needed, instead of making questionable improvements to existing drugs, as most pharmaceutical firms did. During Vagelos's tenure, 10 major new drugs were launched, such as Vasotec and Prinivil for hypertension and Pepcid for heartburn. When Vagelos retired in 1994, Merck had the best and largest marketing staff, and led the pharmaceutical industry in sales.

However, Vagelos's replacement, who was chosen by the board (and not Vagelos), was Raymond Gilmartin, who joined Merck from Becton Dickinson, a medical device maker. He was an outsider who simply did not understand the culture of innovation. As a result, the talented scientists left the business, and Merck's ability to develop new drugs suffered dramatically.[8]

Similarly, take a look at General Motors. Alex Taylor documents the decline of GM in his book *Sixty to Zero: An Inside Look at the Collapse of General Motors—and the Detroit Auto Industry*. Taylor writes that GM's best years were when it was led by such innovators as CEO Harlow Curtice, who led GM from 1953 to 1958. Curtice had started out as a bookkeeper, but he gradually became a super sales-man who developed a shrewd understanding of how design created buzz and sold cars. Under his tenure at Buick, sales doubled. As Taylor notes, "Curtice may have been the last GM CEO who wielded so much power in the design studio."

After Curtice, GM was run by managers who were mainly accoun-tants and who therefore placed more emphasis on cutting costs, instead of worrying about what was coming out of the design studio. For example, Fred Donner was an accountant who directly succeeded Curtice, and he spent his entire career operating GM from New York City instead of Detroit. He seldom visited car factories, and most of what he knew about the operations was from executive meetings, bal-ance sheets, and reports. He was focused on cost-cutting rather than designing cars that sold well. Taylor makes a good case for the idea that GM's failure took root during this period as these cost cutting CEOs kicked down the road many of GM's problems.

How Much Experience Does the Manager Have with the Customer Base?

If a business's success hinges to a great degree on management's capabilities, as it does in restaurant chains, you will typically take less risk if you invest in managers who have a lot of experience with the customer base. Avoid those who have spent most of their careers in the corporate suite or who have served customers in a different type of industry.

For example, in 2002, Jack Stahl left his job as president of The Coca-Cola Company to attempt a turnaround at cosmetics company Revlon. Stahl had been at The Coca-Cola Company for 22 years and Revlon's board had great faith in him, believing that his disciplined approach to operations was just the thing Revlon needed. He brought in financial experts and statisticians, and reduced the company's debt. Unfortunately, he also changed the way Revlon marketed its products. As Revlon launched new products, it lost many of its old customers. Some of the new products had higher prices and didn't use the powerful Revlon name. In the four years after Stahl assumed control of Revlon, the company suffered continued losses as well as a two-thirds decline in Revlon's share price. Stahl left Revlon in 2006.[9] Although Stahl had done an excellent job at The Coca-Cola Company, he was ill-equipped to deal with the nuances of running a cosmetics company.

Does the Manager Have Experience with Most Operations of the Business?

You want to get a sense of the manager's understanding of all the divisions and functions of the business. Ideally, a manager would have experience in multiple positions.

For example, Tom Folliard, CEO of used-car retail chain CarMax, joined CarMax in 1993 as a senior buyer and became director of purchasing in 1994. He was promoted to VP of merchandising in 1996, SVP of store operations in 2000, EVP of store operations in 2001, and president and CEO in 2006.[10] Therefore, he has led most of the major divisions at Carmax, and he understands what it takes to operate each division effectively. This experience reduces the risk to investors that Folliard will fail to execute. Even more important, it improves his credibility with employees within the company because he has managed most of their departments in the past.

What Is this Manager's Previous Track Record in Operating a Business?

As you read articles written about a manager, be sure to learn about their past accomplishments or lack of accomplishments. For example, James Adamson became CEO of retailer K-Mart when it entered bankruptcy in early 2002. Previously, he was a member of K-Mart's

Board of Directors. To determine whether Adamson had the ability to lead K-Mart, you could have reviewed his past history by reading both the proxy statement and historical articles. From 1995 to 2001, Adamson was CEO of the Advantica Restaurant Group, which owned Denny's. He was brought in when Denny's faced many lawsuits for discriminating against black customers, and he successfully transformed Denny's public image issues into a number-one ranking in *Fortune* magazine's "Best Companies for Minorities" category in 2000 and 2001.

However, during Adamson's tenure at Advantica, the company lost $98 million in 2000 and $89 million in 2001. After Adamson assumed control of K-Mart, he was equally unsuccessful at returning the retailer to profitability. Adamson's track record of losing money should have alerted investors that he was probably not the best choice for leading K-Mart through a restructuring.[11]

This wasn't the first time K-Mart had missed the mark on manager appointments. Before Adamson was promoted as CEO, K-Mart had brought in Charles Conaway as CEO and Wal-Mart veteran Mark Schwartz as CFO. Conaway was past president and COO of pharmacy retailer CVS Corporation and Schwartz joined from Wal-Mart (K-Mart's biggest competitor) where he had worked for 17 years. Many investors were excited to hear that Schwartz had joined the business because of his experience at Wal-Mart. Schwartz made many bold statements to investors on how he was going to tackle Wal-Mart head on.

However, Schwartz's track record wasn't as encouraging as his rhetoric. Had you studied his resume, you would have seen that two of the companies he ran before working at Wal-Mart—home products business Hechinger's and Big V Supermarkets—had landed in bankruptcy. Two years after Conaway and Schwartz were brought in, K-Mart declared bankruptcy.[12, 13]

Why Was the Manager Promoted?

You need to determine why a manager was promoted to his or her current position. For example, in 2010, Merck promoted Kenneth Frazier to CEO. Frazier had been with Merck since 1992, and had served in several roles including that of General Counsel. He was known for developing the controversial legal strategy of fighting every case filed against Merck's pain drug Vioxx, rather than settling all the cases jointly in a class action lawsuit. This strategy had helped save Merck hundreds of millions of dollars.[14]

In fact, Frazier was promoted to CEO because he helped Merck defend itself from lawsuits, not because he was successful in helping Merck develop new drugs. Frazier's background was in the corporate suite, and even though he was head of the global human health division (which is Merck's largest unit) from 2007 to 2010, Frazier's experience running the operations of the business was more limited. Therefore, this increases the risk that Frazier will fail to execute as CEO.

What Was the Culture Like at Businesses Where This Manager Worked in the Past?

You need to understand the culture of the businesses where the manager has worked in the past. For example, software and hardware business Oracle is known for a take-no-prisoners culture that is results oriented, whereas British Airways is known for an excessively bureaucratic culture.[15] This will give you tremendous insight into how he or she is likely to manage the current business, especially if the manager worked at the prior business for a long period of time.

Start by reading articles about the culture of the former business where the manager worked, as well as articles about the CEO this manager worked for. Were the CEO and the culture aggressive and hard-charging, or transparent and authentic? For example, if a manager worked at General Electric (GE), take a look at any of several books and articles written about "the GE Way." The GE Way is taught at GE's management school: It involves rotating managers through many jobs, teaches them how to grow a business through acquisitions, and teaches productivity and quality-control tools such as Six Sigma.

When Jim McNerney was passed over as CEO of GE, he was immediately recruited by 3M to be CEO (in 2001). Once he was CEO of 3M, he immediately began to look for acquisitions to make, and he instituted money-saving Six Sigma process-management systems companywide.[16] By reading about the GE Way, you would have had a great insight into how McNerney would likely manage 3M.

☐ 37. How are senior managers compensated, and how did they gain their ownership interest?

It is important to spend time reviewing the compensation and ownership interest of management by viewing the proxy statement.

You can gain great insight into the character and motivation of managers by understanding how they are compensated. You want to understand if the compensation package rewards for long-term or short-term performance. For example, if a CEO owns $100 million of stock, and he is paid $100,000 per year, then he is more likely to make long-term decisions. In contrast, if a CEO gets paid $5 million a year and owns $1 million of stock, then he will likely value his job more than the value of the company's stock.

Let's take a closer look at different compensation scenarios and what aspects you should pay attention to.

Look for CEOs Who Have Low Salaries and High Stock Ownership

Some of the best long-term performing stocks have been run by CEOs with low cash compensation and high stock ownership. These managers generally have a long-term view. Here are a few examples:

Robert Kierlin, founder of Fastenal (a distributor of industrial products), and his successor as CEO, Willard Oberton. Fastenal consistently ranks at the bottom of CEO compensation: For example, Kierlin made $63,000 in total cash compensation in 2001 and owned 5.87 percent of the business.[17] But take a look at how well the stock has performed: The stock price has appreciated from $0.32 per share on September 1, 1987 to $60 per share on December 31, 2010—that's a *huge* increase![18]

Dave Gold, co-founder of 99 Cent Only Stores, was paid $62,000 to $180,000 in total cash compensation (and did not receive any stock options or bonuses) when he was CEO, yet he owned approximately 40 percent of the business.[19] Under his tenure, the stock price increased from $3.81 per share at its initial public offering (IPO) on May 23, 1996, to $15.32 per share when he stepped down as CEO in January 2005—again, a huge increase: more than 400 percent.

Joe Mansueto, founder of Morningstar, is paid $100,000 in total cash compensation and owns 52 percent of Morningstar.[20] The stock price has increased from $21 per share at its IPO in May 2005 to $53 per share in December 2010—in other words, more than double in a little more than five years.

Russel Gerdin, CEO of trucking firm Heartland Express, earned $300,000 per year in total cash compensation, a salary that hasn't changed since 1986. He also owns 34 percent of shares and does not receive stock options. The stock price has increased from $0.43 per share in 1986 to $16 per share in 2010[21]—another enormous increase.

Be Wary of Managers Who Hold Stock Options

One of the most common ways that management is compensated is through stock options, which give the owner the right to buy shares at a specific stock price. They represent a potential payoff to the manager with no risk: The downside is zero (if the stock price doesn't increase, there's no payout to the managers, and if the stock price does increase, then they benefit). Investors believe that giving stock option grants to managers will motivate them to create shareholder value, because it gives them an ownership interest in the business.

The problem is that stock options often reward managers for things that they are not responsible for, such as broad economic gains or industry growth. As one investor said: "The argument that someone is worth tens of millions of dollars in compensation per year because his or her company's market value went up many times is so ludicrous that I've always been amazed anyone can espouse it as fair with a straight face."

In reality, most stock-option programs reward managers for short-term gains. This is because managers with a lot of options rather than actual shares are prone to adopt Wall Street's short-term focus in order to increase the stock price and therefore the value of their options. They can take several harmful actions to drive the price of a stock up in the near-term to the detriment of the long-term health of the business. Examples would be making acquisitions to boost short-term earnings or cutting too many costs. These short-term decisions can eventually cause the value of the business to deteriorate as one bad decision piles up on top of another.

Be Wary of Companies that Offer Mega-Equity Grants to CEOs or Other Managers

The highest pay packages are typically given to managers who are brought in from another company or industry. You need to be cautious of management compensation schemes that give out mega-equity grants that are out of proportion to the CEO's contribution, such as when Robert Nardelli was given $30 million in restricted stock awards plus $7 million in cash when he joined Home Depot as CEO. Furthermore, after pulling in $38 million in 2006, Nardelli was also given an astronomical $210 million in severance when he exited the business. This was money that would otherwise have benefited shareholders. The stock price under Nardelli's tenure was $45 per share when he joined (in December 2000) and $39 per share when he left (on January 2, 2007).[22]

When Nardelli landed at Chrysler later that year, he also landed another lucrative compensation package. Under Nardelli, 35,000 workers at Chrysler were laid off and Chrysler headed for bankruptcy. Nardelli left after only 21 months. In both of these instances, Nardelli was paid not on the performance of the business, but instead was paid to join the business.

However, large compensation packages do not always necessarily indicate that a stock will underperform. For example, Larry Ellison, founder and chief executive of software maker Oracle, has been one of the highest-paid CEOs of any publicly traded business, earning in excess of $78 million in option awards alone in 2009, yet investors in Oracle would have made 3.5 times their money in the last 10 years ended 2010. (However, it is still difficult to argue that Ellison needs additional stock options to motivate him to do his job, as he owns 23.4 percent of Oracle, as of August 9, 2010.[23])

Look for Managers Who Don't Monopolize Stock Options but Offer Options to All Employees

You need to determine if the stock option plan of a company is geared to only a few of the top executive officers or if options are widely distributed among employees. This will give you an insight into the character of senior managers, because if they share the wealth with all of their employees through a widely distributed plan, this means they care about their employees. If, instead, they only award themselves a large option package, this means they care more about themselves.

For example, in a letter to shareholders, Richard Reese, former CEO of document-management company Iron Mountain, explained why he would not accept any stock options, saying that he preferred to use them to retain good people rather than compensate himself.

To find information on a company's stock option-program, look for a table in the proxy statement that lists the total number of options awarded to the top five executive officers. Add up the total number of options awarded to the top five executive officers. Then, in the 10-K or proxy, find the total number of options awarded to all employees. Calculate the percentage of options given to the top five executive officers compared to all employees. Determine if stock options are widely distributed or if they are concentrated within the top group.

For example, at Whole Foods Market, approximately 92 percent of the stock options granted under the plan since its inception in 1992 have been granted to employees who are not executive officers.[24] On the other hand, the management team at bond-rating firm Moody's awarded itself a large percentage of stock options when it was spun off from Dun & Bradstreet. Moody's 2000 proxy statement shows that CEO John Rutherfurd received 4.1 percent of all options granted to employees in the fiscal year, followed by Donald Noe, SVP of Global Ratings and Research, who received 3.0 percent. These two executive officers received about the same percentage of stock options as all of the top executive officers at Whole Foods Market *combined*. This should serve as a warning signal because it indicates that senior managers at Moody's view the business as one where they can personally benefit without sharing those benefits with their employees.

Look for Compensation Plans that Reward Long-Term Performance

In order for a compensation program to reward long-term performance, it must tie compensation to long-term results. For example, at ExxonMobil, half of an executive officer's restricted shares vest over five years, and the other half must be held for 10 years or until retirement, whichever is greater. This rewards management for long-term results.

The ideal compensation structures are those that award for long-term value-creation factors, such as operating income or book value per share, instead of the stock price. Determine if the compensation is tied to variables that make the business better, rather than just bigger. For example:

- Expeditors International (a global logistics company) bases its bonuses on operating income, and these bonuses make up the majority of executive officer compensation.
- Reckitt Benckiser Group (a global manufacturer of household and healthcare products) links performance-based compensation for all executive officers to economic value added.

- Markel Insurance (a specialty insurer) uses growth in book value per share over a five-year measurement period to base its total compensation package.

Let's look at each of these companies' compensation structures in more detail.

Expeditors International's Compensation System   Expeditors International ties its compensation system to operating profit instead of stock price by paying its top executive officers from a pool of 10 percent of pre-bonus operating income. This system has been in place since Expeditors International went public in 1984. If operating income drops (as it did in 2009, when operating income dropped 19 percent compared to 2008), then incentive compensation also drops by the same amount. Furthermore, the compensation system is also based on cumulative operating income, so if any operating losses are incurred, then these losses must be recovered before the executive team can earn a percentage of operating profits. This gives senior managers a longer-term incentive because if they engage in activities that increase short-term profits at the expense of long-term profits, then they will receive a lower bonus down the line. This creates a direct alignment between corporate performance and shareholder interests because the compensation is directly proportional to the profit responsibility of each manager.

Reckitt Benckiser Group's Compensation System   Reckitt Benckiser Group links performance-based compensation for all executive officers to economic value added, measuring net sales growth, profit after taxes, and net working capital. The long-term incentive program requires that EPS has to grow by 30 percent over three years for the options and the shares to fully vest. When Chairman Peter Harf was asked why the compensation plan did not reward for stock price increases, he said, "We have stayed away from that [performance tied to total shareholder return], because it can lead to outcomes that are completely uncoupled from the company's performance."[25]

Markel Insurance's Compensation System   Markel Insurance chose growth in book value per share over a five-year measurement period to set its compensation program for its executive officers. The executive officers at Markel believe that the primary creator of value for an insurance business is its book value per share, not the stock price. Markel uses a five-year period in order to discourage managers from taking unnecessary risks.

There are various other forms of compensation that are positive indicators that the compensation package is based on long-term results, such as restricted stock awards. Stock-ownership requirements also align management interests with the long term.

Look for Restricted Stock Awards because They Reward Long-Term Value Creation

Restricted stock awards reward long-term value creation more than stock options because they often are conditioned on such factors as longevity or performance. In other words, a manager must be employed by the company for a certain length of time or must meet specific performance goals. This is meant to encourage long-term ownership in the firm.

For example, at Goldman Sachs, 40 percent of the restricted stock an employee receives typically vests immediately, but it isn't delivered for three years. Therefore, if an employee leaves, then that employee risks losing his or her restricted shares.

Similarly, at insurance underwriter Markel Insurance Company, restricted stock is given to senior managers after they meet pre-established performance goals, which are granted based on growth in book value per share, over a five-year period. Markel believes that by paying a substantial portion of incentive compensation in restricted stock units (RSUs), it has both the advantage of increasing management's equity ownership and creating a retention incentive, because the manager must remain employed by the company to receive the stock.

Look for Companies that Require Stock Ownership

Some businesses have stock-ownership and retention guidelines that require management to own a certain amount of stock. For example, the 2009 proxy statement for Markel Insurance Corporation states:

> The Company places a strong emphasis on equity ownership by executive officers and other members of senior management. The Board of Directors has adopted stock ownership guidelines

that require executive officers to acquire and maintain ownership of Common Stock with a value at least equal to five times base salary and other members of senior management to acquire and maintain ownership of Common Stock with a value at least equal to two or three times base salary, depending on position. Newly hired or newly promoted executive officers are expected to reach these minimum levels of ownership within five years.

If you find this type of compensation program in the proxy, then it is likely that the management has an incentive to perform over the long term.

Other Valuable Insights You Can Glean from Reading the Proxy Statement on How the Compensation System Is Set Up

The way a compensation system is structured can gave you valuable insights into the character and motivation of management. Rather than focusing on *how much* executive officers are paid, it is more useful to understand *how* an executive compensation plan is structured. Start by viewing the proxy statement section titled Compensation Discussion and Analysis, where the compensation committee of the board of directors communicates how it sets the compensation package for the top executive officers and employees. For example, an executive officer might be compensated even if he or she did not meet the performance targets. The former CEO of Shell, Jeroen van de Veer, received a $1.9 million bonus from an incentive program where he failed to meet the performance targets set for three years. Running across a compensation arrangement such as this would certainly provide insight into the type of management team you are thinking of partnering with.[26]

In contrast, the 2009 proxy statement for Morningstar states:

> In consideration of his status as our principal shareholder, Joe Mansueto believes his compensation as our chief executive officer should be realized primarily through appreciation in the long-term value of our common stock. Accordingly, at his request, he doesn't participate in our equity or cash-based incentive programs. In addition, since resuming his role as our chief executive officer in 2000, his annual salary has been fixed at $100,000.

You can evaluate Mansueto's character and that he manages the business in the interest of his shareholders, because he refuses to accept stock options. This gives you great insight into his character, and this is the type of CEO you should look for as a long-term partner.

Beware of Companies that Use Compensation Consultants

If a compensation package is determined by consultants hired by the board of directors, this should serve as a red flag. This kind of compensation benchmarking is usually not about the performance of the business, but rather a comparison to what others in the industry make. However, the peer groups used are often in completely unrelated business lines. You will find that the majority of compensation plans are determined in this way.

For example, in FY 2010, jewelry retailer Zale hired a compensation consultant who put together a list of 21 companies as a peer group. The consultant included such companies as Abercrombie & Fitch, American Eagle Outfitters, and Children's Place, which are specialty apparel companies, not jewelry retailers. The consulting firm then targeted compensation within a certain percentile range of the peer group. For example, the 2009 Zale proxy states: "Accordingly, base salaries generally were targeted between the 25th and 50th percentile of market, and annual performance-based bonuses generally were targeted between the 25th and 50th percentile of market."

Two red flags are raised here: That compensation was determined by comparison to loosely related peers, and the fact that base compensation does not have anything to do with the performance of the business.

Beware of Companies that Use Employment Contracts

Another red flag is when you find employment contracts in the proxy statement that guarantee that a manager will be paid a certain amount in total cash compensation. This guarantee of compensation does not directly align the executive officers with the long-term interests of the business.

For example, K-Mart handed out roughly $30 million in retention loans (retention loans are given when the company is failing, but often they are awarded after a bankruptcy filing) to its 25 top managers, including $5 million to then-CEO Chuck Conaway.

The loans were given to entice the managers to stay at the business. At the same time, however, management was firing thousands of employees and cutting the salaries of other managers. This likely decreased morale among the employees at K-Mart, and these managers were ultimately unsuccessful in turning around the business. Eventually, these executive officers were fired by the board of directors, but they had already been given millions of dollars in compensation because it was guaranteed.[27]

You should always watch for managers who demand extremely high compensation packages before joining a business or who demand them to remain at the business. There is a saying that people who demand the most up front are usually the ones who deliver the least at the back end. This is generally true because those who receive guaranteed salaries and bonuses, regardless of the performance of the business, do not have any incentive to create long-term value.

For example, the CEO and founder of an energy company was awarded a $75 million-option package to renew his employment contract with the company for five years and not pursue other entrepreneurial ventures. This is a warning signal. Why would a CEO demand to be paid $75 million to remain at a business he founded? If he were truly passionate about the business, it is likely the board of directors would not need to entice him to stay at the business with financial incentives. This is just plain common sense. Clearly, the interests of the shareholders and management were not aligned.

Look for Managers Who Continually Increase Their Ownership Interest in the Business

The best managers to partner with are those who continually increase or retain their ownership in the business. For example, the following CEOs have sold very limited quantities of their companies' stock during their tenures:

- Warren Buffett, CEO of Berkshire Hathaway;
- Bruce Flatt, CEO of Brookfield Asset Management;
- Dave and Sherry Gold, founders of 99 Cent Only Stores; and
- Henry Singleton, former CEO of Teledyne.

Singleton, for example, did not receive any option awards and only sold stock in 1987 and 1988 after continuing to buy it for more than 20 years.[28] Bruce Flatt was once asked what his hobby was, and he responded that it was collecting shares of his stock. All of these businesses have created tremendous value for shareholders over the long term.

Use the proxy statement to construct a manager's ownership of the stock by viewing the stock ownership section over a 5- to 10-year period. Note how the shares were acquired, either through direct purchases or through option issuances. Determine if the manager is increasing his or her ownership interest in the business rather than decreasing it. If the manager's ownership interest is declining over time, this is not a positive sign. Many times, managers will claim they are selling for diversification purposes: This is reasonable and certainly believable, but remember that at the end of the day, a sale is a sale.

☐ 38. Have the managers been buying or selling the stock?

It is important to keep up with the purchases and sales of stock made by management by continually monitoring Form 3, 4, and 5 filings (which are SEC filings related to insider trading) and schedule 13-D filings (which are required for anyone who acquires beneficial ownership of 5 percent or more of a public company). Insider transactions signal where senior managers really believe their companies are going, without the corporate spin. They can also be a useful indicator of whether a stock will out-perform or under-perform. In his 1998 book *Investment Intelligence from Insider Trading*, Nejat Seyhun examined insider activity from 1975 to 1995 and discovered that stocks bought but not sold by insiders outperformed the market by 7.5 percent, on average, during the 12 months that followed the insider purchases. In contrast, companies with insider selling underperformed the market by 6.1 percent.

You must be careful not to jump to conclusions from an executive officer who is buying or selling stock without first examining the motivation behind the purchases or sales and whether the buying and selling is material to the total net worth of that executive officer. For example, insider purchases have become less useful indicators than they were in the past. Many executive officers have learned that by buying stock, they can increase the price of the stock, because the media reports these purchases. You have to be aware that the top executive officers may be attempting to manipulate the stock.

In order to be a useful signal, the insider buying or selling must be significant compared to the total net worth of the insider—for example, representing 15 percent or more of their total ownership. Unless you see these high-conviction purchases, then purchases and sales are just noise, and you need to be careful not to regard them as useful indicators.

For example, one CEO bought $100 million worth of stock in 2008, which sounds like a big sum. However, when compared to his total net worth, which was estimated by *Forbes* magazine to be $17.3 billion in 2008, it represented a small amount.

Here are a couple examples where insider purchases were useful indicators:

- A good example of a strong buy signal is the insider purchases of Carl Kirkland, founder of specialty retailer of home décor Kirkland's. On March 23, 2006, Kirkland owned 1.3 million shares. A few months later, on September 10, 2008, in a 13-D filing, Kirkland disclosed that he purchased 3,464,032 shares of stock for $6,754,862 (i.e., at an average price of $1.95 per share) by taking out a loan using an airplane he owned and his vacation home as collateral. The 13-D filing listed a business loan agreement between Bank of America and Kirkland Aviation, which owned a Hawker Beechcraft B200GT for a loan in the amount of $4 million. He also took out a loan in the amount of $3.5 million, using his Avon, Colorado, vacation home as collateral. Whenever you see a former founder buying so much stock using loans to fund his purchases, this is a strong buy signal. The stock price of Kirkland's shortly increased in price to more than $14 per share at the end of 2010.
- Three days before Jamie Dimon joined Bank One as CEO, he acquired two million shares for nearly $60 million, using his own capital. When asked why he bought so much stock, he said he felt a CEO should eat his own cooking. This is a clear signal that you and the CEO are aligned. The stock price increased from $30 per share when Dimon joined in March 2000 to $51 per share when Bank One was acquired by J.P. Morgan on January 15, 2004.[29]

Examples of Good Sale Indicators

If you see senior managers or board members selling a lot of shares, this is not a signal that you should sell your stock, but it *is* a signal that you should question their long-term faith in the business. You are looking for extremes rather than an insider selling a portion of his or her holdings: After all, that manager could be remodeling a house or have other reasons that have nothing to do with his or her confidence in the business. The following are a few examples of useful warning signals:

- If you see a stock whose price is continually dropping, yet insiders are selling, this is a warning sign.
- In two quarters alone, nine executives and directors of Novatel Wireless sold more than half of their holdings in 2007, at prices ranging from $17 to more than $20 per share. One year later, the stock price dropped below $10 per share and traded as low as $3 per share on December 1, 2008.[30]
- Five board members at Jones Soda Company disposed of nearly all of their shares of company stock over a three-month period in 2007 as the stock price reached $27 per share. That year, Jones Soda was developing into a mainstream brand with a national distribution contract, and the company had just announced strong fourth quarter earnings. The CEO also announced that the company would be in 25 percent of the retail market by selling at stores such as Wal-Mart, Kroger, and Safeway. Shortly thereafter, Jones Soda released 2007 first and second-quarter earnings that disappointed investors, causing the stock price to drop to $7 by the end of 2007. Most of the directors were able to sell their shares at prices ranging from $10 per share to $25 per share, while those stockholders who kept the stock suffered a decline in their net worth.[31]
- CEO John Hammergren of McKesson (a healthcare information technology company) owned 4.5 million shares as of June 1, 2010, including options and restricted stock holdings. He sold more than 2.9 million of these shares in 2010 (64 percent of his holdings), realizing more than $98 million in profits, according to SEC filings. This significant reduction in Hammergren's ownership should serve as a warning signal to investors that he does not have long-term confidence in the business.

Determine the Motivation When Management Purchases or Sells Company Stock

You should also examine further the motivation of stock purchases or sales. To gain full perspective on insider purchases and sales, read the notes to Forms 3, 4, and 5, which often disclose the reason for the purchase or sale. If you are unable to determine the motivation behind the purchases or sales, then you do not have enough information to draw a conclusion, and you need to be careful to not make assumptions. Some of the most common reasons are listed here and described in more detail in the following paragraphs:

- 10b5–1 programs
- Tax purposes
- Margin calls
- Personal reasons, such as commitments to charities that need to be funded

Executive Officers Who Sell Shares under the Terms of a 10b5–1 Program   A 10b5–1 program is set up under SEC regulation designed to allow insiders to buy or sell company shares in an orderly pattern without having to worry about allegations of improper use of insider information. The plans vary in complexity, but they generally specify the amount, price, and date of the purchase or sale of a stock. Many investors make the mistake of ignoring purchases and sales of stock in a 10b5–1 program because they believe there is an orderly pattern to trading the stock, but the executive officers have the ability to change the terms of the program at any point. Whenever you note significant deviations from the trading plan, this should serve as a warning signal.

For example, the co-founder of subprime mortgage lender New Century Financial Corporation, Edward Gotschall, sold more than $15.4 million in stock from August 2006 to the first quarter of 2007, just before the company disclosed accounting problems related to reserves, and the business eventually filed for bankruptcy. This sale was conducted under a 10b5–1 plan and was ignored by most investors[32]—but it shouldn't have been. If investors had paid attention to the historical sales pattern in the 10b5–1 program, they would have noticed that Gotschall changed the terms of the plan to dramatically accelerate his stock sales.

Managers also sell stock for reasons that are unrelated to their confidence in the business. The following two examples represent two of the most common reasons.

Managers Who Sell Stock for Tax Purposes   When a manager exercises a stock option, it generates a tax liability for the difference between the price the option was originally granted and the price the stock is sold for. Therefore, the manager has two ways to handle this. One way is for the manager to sell all or a portion of the exercised stock and use the proceeds to pay the tax. The other way is for the manager to take out a loan, using the stock as collateral, to pay the tax, which has the effect of deferring the tax. The main risk to this is that if the stock price drops below a certain price, the manager will face a margin call.

Managers Who Sell Stock to Meet Margin Calls   During 2008, when the S&P 500 dropped by more than 37 percent, many managers had to sell stock to meet margin calls. One of the more noteworthy sales during this time was from Aubrey McClendon, co-founder and CEO of Chesapeake Energy Corporation, who was forced to sell 94 percent of his holdings for $569 million to meet margin calls when Chesapeake's stock price dropped 65 percent.[33]

Key Points to Keep in Mind

Learn about the Background of Senior Managers

- The most logical predictor of the future success of a business is its management.
- If you are investing in a manager who has a long track record (i.e., more than 10 years) of successfully managing a business, the odds that he or she will continue to manage the business successfully are in your favor. It's easier to predict what managers will do in the future if you have already seen what they do in both difficult and favorable environments.
- Outside managers who join the business and make major changes immediately, without fully understanding the customers and soliciting input from the employees, are more likely to fail.
- You can quickly judge several qualities in managers by using the lion/hyena metaphor.

(continued)

- Managers who have risen from inside the corporate suite (e.g., CFOs and General Counsels) often do not make good operators because they have less experience with the day-to-day operations of the business; they have a constricted way of thinking; and their past interaction with the employees of the business is limited.

How Managers Are Compensated Is Important

- Some of the best long-term performing stocks are run by CEOs with low cash compensation and high stock ownership.
- If a business has a widely distributed stock-option plan, this indicates that managers care about employees rather than just themselves.
- The ideal compensation structures are those that reward for long-term value creation factors, such as operating income or book value, instead of just the stock price (e.g. stock options).
- If a compensation package is determined by consultants hired by the board of directors, this should serve as a warning signal. This kind of compensation benchmarking is usually not about the performance of the business, but rather a comparison to what others in the industry make.
- People who demand the most up front are usually the ones who deliver the least at the back end. Watch for those managers who demand high compensation packages before working at the business.
- Insider transactions signal where managers really believe their companies are going, without the corporate spin.

8

Assessing the Quality of Management—Competence: How Management Operates the Business

In addition to researching the backgrounds of senior managers, so that you'll know more about their careers, how they were promoted, what functional experience they have (or don't have!), and the corporate culture of the companies they worked at previously—all of which Chapter 7 focused on—it's also helpful to assess how managers actually operate the business, which is the focus of this chapter. Here, we'll look at management styles; strategic planning and day-to-day operations; organizational structures (i.e., centralized versus decentralized); how managers treat their employees and whether they know how to hire well; whether management knows how to intelligently manage its expenses; and whether management is disciplined or undisciplined in making capital allocation decisions.

By looking at how managers actually operate, you will be better able to assess how competent they are. Competency matters for many reasons, but one of the most compelling is that truly competent managers are able to quickly adapt to changing environments. For example, during the stock market downturn in 2008, when the S&P 500 dropped 37 percent, my firm strictly maintained its commitment to investing in proven and competent management teams. With so much uncertainty in the economy, there was very little visibility into the future earnings power of many companies. Therefore, we partnered with management teams that had the ability to adapt their businesses to the changing economic environment. And we avoided investing in management teams that had a limited track record running their business.

For example, we did not invest in an online retailer of diamonds and fine jewelry, because the founder had recently passed the chief executive officer (CEO) title to the chief financial officer (CFO) (February 2008). Even though the CFO had been at the business since 1999, we could not judge her competence in running the business in her new role.

In contrast, we had strong conviction in regard to the competence and abilities of the management team at Whole Foods Market, because that team had operated successfully together since 2001. Faced with declining same-store sales, which the management team had never encountered before, management strengthened the balance sheet and increased free-cash flow.

Another less direct but substantial benefit of partnering with proven and competent management teams is that it frees your time to focus on other investment opportunities. If you partner with incompetent management teams, you have to spend a lot of time monitoring their actions.

I once invested in a business because the stock was cheap, but I knew the management team was somewhat incompetent. I continued to hold the stock because I believed it was substantially undervalued. Each time the business issued a press release, my stomach churned, as I anticipated bad news. The CEO never let me down and continually reported bad results. This investment failed to create any value for my fund.

In contrast, when I have partnered with competent managers such as Bruce Flatt, CEO of asset-management-holding company Brookfield Asset Management, I do not have to scrutinize each management decision in detail. I know that if the top managers make a mistake, they will quickly recognize the mistake and correct it. By investing in proven and competent management teams, you will rarely be disappointed. This will help you maintain an opportunistic attitude.

Now let's take a look at questions that will help you determine if the management team is competent.

❐ 39. Does the CEO manage the business to benefit all stakeholders?

If you were to ask investors whether shareholder value is more important than customer service at a business, most would answer that it is. What they fail to consider is that shareholder value is a byproduct of a business that keeps its customers happy. In fact, many of the best-performing stocks over the long term are the ones that balance the interests of *all* stakeholder groups, including customers, employees, suppliers, and other business partners. These businesses are managed by CEOs who have a purpose greater than solely generating profits for their shareholders.

In the book *Firms of Endearment*, David Wolfe, Rajendra Sisodia, and Jagdish Sheth studied 30 companies that view success as more than just maximizing shareholder returns. These companies instead try to maximize value for all stakeholders. Interestingly, these companies outperformed the S&P 500 over the 10 years that the authors tracked them. The companies returned an astonishing 1,026 percent for 10 years ending in 2006—the S&P 500 returned only 122 percent.

It is surprising how few CEOs manage the business for the benefit of all stakeholders. The reason is that it is harder to do. It is easier to focus on one constituency, such as stockholders, rather than many.

John Mackey, co-founder and CEO of Whole Foods Market, has coined the term *conscious capitalism* to describe businesses designed to benefit all of their stakeholders, such as customers, employees, investors, and suppliers. Instead of subscribing to the theory that the only purpose of a business is to maximize profits, conscious capitalism proponents believe that increases in shareholder value are the by-product of helping customers, employees, and vendors reach their highest potential.

Mackey compares profits to happiness to illustrate his point. Just trying to be happy doesn't usually work. Instead, we're happy due to a host of other reasons: a strong sense of purpose, meaningful work, good friends and good health, loving relationships, and the chance to learn, grow, and help others. Like happiness, profits are also the result of other things, and aren't achieved by making them the primary goal of the business. "Long-term profits," says Mackey, "come from having a deeper purpose, great products, satisfied customers, happy employees, great suppliers, and from taking a degree of responsibility for the community and environment we live in. The paradox of profits is that, like happiness, they are best achieved by not aiming directly for them."[1]

Some examples of businesses that manage the business for customers and other stakeholders instead of maximizing profits are below:

- At Costco, CEO Jim Sinegal says that by treating employees fairly and making sure that customers receive a good value, shareholders will benefit over the long haul.
- Robert Wilmers, CEO of M&T bank, lived a business philosophy that could be a primer for sound banking: "Know your markets and employees, watch credit quality relentlessly, don't gamble with interest rates, and focus on serving your community."[2] You will note that none of the goals were to increase shareholder value. Even Warren Buffett, CEO of Berkshire Hathaway, held a long-term stake in M&T.[3] Under Wilmers' tenure, the stock appreciated from less than $3 per share when he joined the bank in 1983 to $87 per share on December 31, 2010,[4] making it one of the best-performing bank stocks in the last two decades. Wilmers did not focus on the profits of the bank, but instead focused on those things that *generated* the profits.
- David Packard, co-founder of Hewlett Packard, was also known for taking a broader view of stakeholders. One story describes the 37-year old Packard in 1949 listening to a group of business leaders who were apparently focused solely on profits. Uncomfortable with their views, Packard told them plainly, "A company has a greater responsibility than making money for its stockholders!" Of course, Hewlett-Packard went on to become the premier technology company under Packard and Bill Hewlett.[5]
- Similarly when Robert Silberman took over as CEO of Strayer Education in 2001, he said he was not going to focus on any of the metrics that generally drive public company valuations, such as revenue growth, operating income growth, and margin expansion. In an interview, I asked him why he focused on academic outcomes instead of profits, and he said, "It evolved from looking at the asset of the enterprise. It was pretty clear to me that the only thing that was going to drive real sustainable long-term value to my owners was the intangible value of Strayer University. So then I sat back and said, how do you increase the intangible value of Strayer University? And the answer to that is, you increase the level of learning outcomes."[6]

☐ 40. Does the management team improve its operations day-to-day or does it use a strategic plan to conduct its business?

Most investors seek out superstar CEOs who can seemingly change the business overnight with a well-planned strategy. In essence, the investor believes that business transformation is the result of brilliant ideas and clever plans. One reason investors think great performance results from brilliant strategy is that it is often reported to seem that way in the popular business media. These stories are popular for a couple of reasons: First, they are easy to write; second, people enjoy stories about flash and charisma far more than stories about CEOs who grow their business through continuous improvement. These articles often contribute to increases in the stock price as investors buy into the hopes and dreams of the charismatic CEO. Investors tend to have short memories, and they forget that many of these businesses eventually derail in dramatic fashion later on.

Beware of the CEO who believes that one strategy or a single stroke will transform their business. These CEOs typically make big announcements, such as they will take their business from the number-three position to number one in five years, by revolutionizing the way they conduct business, by making a transformational acquisition, or by leaping into a hot new market. These ambitious plans hinge on making rapid, sizable market-share gains.

For example, Nortel's strengths had traditionally been in voice transmission when CEO John Roth decided that he would transform the company into a much bigger data networking company. He did this by quickly acquiring 19 new businesses from 1997 to early 2001. Nortel's stock price rose, reaching a market cap of $277 billion in July of 2000. By the end of 2001, the stock price had fallen 90 percent from its peak the previous year. Most of the 19 acquisitions were eventually sold for less than Nortel originally paid or were written off entirely.[7]

A strategic plan is a detailed roadmap to success, such as a five-year plan that sets specific targets that must be met. As a result, a strategic plan can also be an inflexible plan that outlines how a business will operate for the next 2, 5, or 10 years. If a project or product does not meet the goals of the plan, then it is dismissed. Therefore, seizing opportunities becomes less of a priority for the business.

Contrary to popular belief, most successful businesses are built on hundreds of small decisions, instead of on one well-formulated strategic plan. For example, when most successful entrepreneurs start their business, they do not have a business plan stating what their business will look like in 2, 5, or 10 years. They instead build their business day by day, focusing on customer needs and letting these customer needs shape the direction of their business. It is this stream of everyday decisions over time that accounts for great outcomes, instead of big one-time decisions. These businesses don't attempt new initiatives until existing ones are thoroughly absorbed by the employees of the company. For example, Apple's approach is to put every resource behind just a few products and make them exceedingly well. Can you even imagine Apple making a cheap, poorly made product?

Another common theme among businesses that improve day by day is that they operate on the premise that it is best to repeatedly launch a product or service with a limited number of its customers so that it can use customer reactions and feedback to modify it. They operate on the premise that it is okay to learn from mistakes and that it is critical to obtain customer feedback to shape their strategies.

For example, Coach conducts more than 10,000 customer interviews every year before it launches new luxury handbag and accessory products. Based on the information it collects, Coach will alter the design of the product or drop items that test poorly. As a result, Coach has a direct line to the pulse of its customers and is able to avoid numerous market misfires. Coach believes that the millions of dollars it spends on customer interviews represent a low-cost form of insurance against getting blindsided by customers' shifting priorities. Instead of setting up a strategic plan, Coach lets customer input shape its strategies.[8]

You need to determine if the management team you are investing in works on proving a concept before investing a lot of capital in it or whether it prefers to put a lot of money in all at once hoping for a big payoff. Proving a concept does not need to be expensive. For example, Reed Hastings, founder of movie-rental-by-mail business Netflix, mailed himself a CD in an envelope when he was developing the business. When the envelope arrived undamaged, he had spent only the cost of postage to test one of the business's key operational risks.[9]

Similarly, Tom Perkins, founder of Kleiner Perkins, an early investor in companies such as biotechnology business Genentech, counsels, "First, eliminate the risk. Then, grow the business." Perkins would not make any significant financial commitments to a new venture until certain risks were reduced. This model is commonly used in the Venture Capital (VC) industry where startups are given capital in multiple rounds. After a start-up reaches certain milestones, then the VC investors will invest more money. For example, Genentech outsourced a lot of its work to labs instead of investing in its own lab as it developed its products. As Genentech became more successful and proved its product it then invested in its own lab.[10]

In contrast, businesses that rely on strategic plans often spend millions of dollars on research data compiled by consultants (instead of customers) over a long period of time before they launch a product or service.

For example, when Motorola launched its Iridium phone, only 50,000 people subscribed to its services instead of the millions of subscribers that Motorola had anticipated. It was one of the largest fiascos in business history, and Iridium declared bankruptcy in 2000. Motorola had devised a long-term strategic plan to develop a service where customers could make cellular phone calls from anywhere on earth. This technology took more than 10 years to develop and Motorola invested more than $5 billion in the project to launch 66 low-flying satellites.

Unfortunately, when the company was ready to launch the service, the phone needed to receive the satellite signal was the size of a brick and users had to be outdoors to get reception. Both of these were major stumbling blocks that Motorola had not fully considered when it was developing the service.[11] Motorola had focused so much on achieving its strategic goal that it neglected the basics of getting good customer feedback early on.

Here are a few examples of businesses operated by CEOs who do not follow well-formulated strategic plans but instead improve the business day by day.

- Henry Singleton, CEO of Teledyne Inc. from the 1960s through the 1980s, believed the best plan was no plan. Under his tenure, Teledyne's stock compounded at more than 20 percent for more than 20 years. He believed it was better to approach an uncertain world with an open mind. Singleton once remarked at a Teledyne annual meeting, ". . . we're subject to a tremendous number of outside influences, and the vast majority of them cannot be predicted. So my idea is to stay flexible. I like to steer the boat each day rather than plan ahead way into the future."[12]

- Dave and Sherry Gold, co-founders of 99 Cent Only Stores, started the business in 1982 and grew it to more than $1 billion in sales in 2005. Dave Gold said, "The people who are making long-term projections usually do not have accountability, and people often forget what they said years before. If you have a strategy for growth for the next 5 or 10 years, it gets changed so much in that time period. I don't think you can plan out more than 2 years from now. I don't think that far ahead. If you do, you just get into dreaming."[13]

- Thomas Stemberg, founder of office retail chain Staples, said, "I don't get hung up on business plans. I read them, of course. But whatever the plan says, the company will end up looking different. When we started Staples in 1986, for example, our business plan proclaimed we would never deliver. Delivery added costs; we figured we couldn't afford it." Today, a large portion of Staple's profits are derived from its delivery operations.[14]

- Bob Graham, co-founder of AIM Management Group Inc., one of the nation's largest mutual fund companies said, "When we started AIM Management Group Inc., we never had a plan. We followed opportunities as they came along. Our plan changed along the way, depending on what opportunities presented themselves. We had no idea that we would be in the money market funds business or in the equity funds business, nor did we have an idea of how big they would get."[15]

Why Do Strategic Plans Fail?

When CEOs set a strategic plan, they risk becoming committed to it and may fail to consider other alternatives. In the book *Influence*, author Robert Cialdini writes about "the commitment and consistency principle." After making a commitment or taking a stand, people are more willing to agree to requests that are consistent with their prior commitment. In other words, once you make a public statement, it makes it difficult for you to change your mind. Setting strategic plans has the same effect: A CEO is very likely to do things to remain committed to meeting his or her stated plans because the consequences of not meeting them are that the stock goes down, thereby reducing the value of stock options or tarnishing the reputation and credibility of the management team. The management team thus becomes committed to only one way of doing business.

Strategic plans fail because they often shut out other opportunities. When an opportunity comes up and it does not fit into the strategic plan of a business, then the management team will likely pass it up. The truth is that most management teams often stumble upon their best ideas.

For example, in the 1990s, Pfizer stumbled upon one of its bestselling drugs, Viagra. The company was developing a treatment for angina (the painful heart condition caused by constricting or clogging of heart arteries), when the users of this drug began to report that it improved their ability to have erections. So Pfizer made a very smart move and refocused on the newly discovered opportunity.[16]

Another reason they fail is that a business may focus on strategic targets instead of on what the customer wants. This is the same as telling a customer "That's not how we do things," instead of asking "How do you want it done?"

For example, Fannie Mae and Freddie Mac bought billions of dollars' worth of sub-prime mortgages. Instead of focusing on the true needs of the customers, they helped banks lend money to customers who could not afford the loans. Later, as these sub-prime mortgages defaulted, both of these businesses had to be bailed out by the government.

Do Not Confuse Strategic Plans with Long-Term Planning

Do not confuse a strategic plan with goals or long-term planning. You can think of long-term planning as a vision that is always in the head of the CEO as he or she builds the business. For example, a CEO may have a long-term plan to become the highest-rated business in customer satisfaction or to have the lowest employee turnover rate in its industry.

Highest-Risk Strategic Plans: Setting Financial Goals

The strategic plans that are most prone to failure are those that have an overly narrow focus, such as those that set a financial target. Many CEOs often make such announcements as "the business will generate $100 million in revenues in three years" or "we will sell 1,000 units per week by the year 2012." However, what happens in most of these cases is that when the CEO focuses on a specific financial target, they neglect other areas or take on more risk. The single plan will dominate all of the activities of the business at the expense of other important areas.

For example, in 2003, General Motors executives wore lapel pins and buttons with the number "29" as a reminder of the company's goal of obtaining a 29 percent U.S. market share. To meet the number that year, GM even offered rebates of up to $5,500 and 0 percent loans over 6 years on some of their cars. Six years later, GM's U.S. market share was below 20 percent, and the company was bankrupt. Why?[17]

The reason GM failed is because it focused on market share, and it had built a cost base structured for at least that level of market share. In other words, it was locked in. To try to make that number, the company burned through billions of dollars, launching new models in many market segments. By 2005, their U.S. share was at 26 percent—which was the lowest since 1925. By 2007, they were down to 23.7 percent, only barely ahead of Toyota. Furthermore, GM's cash losses during its high-growth years had left few cash reserves for years with declining car sales, and little or no cash to deal with the downturn of 2008 to 2009. By competing in too many market segments, and not leaving the segments where they couldn't adapt quickly enough to make money, GM lost the gamble it had made to try to gain market share from Toyota and the other import companies.[18]

Paul Larson, editor of Morningstar *StockInvestor*, offers a great analogy of why it is dangerous to set specific financial targets: "It's like you're driving somewhere and you tell yourself you will drive to a certain destination at an average speed of 63 mph. Instead, the way you should do it is to go as fast as road conditions will allow. If you have a set projection, you might go too fast and crash, or maybe it is a wide open road and you can gun it."[19]

When a management team sets specific financial goals, it may resort to such actions as managing earnings to meet those goals or making costly acquisitions. Some examples of CEOs who have failed after setting specific financial targets are:

- Hugh Grant, CEO of agricultural biotechnology company Monsanto, once declared that his goal was to double profits within five years. To meet this goal, he needed to shift the businesses focus away from herbicides to its more profitable biotech seed business. By 2010, Grant announced that they were unlikely to meet such a goal and that he was abandoning those plans. Grant later declared, "I'll tell you from the school of hard knocks, I don't think you're going to be seeing us laying out long-term targets."[20]

- In 1976, Continental Bank was the eighth-largest bank in the United States. The chairman of Continental announced that within 5 years, the bank's lending would match that of the other largest banks. To reach this goal, Continental shifted its strategy from conservative corporate financing to aggressively pursuing borrowers. Continental did become the largest commercial lender in the country, and it became a much larger bank, but in the process, it made several critical mistakes. Continental took in more volatile foreign deposits, loosened lending criteria, and sent the wrong message to its employees, who relaxed documentation standards. The bank also lost its historically conservative discipline and cut its pricing on loans. By 1984, Continental was in trouble, and it needed the largest bailout in U.S. history up to that time.[21]

- In the late 1960s, Ford had begun to lose market share to its competitors who were making small fuel-efficient cars. Ford CEO Lee Iacocca decided to challenge his engineers to produce a car that would cost less than $2,000, weigh under 2000 pounds, and complete it by 1970. Talk about specific goals: This was a trifecta! The result was the Ford Pinto, best known as the car that could ignite on impact. Not only was the car design defective, lawsuits later revealed that Ford's top managers knew that the car could ignite. So committed were Ford's managers to their strategic plan that instead of fixing the faulty design, they decided to go ahead and manufacture the car. They figured the costs of the lawsuits from the Pinto fires would be less than the cost of fixing the design.[22]

☐ 41. Do the CEO and CFO issue guidance regarding earnings?

Guidance is when management predicts earnings per share or other business metrics over the next quarter or next year and shares this information with investors, either through a press release or a conference call. Wall Street analysts then tend to fixate on whether a business will meet or beat these quarterly earnings estimates. The majority of businesses that are publicly traded give guidance. The National Investor Relations Institute (NIRI) compiles responses from more than 500 public companies regarding earnings guidance and reports that 60 percent of companies provided quarterly earnings guidance in 2009.[23]

Guidance can have the most damaging effects on a business when it begins to represent the organizational goals of the whole business. If meeting guidance represents the only goal the business has, then other valued activities will not be prioritized and are often ignored. Meeting guidance will therefore *drive* the operations of the business, rather than the earnings of the business being a byproduct of the business's operations. For example, a CEO and CFO who give guidance may be tempted to achieve dependable period-to-period growth by masking the volatility inherent in a business. Unfortunately, in the real world, a business does not grow in a constant fashion. The majority of businesses face a lot of volatility that CEOs and CFOs cannot make disappear. Growth is almost always subject to seasonality, cyclicality, and random events.

Once a business begins to set guidance, it may also adopt a short-term outlook at the expense of long-term growth. A CEO and CFO may fear disappointing Wall Street analysts because if they do, their stock price plummets. If management falls short of a guidance goal, they may do things that are not in the best interests of the business to make up the difference. Once they start this process, it is difficult to stop it. Then management begins to borrow from the future in order to sustain the present and begins to participate in the earnings game. The game has little to do with running a business and instead becomes a major distraction that detaches the CEO and CFO from the fundamentals of the business.

For example, a CEO may push more products onto its customers in order to meet the current quarter's guidance. Or the CEO may refuse to invest in long-term capital projects that do not contribute to profitability in the short term. At some point, it becomes impossible to manage earnings as usual, and the stock price falls. The CEOs and CFOs at such failed businesses as Enron, WorldCom, Tyco, Adelphia, and HealthSouth, which were stellar performers, succumbed to the pressure to meet the numbers.

Enron is a case in point. At one time, it had strong global assets such as pipelines, but it then sought to transform its business model by becoming a market maker of natural gas and energy. As Enron's stock price increased due to the company's ability to continually exceed its guidance, it had to seek new avenues for growth and moved away from its core competence to areas where it had no expertise, such as broadband, water, and weather insurance. As these operations began to generate losses, Enron's management began to use off-balance-sheet partnerships in order to continue increasing their earnings per share by taking debt off of its balance sheet. At its peak in August 2000, Enron had a valuation of $69 billion[24]—yet it declared bankruptcy in 2002.

You need to be cautious with businesses that issue guidance. Ideally, you should look for managers who promise only what they can realistically deliver and do not bow to analysts' demands for highly predictable earnings. If management is constantly worried about its stock price, then this is an indicator that management is worried more about managing the perception of the business than operating the actual business. Instead, management should be clear about all of the risks and uncertainties involved and should outline how a business is progressing toward meeting its long-term objective.

Some businesses have even stopped issuing quarterly financial targets because they no longer want to subject themselves to the unnecessary pressure to meet external goals. Here are just a few examples:

- Gillette: At one time, Gillette promised investors that it would grow its earnings at 15 percent to 20 percent. But after it acquired Duracell in 1996, it began to have problems meeting this goal. Gillette's management began to resort to such actions as channel-stuffing products to its distributors in order to meet its projections. When James Kilts took over as CEO in 2001, he quickly dropped the practice of issuing earnings guidance entirely.[25]
- Newell, a global marketer of consumer products: Newell used to state in its annual reports that it aimed for earnings-per-share (EPS) growth of 15 percent a year; however, after Newell acquired Rubbermaid and its earnings fell, this line disappeared from the annual report.
- Unilever, a consumer goods company: As CEO Paul Polman explained, "What mattered far more than goals and targets

was consistent delivery over time. Anything more specific only caused trouble."

If a business does issue guidance, you need to be careful that managers are not managing earnings. Start by comparing the quarterly or annual earnings estimates to the actual earnings per share of the business. Create a chart that shows the guidance given by management, and count how many times they beat their estimates. If management is consistently beating its own estimates, you can classify these management teams as "dedicated guiders." This should serve as a warning signal, and you should closely scrutinize its accounting to understand how the business is consistently beating its guidance.

☐ 42. Is the business managed in a centralized or decentralized way?

It is important for you to determine if top management operates a business using a centralized or decentralized structure. If it is centralized, the business is managed using top-down hierarchies with rigid reporting structures, which create bureaucracies. A centralized management team often tells employees exactly what tasks to do. These businesses also have very narrow decision-making processes, and they mainly get compliance from their employees rather than genuine commitment. This may lead employees to not feel trusted and make them less likely to internalize responsibility. They are afraid to make mistakes and sometimes they will not do the right thing because of that fear.

Bureaucratic businesses also tend to have difficulty recruiting and retaining competent employees because competent employees don't want to just take orders without understanding the reasons behind them. Rules and restrictions cause the most innovative people to run from the business or start their own companies. This means that a business's pipeline of future leadership will often be limited.

In contrast, if a business has a decentralized management structure, those employees who are closest to the customer are empowered to make decisions. These employees often feel as if they are running their own business. An added benefit is that it's much easier for front-line employees to convey valuable information about their customers to top managers. Because it's much easier for information to flow up, managers know more about their customers.

Many of the best-performing stocks in history—that is, those that have compounded at rates greater than 20 percent over 15 years—have used decentralized operating structures; for example, Teledyne, Berkshire Hathaway, Penn National Gaming, Expeditors International, Fastenal, Capital Cities ABC, and Bed Bath & Beyond. One reason for their success is that this type of business attracts independent thought and a diverse workforce, which encourages innovation. The greatest financial benefit is that decentralized businesses have reduced corporate overhead. For example, Penn National Gaming, a regional casino company, has one of the lowest corporate overheads of any publicly traded casino.

Let's take a closer look at Fastenal (another company with a decentralized management structure), whose stock price increased from $0.27 per share on September 1, 1987, to more than $60 per share on December 31, 2010. Fastenal doesn't operate using strict, top-down corporate hierarchies. Instead, this company treats its branch managers more like individual store owners, giving them wide latitude in decision making. Company founder Robert Kierlin always felt that because most customer interaction happens at the store level that it made sense to transfer the decision making to that level. Branch managers know the customer best, so Fastenal's store level managers make decisions about what inventory to carry, and what price to charge for their products. In fact, some managers negotiate directly with corporate suppliers. The compensation structure is also matched to the store level, with branch managers receiving commissions and profit sharing from their stores.

Similarly, Louis Vuitton Moët Hennessy's (LVMH) stock price has increased more than 10 times in value from 1989 to 2010, under the leadership of Chairman and CEO Bernard Arnault. Arnault attributes much of this success to the company's management structure, stating, "One key element of management of a group like this (LVMH has 83,542 employees[26]) is decentralization. You need the right team of inspired managers. I want all of my managers to take charge of their divisions as though they were family enterprises."[27]

How Do You Identify a Business That Is Managed in a Centralized or Decentralized Way?

First, determine who has the responsibility for selecting and hiring employees. Is it the Human Resources (HR) department or the managers who the employees will be working under? If it is the group where the employee will be working, then it is decentralized, but if all hiring is done through HR, then it is bureaucratic. Ideally, the responsibility of selecting employees should rest primarily with those holding authority over the department in which there is an opening. Herb Kelleher, founder of Southwest Airlines, brought model employees into the hiring process. For example, pilots made hiring recommendations for new pilots because they were in the best position to judge the abilities of potential candidates.[28]

Second, speak with the customers of a business. You need to determine how the business solves customer issues. Do employees have to resort to a bureaucratic process to resolve customer issues? Or do they have the authority to solve a customer issue without getting supervisory approval? Think about how frustrating it is when you have to return a product to a store and the manager has to approve the return or you have to fill out lots of paperwork. In contrast, Four Seasons Hotels encourages all of its employees to solve problems themselves, and it rewards employees who go beyond the call of duty in helping a hotel guest.

Third, note what the difference is in compensation among the top five executive officers by viewing the proxy statement. This will help you determine whether the business is run by a top-down CEO or if it is a flat organization. For example, the proxy statement of one business revealed the following:

- CEO received a salary of $2,164,423; the next highest paid executive received $690,577.
- CEO's bonus was $7 million; the next highest was $825,000.
- CEO was also given 590,000 stock options, as compared to 90,000 options for the next-highest-paid executive.

You can clearly see that the CEO had a significantly higher compensation package than the rest of the management team. This indicates that the business is being run by a top-down CEO.

By comparison, the 2009 proxy statement for Expeditors International shows that CEO Pete Rose received total compensation of $4,782,892, and the other 4 top executive officers earned similar amounts. This indicates that it is probably a decentralized operation.

Fourth, talk to salespeople who sell products and services to the business. Salespeople have to determine whether a business is managed in a centralized or decentralized way because they need to identify the primary decision maker in order to make a sale. For example, experienced salespeople will try to determine how important job titles are at a business. If titles are not important, then this is a sign it is decentralized. Salespeople will also look at the environment of the business they are selling to. For example, they look to see if the cubicles or offices of the employees are sterile (centralized) or if they are customized to the tastes of the employees of the business (decentralized).

☐ 43. Does management value its employees?

Most investors view the CEO as the sole person who operates the business, while the employees are viewed as commodities that can be downsized at any point. Nothing is further from the truth. The primary function of a manager is to obtain results through people. If a manager is unable to achieve results through people, he or she is not a good manager. Try to understand if the management team values its employees because the only way it will obtain positive results is through these people.

When employees feel they are partners with their boss in a mutual effort, rather than merely employees of some business run by managers they never see, morale will increase. Furthermore, when a business has good employee relations, it typically has many other good attributes, such as good customer relations and the ability to adapt quickly to changing economic circumstances.

Great Employee Relations Can Translate into High Stock Returns

Great managers know that if they treat their employees well, employees will, in turn, treat their customers well. Some of the highest-performing stocks within the S&P 500 have been run by CEOs who value their employees. One of the top performers is Expeditors International, whose stock price has increased 83-fold (up to July 2010) since CEO Pete Rose took over the freight forwarder in 1988. As Pete Rose once said, "You take care of employees. They take care of customers. And that takes care of Wall Street."[29]

HCL Technologies CEO Vineet Nayar instituted a new way of thinking about employees and customers at his company in 2005. In the book *Employees First and Customers Second: Turning Conventional*

Management Upside Down, Nayar discusses his idea that employees create the most value at a company, because they end up knowing the most about the customer. His company, which provides global IT services, focuses its effort on making sure that employees are able to meet customer's needs. Because employees understand the customer's problems and how to fix them, Nayar makes sure that employees have what they need, and even makes managers account- able to employees. His results are impressive: From 2005 to 2009, revenues have increased by 3.6 times and operating profits by 3.4 times. HCL was one of the few companies that grew during the global recession beginning in 2008, and it also increased revenue by 23.5 percent in 2009.

Read Articles Written about the Business

As you read articles about the business, look for specific situations where the managers demonstrate they care about their employees. Here are a few examples:

- Howard Schultz, founder of Starbucks: Howard Schultz was asked in a 2010 interview about decisions that he had made that turned out to be unpopular with investors. He imme- diately brought up healthcare: Schultz estimated Starbucks had paid around $300 million in healthcare costs that year. Many investors wanted him to cut that cost, and one institu- tional investor even called him and suggested he had cover (meaning no one would criticize him) to cut healthcare costs because times were tough. Schultz decided not to cut the healthcare plan, saying he'd rather have the respect of his employees.[30]
- Richard Galanti, CFO of Costco: In an interview during the recession of 2007 to 2009, Galanti was asked whether he considered increasing the amount that employees pay for healthcare from 10 percent to a higher amount in order to save Costco $10 million to $20 million per year. Galanti and the other Costco managers declined to pass the cost along to employees, saying that in tough times they wanted to give their employees as much as they could.[31]
- Herb Kelleher, CEO of Southwest Airlines: When Southwest Airlines was founded, it struggled and was losing a lot of

money because there was inconsistent ridership. Founder Herb Kelleher faced the dilemma of laying off employees or selling a plane. Kelleher said, "We've always taken the approach that employees come first. Happy and pleased employees take care of the customers. And happy customers take care of shareholders by coming back." So Southwest Airlines sold a 737 plane and instituted a "no layoff" policy.[32] This policy contributed to the success of Southwest Airlines: By 2010, Southwest Airlines was the biggest domestic airline in the country, with a market capitalization greater than *the combined market capitalization of all its domestic competitors.*

In contrast, if you see management taking big bonuses at the same time they are cutting the benefits of the employees, this is an obvious warning signal. No matter how much managers say they value their employees, they will have no credibility.

For example, when American Airlines was on the edge of bankruptcy, it successfully negotiated with unions for concessions in their contracts. Just days after those negotiations, former Chairman and CEO Don Carty made arrangements to protect the pension plans of senior executives. Carty later resigned because he had not disclosed these activities.[33]

Does the Business Have Good or Bad Employee Relations?

There are many questions you can ask to determine if a business has good or bad employee relations:

- Does management treat its employees as assets or liabilities?
- Does management talk about the contributions of their employees?
- Does management believe that retaining employees is critical?
- Does the business promote from within?
- Does management show employees how they can get promoted?
- Does the business invest significant resources in employee training?
- Does the business attract a great number of applicants?
- Are employees avidly recruited from the business?

- Are there large differences between the benefits that the top managers receive versus employees?
- Does management treat employees with respect when they lay them off?
- Does management listen to its employees?
- Does the business have a strong culture?
- Does the business have identifiable, shared values?
- What is the employee-retention rate?

The following sections take a closer look at each of these questions.

Does Management Treat Its Employees as Assets or Liabilities?

To answer this, look for articles and note how the managers refer to their employees. For example, Michael Bloomberg says in his book *Bloomberg by Bloomberg,* "the main asset is not our technology, our databases, our proprietary communications network, or even our clients. It is our employees. Business must recognize employees as assets."

Does Management Talk about the Contributions of Their Employees?

Nucor Corporation, a steel manufacturer, puts the names of all of its employees on the cover of its annual report. This gesture is a good indicator, and another is that Nucor always shows up on *Fortune* magazine's list of "Best 100 Companies to Work For." Good employee relations have likely helped Nucor become one of the best-performing stocks within the steel industry.

Does Management Believe That Retaining Employees Is Critical?

Shipping company UPS learned that it was critical for it to retain its drivers because experienced drivers learned the fastest routes and were more efficient in making deliveries. At one point, UPS management discovered that part of the reason for the high turnover rate for drivers was that loading the trucks was so physically demanding. When it discovered the problem, UPS promptly hired part-time workers to load packages: This way, the drivers could concentrate on their core competence, which was finding the best routes. As a result, the turnover rate of UPS declined. Anytime you see a management team focusing on the well-being of its employees so they can focus their time productively, this is a great sign.[34]

Does the Business Promote from Within?

A business that promotes from within has a better chance of retaining valuable employees because talented employees typically like to work in growing organizations with opportunities for advancement. A business that promotes from within will hire outsiders only when it needs to fill a specialized position. You can obtain this information by interviewing employees and asking them if most positions are filled with internal candidates or if the company actively recruits outsiders. You can also call the HR department and ask if the company has a policy of promoting from within. Most often, when a company promotes from within, it will highlight this in investor presentations found on the company website or on its employment websites.

Does Management Show Employees How They Can Get Promoted?

A manager's job is to help his or her people grow. Great business leaders have sometimes measured their own success by the positive impact they've had on others, especially in helping employees reach their highest potential. In turn, this inspires employees to do great things for the manager and the company.

In the book *First, Break All the Rules: What the World's Greatest Managers Do Differently*, research firm Gallup sought ways to increase employee engagement. The study represents the largest worldwide effort to understand employee engagement, and was based on Gallup's analysis of 10 million workplace interviews. Gallup found there are two employee sentiments that best predict engagement: "my opinion matters—I have a voice" and "somebody here cares about my advancement."[35]

If managers focus on themselves rather than developing their employees, this will cause employees to disengage from the business, and the managers will fail to develop a pipeline of future leadership at the business.

Does the Business Invest Significant Resources in Employee Training?

If managers are committed to employee training, this is a great sign that they have a long-term orientation. In contrast, a short-term oriented manager considers spending money on training employees a waste of money and a discretionary cost that can be eliminated.

Look for examples where the business is investing in its employees through training by reading articles written in trade journals, such as *Training Magazine.*

For example, Kip Tindell, Chairman and CEO of The Container Store, believes that putting employees first is a profitable strategy. He believes that one great employee has the same productivity as three good employees. Great people are hard to find and even harder to keep. So when The Container Store finds them, it pays them well and spends a lot of money training them. In fact, the average amount of time a first-year, full-time employee spends in training is 263 hours versus the retail industry average of 7 hours. This investment in employees contributes to low turnover. The average turnover in the retail industry is 110 percent, whereas at The Container Store it has historically been below 10 percent. This lower turnover decreases costs over time.[36]

Does the Business Attract a Great Number of Applicants?

Many people hear about good places to work and want to work there. *Fortune* magazine and regional magazines such as *Texas Monthly* publish lists of the best places to work. Whenever a business makes the list, it has more job applicants.

Are Employees Avidly Recruited from the Business?

During the 1980s, the most actively recruited managers in banking were at Wells Fargo.[37] Finding a business with this characteristic is a positive sign because it means the business typically has a strong culture focused on execution. This does not mean employees would be successful at another business, but if they are avidly recruited, this is a sign that the business is well respected. Talk to headhunters who work in a particular industry and ask them what businesses they believe are the best places to recruit employees from and why.

Are There Large Differences between the Benefits That the Top Managers Receive versus Employees?

A successful CEO once told me, "If you are constantly reminding people at the bottom that they are not at the top, do you really expect them to be gung ho about the company?"

Does Management Treat Employees with Respect When They Lay Them Off?

One of the most revealing times to observe managers is during layoffs. You will gain a great deal of insight if you watch how they lay off employees. When a company fires employees, does it do so with respect, or do security guards escort employees out? If you learn that security guards escort employees out, this is a warning signal that management really does not care about its employees.

The best-performing managers have always told me that when they have to lay off employees, they treat them with respect. One CEO told me that he would want the former employee to still feel close enough to the company to remain a company advocate and customer. These managers conduct layoffs or firings in an open manner and always disclose the reasons and rationale behind their decisions. They often give furloughed employees assistance in finding a new job. This way, the management team is able to instill a sense of security and confidence in those employees who are left behind, helping to keep more valuable employees from leaving.

In contrast to this approach, you will often see a degree of insincerity by CEOs even as they announce layoffs. For example, one CEO stated, "Loyal and committed employees are critical," yet at the same time, he was laying off thousands. Look for these negative signs when assessing whether a business has good employee relations.

Watch out for those management teams that quickly announce layoffs the moment their business encounters a setback, such as a temporary drop in demand for its goods and services. There are many examples of businesses in the financial-services, retail, or real estate industries that quickly lay off employees when they encounter a downturn, but as soon as things start to pick up, they look to re-hire the same people—often at a higher pay rate. Instead, look for those management teams that attempt to hold on to their employees by taking the following actions:

- eliminating overtime;
- freezing hiring;
- offering voluntary retirement packages;
- reducing hours;
- reducing everyone's salary;
- delaying raises;
- trimming spending on training, travel, or marketing;

- cutting temporary staff;
- delaying capital investments;
- and using less-busy employees to balance workloads elsewhere in the company.

For example, in 2008 before Federal Express resorted to layoffs, it instituted pay cuts and temporarily halted retirement contributions.[38] In 2000, under similarly slowing economic conditions, FedEx Freight also resisted layoffs on a large scale. In 2003, Pat Reed, CEO of FedEx Freight East, said they juggled hours and kept people working. He called the long-term payoff "indescribable," saying it created loyalty and reduced turnover. Another benefit: "It gives you the ability to hire the best of the best."[39]

Does Management Listen to Its Employees?

Managers can learn more by listening to the conversations of a few employees than by spending time setting down strategic visions. Many of the best ideas come from employees who are in the field, so it is critical for management to listen to them and have avenues for employees to channel information to headquarters. For example, the idea for the Post-it note® developed by the 3M Company came from an employee, and the Frappuccino® at Starbucks was invented by a store manager.

Does the Business Have a Strong Culture?

A culture is an organization's shared values and beliefs, and it sets the tone for how employees treat customers. It is found in all businesses and varies from "this is just a job" mentality to "I love my employer." For values and beliefs to be shared, they must be made clear and they must be modeled. A culture is typically built through the example of the top management of a business; employees will watch how top management acts as a cue for how they should act.

An identifiable culture will attract employees most likely to agree with those values and beliefs. It also informs new employees about what is important at the company. For example, Whole Foods Market's culture is so important to the success of the company that management sends existing Whole Foods Market employees to work at new store locations. They do this not just to help set up systems or train, but to help new employees understand which things are most important to Whole Foods Market. They call this transfer *yogurt culture.*

One of the main advantages of a strong company culture is that a business is able to attract great employees and does not need to pay the highest salaries in order to recruit them. Most talented employees will gladly sacrifice pay for the right work environment. Furthermore, when employees feel like they are part of something important, they are more loyal to the business.

In contrast, a business without a strong culture may be one where failures are not tolerated or where there is a lack of trust among management and employees. Businesses with weak or negative cultures may be inwardly focused and often do not possess good customer service. Employees are there to collect a paycheck, and most employees are not looking to develop their careers at the business.

For example, HealthSouth (an owner of rehabilitation centers) had a hard-charging culture and was known for weak employee relations. When CEO Richard Scrushy performed audits of the rehab centers, he often performed a white glove test of the picture frames: After wiping his finger on a hanging picture, he would then wipe his finger on the clothing of the manager of the center. Any dust marks resulted in lower audit scores.[40] Even though HealthSouth was quickly growing and its stock price was increasing, management-employee relations would be suspect based only on this or similar anecdotes. Regardless of short-term growth, a weak or demeaning culture is usually representative of a weak firm, and it should be a warning signal to investors.

As you determine whether or not a business has a strong culture, look for engaged employees, because the happier employees are in their jobs, the more they will typically try to satisfy customers. The company grapevine is the swiftest means of communication, so tapping into it with a few employees can net you valuable information. The best way to determine if a business has a strong, healthy culture is to talk with mid-level and lower-level employees of a business. These are the people who interface with customers most often. It is one thing for management to say something is important, but if the rest of the company doesn't buy it, it isn't part of the culture.

For example, if you could take the staff from, say, Dunkin Donuts, and plunk them down in a Starbucks, do you think you'd receive the same level of service? Not a chance. The Dunkin Donuts employees would not have been selected and trained to provide individualized attention and service: The entire atmosphere would be different. This difference shows up in your customer experience, and is one reason that Starbucks is able to charge a premium for its products.[41]

To learn more about how a culture is built, I interviewed Bob Graham, co-founder of AIM Management Group, one of the nation's largest mutual fund companies. AIM grew from a firm with five employees and no assets in 1976 to a firm with more than $57 billion in assets under management and a valuation of $1.6 billion in 1997 (when it merged with Invesco). One of AIM's greatest strengths as it grew into a top asset manager was its extremely low employee turnover rate, which was (and still is) rare for a business in the investment management industry. The main reason for such low employee turnover was that AIM was well known for having a strong and energized culture. This allowed it to attract talented employees, and more important, to keep them. Graham recalls, "There was a sense of excitement working at AIM. It was known as a people-friendly company, and people wanted to come work there. It was fun and people didn't leave because they had the excitement of building something everybody was proud of."

This was critical to the success of AIM and its growth. In the book *People Are the Product: A History of AIM*, co-founder Ted Bauer observed that, "In the investment business, people are the product. Your inventory goes down the elevator every night and comes back in the morning. If people are happy, they work more productively."[42]

I asked Graham how AIM was able to build such a strong culture when other companies couldn't. Graham says that in at least one way, they modeled their business on friendships. "To build any successful enterprise requires people. You attract good people through the culture. Our philosophy from the beginning was that we wanted the business to operate in the same way our friendships did. The three of us [Bob Graham, Gary Crum, and Ted Bauer] were all friends, and we all got along so well together. In fact, we hired people we wanted to be friends with. If we felt we would not enjoy spending time with them outside of work, then we would not hire them. When you hire these types of people, a big benefit is that whenever you run into inevitable disagreements, they will always be amicably resolved."

As Graham and his co-founders were building the culture, Graham said they wanted to offer a different type of work environment that gave employees a chance to be part of a small family operation. But they also wanted employees to have opportunities.

Graham explains some of the ways that AIM's culture supported its growth. "We offered a more entrepreneurial environment. We wanted people to have a sense that they could control their destinies." Graham credits Ted Bauer with helping to develop employees: "Ted was always willing to give younger people a lot of responsibility. This was a great way to develop people because they really appreciated the responsibility." By constantly promoting and giving more responsibility, Graham says they also avoided becoming stagnant.

In addition to offering entrepreneurial opportunities, AIM attracted employees who appreciated what is now called work-life-balance. Graham says, "We believed that employees should live a balanced life where family was important. We expected employees to have a life outside of work."

I also asked Graham how AIM had managed to avoid the pitfall of an overly competitive culture, which was dominant in most Wall Street firms. In other words, what did they do to foster a cohesive team environment? He told me they weeded out people who were bad apples or who just didn't fit in well with the culture. This made it much easier on those who stayed. These employees made extremely impressive contributions, and they did it together. Graham said, "We wanted to avoid employees who had the attitude that they needed to beat the guy sitting next to them. AIM's culture was not cutthroat. Employees did not worry about who got credit."

AIM's business and cultural growth shows a cycle of benefits that would be hard to reproduce. The results were that AIM was able to attract talented, entrepreneurial employees and keep those same employees happy by giving them a healthy work environment. In turn, these entrepreneurial employees were the engine that helped AIM grow, which then offered more opportunities for others to move up the ranks.

Look for similar elements in businesses you evaluate. When you locate one with the cultural elements that AIM cultivated—that is, talented, happy, energized managers and employees attracting more of the same—you have discovered the foundation of a successful business.

Does the Business Have Identifiable, Shared Values?

The strongest cultures have shared ideas about what is most important; these are *shared values*. For example, senior managers may value the long-term benefits of training over the savings they would have from not training employees. Similarly, a business may value having great service and generous return policies over the benefits of reducing its service staff or reducing its restocking efforts. Managers and leaders play a central role in communicating and demonstrating what is important for the business, and they often are responsible for how well employees understand and adopt these values, which create the foundation for day-to-day decisions regarding the operations of a business.

To learn how to identify a business that has strongly held and clearly defined values, I interviewed Lee Valkenaar, Co-Chairman of the Board for Whole Planet Foundation.[43] Valkenaar has been at Whole Foods Market since 1987 in various capacities, including executive vice president (EVP) of Global Support (from 2004 to 2008) and president of the Mid-Atlantic Region (from 2001 to 2004). He helped build the culture that Whole Foods Market is so well known for today. In Valkenaar's opinion:

> When you are explicit about your company's values, it gives employees an opportunity to identify with those values because they identify those values within themselves. When employees see things that resonate within themselves, they can align themselves with those values. One of the main advantages of a business that has values is that it creates buy-in from employees by giving them a form of ownership in the business, which increases the chances of successful execution.
>
> Many companies have values that are expressed through a vision and mission. You need to determine if these values are baked into the policies and procedures of the business or if [they are] just a statement that shows up on the wall. If they are incorporated into the culture—into the policies, procedures, and practices—that is when execution happens. People can and should be held accountable for knowing and adhering to these 'shared value policies' the same as they would an attendance policy.

For example, although you may see it in a mission statement, most businesses do not think employee empowerment is critical. Empowered employees can be intimidating to some senior managers, and empowerment also requires a substantial investment in time and energy to make decisions with more voices. When a business truly considers it important to empower employees, it encourages them to speak up. Whole Foods Market has team meetings every month where employees are solicited for their honest feedback. According to Valkenaar, some of these meetings can be intense, and sometimes employees have personal agendas or just want to vent their personal frustrations. For some senior managers, it is not easy to hear that the employee does not like the policies that have been implemented, but it is critical for senior management to listen.

To identify whether a business really has shared values, you need to ask the following questions:

- How do values show up in the organization? At Whole Foods Market, one shared value is that there should be more equitable levels of pay across the organization. To implement this, managers established salary caps for the top executive officers, which limit the amount they can make, compared to a full-time employee. According to the 2010 proxy statement, the compensation was limited to 19 times the annual wage for a full-time team member.
- Are the values identifiable and explicit? Are they found on the company website? Start by looking at the website of the business in the about us tab. If there is nothing there that mentions values or mission, then they are not a central part of the organization.
- Does management continually state them? Reinforcement and public recognition by managers send a message about what's important. Do the employees even know what the company values are? If you were to walk up to any employee at the business and ask what the values are, would that employee be able to answer this question? If not, then it is highly likely the company has not done a good job of expressing what its values are.
- Does the company hold its employees accountable for knowing and incorporating the values? If a supervisor or employee violates the core values, is this behavior tolerated? If a business is serious about communicating, teaching, and operating by using shared definitions of what's important, it won't look away if an employee ignores a shared principle.

Let's say a company, on paper, makes a commitment to an environment of mutual respect, but employees don't buy in. Then that's not a shared value. Many companies have values on paper that say it's important to treat people well, but as Valkenaar notes, "If a business is not proactive in managing assholes, then it is probably not acting in accordance with the values of the organization."

- Are there costs associated with the values? At Starbucks, healthcare costs represent a large portion of costs, but offering great benefits is valued at the company, because that's how it attracts and retains the kinds of employees who keep customers happy. Observing direct investment in something is often the only way to discern its importance to a company.

Finally, Valkenaar gives an example of a business that has not baked those values into its culture. He related a publicized story about a company that encountered a problem because it manufactured a product that said, "Made in the U.S.A." on the outside of the product, but inside, the label stated "Made in China." Visualize the path this product must have taken: As the brainchild of a creative merchandiser, it wound its way from production to the retail stores. Imagine what message is implicitly sent when you brand a product made in the United States and manufacture it in China.

Could that even happen in a company that completely believed in domestic sourcing? Also, if the company were truly committed to open communication, someone likely would have voiced concern even after the item was produced. Finally, if the company thought that customers deserved to know exactly what they were buying, the company would likely have stopped stocking the product completely.

Any company can say it wants open communication with employees, the trust of its customers or that it buys American, but this example shows why saying it isn't the same as doing it. Valkenaar sees a clear disconnect between employees and leadership that allowed this to happen. If the company had really incorporated its values into its business, the snafu would likely have never happened, or at the very least the problem would have been solved long before the product ever hit the shelves.

What Is the Employee-Retention Rate?

If a business has an especially good employee-retention rate, it will often mention this on its website, annual report, or a plaque. For example, Baldor Electric, an electric-motor manufacturer, has a plaque at its headquarters showing the names of its employees who have been with the company for more than 10 years and the date each joined the company. Most of the employees on the plaque have been at the business for 15 years or more. There are many advantages to a high employee-retention rate, including reduced hiring costs, better customer relations, and higher profitability than competitors.

For example, even though Costco pays its employees 40 percent more (on average) than Sam's Club (which is owned by Wal-Mart) and gives its employees better benefits, Costco's profit per employee is much greater than its competitor Sam's Club. Low employee turnover is one of the reasons for this. Whereas Sam's Club turnover is 21 percent in the employees' first year, Costco's is only 6 percent. "Paying your employees well is not only the right thing to do, but it makes for good business," says Costco CEO Jim Sinegal. He further states that if Costco paid rock-bottom wages, it would get what it paid for. "It doesn't pay the right dividends. It doesn't keep employees happy. It keeps them looking for other jobs. Plus, managers spend all their time hiring replacements rather than running your business."[44]

☐ 44. Does the management team know how to hire well?

There are few management decisions more important than those involved in hiring and promoting employees. The number-one job of a manager is to pick the right people and then put them in the right positions. In essence, management is the art of getting things done through other people. Jack Welch, former CEO of General Electric, said, "My job is not to know everything about each business. It is to pick the people who will run the business and to decide how much money Business A versus Business B or C gets—and how to transfer people, dollars, and ideas across those businesses. I don't get into the how."[45]

If the management team has good people it can trust and count on, then executing the plans of the business becomes easier. In turn, talented employees hire other talented employees, who strengthen the entire organization. Therefore, if management is able to hire well, this is a great indication of competence.

You need to determine the caliber and tenure not only of top managers, but also those managers in important operational roles. Begin by identifying all of the key managers at the business by position. You may want to construct a management-timeline report, similar to the one shown in Table 8.1 for regional gaming business Penn National Gaming.

To construct this timeline, use the historical proxy statements to identify the top managers of the business. To identify other managers not shown on the proxy statement, screen for all of the Form 3, 4, and 5s, which you can find on the SEC website. These forms must be filed promptly, and they describe the holdings and transactions of officers, directors, and beneficial owners.

An added benefit of creating a management timeline report is that you will be able to note if there is a lot of manager turnover at the business, which is a negative sign. I have learned that one of the best indicators of a business that is deteriorating is when the most competent top managers of a business begin to look for other jobs or leave the business. You can use your timeline to monitor management turnover to alert you of any potential problems within the business.

After you have finished constructing a timeline report, research the backgrounds of each manager by searching for press releases and historical articles found in news aggregation sites, such as *Dow Jones Factiva* or *LexisNexis*. You will often find a press release issued by the company describing the background of the new management hire. You can then search for other articles by combining the name of the manager with previous employers. As you read through the articles and the press releases, determine whether the managers hired have the experience and knowledge necessary to do the job. Pay particular attention to whether they have dealt with a similar customer base in the past. If the top managers are hiring other managers with a lot of experience with the customer base, then this is a positive sign; however, if they are hiring their former colleagues or other managers who have limited experience with the customer base, this should serve as a warning signal.

For example, at IMS Health, a pharmaceutical information and consulting company, CEO David Thomas hired managers who had worked at his previous employer, IBM. These new hires did not have

Table 8.1 Penn National Gaming—Management Tenure from 2001 to 2010

	2001	2002	2003	2004	2005	2006	2007	2008	2009	2010
CEO	Peter Carlino	Peter Carlino	Peter Carlino	Peter Carlino	Peter Carlino	Peter Carlino	Peter Carlino	Peter Carlino	Peter Carlino	Peter Carlino
Pres/COO	Kevin DeSanctis (02/01)	Kevin DeSanctis	Kevin DeSanctis	Kevin DeSanctis	Kevin DeSanctis	Kevin DeSanctis (10/06)	x	Tim Wilmott (02/08)	Tim Wilmott	Tim Wilmott
EVP of Operations	x	x	Len DeAngelo (07/03)	Len DeAngelo	Len DeAngelo	Len DeAngelo	Len DeAngelo	Len DeAngelo (08/08)	x	x
CFO	Bill Clifford	Bill Clifford	Bill Clifford	Bill Clifford	Bill Clifford	Bill Clifford	Bill Clifford	Bill Clifford	Bill Clifford	Bill Clifford
SVP/Regional	x	x	x	x	x	x	x	Thomas Burke*	Thomas Burke	Thomas Burke
SVP/Regional	x	John Finamore	John Finamore	John Finamore	John Finamore	John Finamore	John Finamore	John Finamore	John Finamore	John Finamore
VP/Secy/Tr	Robert Ippolito	Robert Ippolito	Robert Ippolito	Robert Ippolito	Robert Ippolito	Robert Ippolito	Robert Ippolito	Robert Ippolito	Robert Ippolito	Robert Ippolito
Corp Development	Steven Snyder	Steven Snyder	Steven Snyder	Steven Snyder	Steven Snyder	Steven Snyder	Steven Snyder	Steven Snyder	Steven Snyder	Steven Snyder

*Burke with PENN since 2002, previously General Manager Argosy Riverside and Bullwhackers

Note: x denotes position not filled

241

pharmaceutical knowledge or experience with the customer base. A sweep of press releases and news stories would have alerted you to the fact that many other IBMers ended up at IMS Health, among them:

- John Schultz, IMS' SVP of European Sales (after 20 years at IBM);
- Bruce Boggs, SVP of IMS' U.S. Sales (after 26 years at IBM);
- Adeh Al-Saleh, President of IMS EMEA, (after 19 years at IBM); and
- David Carlucci, President/COO (after 25 years at IBM). Carlucci later became CEO of IMS Health.

The warning signal to our firm was that it appeared that the CEO was hiring his former colleagues rather than hiring managers who were more qualified or who had experience in the pharmaceutical industry. As one indicator of the success of using this hiring method, note that the stock price when Thomas was appointed in 2000 was around $25 per share. It remained in the $25 to $26 per share range as Carlucci took over as CEO in 2006, and it then dropped to $22 per share when the company was taken private in 2009.[46] In other words, over a nine-year period, the managers at IMS Health failed to create any market value for shareholders.

In contrast, Casey Hoffman, founder of supportkids® (a child-support-services company), mainly hired single parents. These managers understood what it was like to be in their customers' shoes and lived their lives understanding many of the same frustrations and difficulties as their customers. This allowed them to execute more effectively than those who did not understand the customer base. As a result, supportkids grew its revenues at an annual rate of 28 percent during Hoffman's tenure as CEO.[47]

How Do You Determine if the Manager Knows How to Pick Good Employees?

A business will put the odds of succeeding in its favor if it recruits and retains employees who truly want to work there. Employees who are thoroughly engaged are more likely to stay longer. On the other hand, if a business does not hire well, then most of its employees will rotate in and out of critical roles, reducing productivity for the long term. Managers who know how to hire well are disciplined, hiring only those employees that fit their criteria, instead of just hiring the best candidates who are available at the time. Therefore, watch for those businesses that take their time as they hire employees.

Next, determine if the employees are coming from businesses with similar cultures. For example, if an employee has spent 20 years working at bureaucratic British Airways (BA) and has been hired at a decentralized business such as Penn National Gaming, then it is less likely to be a good cultural fit for both the company and that employee. If most company hiring is from businesses with similar cultures, then the odds are better that it will be a good fit.

Managers who hire well typically hire for a certain character trait, such as integrity or attitude, rather than skills. Issadore Sharp, founder of Four Seasons Hotels, said he hired employees for attitude first and then trained for the rest. "I can teach anyone to be a waiter," he said, in the book *Four Seasons: The Story of a Business Philosophy.* "But you can't change an ingrained poor attitude. We look for people who say, 'I'd be proud to be a doorman.'" Herb Kelleher, founder of Southwest Airlines, echoed this sentiment when he said, "You don't have the time, techniques, or enough drugs to change attitudes."[48]

How Well Is the Business Able to Articulate the Values and Attributes of the Firm to Attract the Right Employees?

It is critical for a business to attract the right employees. Businesses attract employees to a degree because of the culture they offer. Employees who enjoy and excel in collaborative environments pick those types of companies, whereas other employees may choose to work in more structured environments. The type of employee a business attracts depends on the type of business. For example, in retail, you must have a strong customer-service culture. If you visit retail stores and find that the employees are not customer oriented, then this is a clear indicator that they are not hiring well.

The only way a business can hire employees who will be enthusiastic about their work and loyal to the business is by clearly communicating the values and attributes of the business to potential employees. This way, employees can self-select into the business if they believe that their values and preferences fit with the business. Some businesses excel at expressing what makes them unique. For example, at Whole Foods Market, potential employees are told that they will have a four-week trial period of working in a team; after that trial period, two-thirds of the team must accept the employee in order for him or her to join the company permanently. Potential employees who do not like team environments will most likely not want to go further in the interview process. Therefore, potential hires at Whole Foods Market self-select into the business.

Employees who thrive in clear-cut, well-defined work environments do not want to work in uncertain environments where there are no hierarchies or predetermined channels of communication. For example, Exxon Mobil does a good job of explaining to employees that it has a highly structured environment and that it will take a long time in order for an employee to be promoted. It expects its hires to remain at the company for long periods of time. Employees who become frustrated with their progress may leave, but those who remain are more likely to make their careers at the company.

One type of employee isn't necessarily better than another, but the business does need to do a good job of communicating what type of firm it is. If you note that the business has high turnover or disengaged and unproductive employees, then this is a sign it is not clearly communicating its values to potential hires.[49]

Do They Hire Managers or Employees Who Are Candid?

You want to determine if the manager hires employees who are candid or those who are not afraid to challenge the top management team. Candid employees will speak up when they think the manager is pursuing a flawed strategy, whereas an employee with a different personality or outlook may just assume the manager knows more than the employees.

Candor is, in essence, the willingness of employees to express their real opinions. Perhaps you have been in a formal meeting where another manager is making a presentation that you know will not work, but you wait for the boss's response before proceeding to question the plan. If the boss approves, it is highly likely you will not speak up. An open CEO encourages others to be open and not agree to things that they have no intention of acting on, or consider poor ideas. Formality thus suppresses candor, whereas informality encourages it. One way to learn if a business hires candid employees is to learn about the type of workplace it has. Ask the employees if the meetings they attend are full of presentations that are prepackaged, well-orchestrated, or stiff. If the meetings are instead open, employees will probably be more comfortable providing valuable feedback.

For example, at DaVita, which operates dialysis treatment centers, CEO Kent Thiry encourages employees to bring him bad news. Thiry regularly surveys employees, and he makes it a point to act quickly on the feedback he receives. He uses the information to avoid mistakes.[50]

Similarly, Motorola was recognized as a great business in the 1980s when it was run by CEO Robert Galvin. During that period, the only way managers got ahead was by challenging existing assumptions and not supporting the status quo. Galvin encouraged his employees to tell him the truth and to challenge him. A story often told is that a young middle manager once approached Galvin and said, "Bob, I heard that point you made this morning, and I think you're dead wrong. I'm going to prove it: I'm going to shoot you down." Galvin's response to a companion was proud: "That's how we've overcome Texas Instruments' lead in semiconductors!"[51]

However, as Motorola's top management changed, these employees no longer felt comfortable being candid. As a result, Motorola developed fewer innovations, and its stock price (even after accounting for spin-offs) increased only marginally over the last 20 years, from 1990 to the end of 2010.[52]

If the top managers are hiring employees who are not encouraged to speak their minds, it is likely the business will encounter problems down the road, making it a bad investment.

What Type of Board Members Does the CEO Choose?

Typically, the CEO plays an important part in bringing board members in, especially if the CEO has been running the business for a long period of time. Is the CEO bringing in cronies, board members with prestige, political figures, friends, consultants, or lawyers? If they are bringing in, say, politicians, many will lack business experience, and this could be an indicator that the CEO is bringing in people because they are loyal to him or her. Viewing the types of board members that have come to the business during the CEO's tenure will alert you to whether the CEO is using the business as a personal vehicle to benefit him- or herself, or if the CEO is running the business with shareholder interests in mind.

Most of the largest frauds in corporate history involved board members whose interests were more clearly aligned with management than shareholders and the business.[53] For example:

- Enron's board was known for rubber stamping the company's deals. Board members didn't often challenge management on the financial reports or any other matters. And why would they? A board member doing so would be risking as much as $380,000 received as an annual board retainer.
- WorldCom, the telecom business embroiled in accounting fraud, had a board almost entirely aligned with CEO Bernard Ebbers: Most were insiders, and even those who were outsiders had strong personal and financial ties to Ebbers.
- At cable business Adelphia Communications Corporation, family members made up the majority of the board. The founders of Adelphia were charged with securities violations.
- Insiders dominated conglomerate Tyco's board. CEO Dennis Kozlowski's board filled 8 of 12 positions with Tyco employees. Kozlowski was convicted of grand larceny related to unauthorized compensation.

Look out for conflicts of interests between directors and the CEO found in the Related Party section of the proxy statement. For example, here's what you would have found in HealthSouth's proxy statement (HealthSouth's CEO was involved in a corporate accounting scandal):

- A director earning $250,000 annually for seven years as part of a HealthSouth consulting contract.
- A director with a $395,000 joint property investment with HealthSouth CEO Scrushy.
- A director whose company received a $5.6 million glass installation contract at a new HealthSouth hospital.
- A company owned by HealthSouth employees (Scrushy, six directors, and the wife of a director) that also did business with HealthSouth. The company, MedCenterDirect, was a hospital-supply company that operated online.

Watch also for donations to charities made by the company on behalf of certain directors as this often serves as a red flag. For example, at Enron:

- Dr. John Mendelsohn was a board member and member of the audit committee: He received substantial donations for the cancer research center he directed from both Enron and Ken and Linda Lay.
- Lord John Wakeham, another audit committee member, was paid $72,000 each year over many years as an Enron consultant.
- Wendy Gramm (another audit committee member) received a $50,000 Enron donation for the program she directed at George Mason University, the Mercatus Center Regulatory Studies Program.

These are potential conflicts of interest, and they serve as clear warning signals.

☐ 45. Does the management team focus on cutting unnecessary costs?

I used to believe that a frugal manager was a good manager. Over time, I learned that although managers who are habitually thrifty will be able to recognize opportunities to lower costs, they may not invest in important projects. Frugality is bad when the company does not spend money for the benefit of customers.

On the other hand, reducing unnecessary costs while continuing to invest in the core business is good. For example, if you visited the headquarters of retailer 99 Cent Only Stores, you would see stained carpeting, broken file cabinets, folding tables used as credenzas, and front pages of newspapers displayed as art. Clearly, founders Dave and Sherry Gold have chosen not to spend money on the headquarters because customers don't care what corporate offices look like. As Dave Gold says, "I don't mind spending money. I just don't like to waste it." Instead, 99 Cent Only Stores invests in the things that benefit the customer, spending money on the stores, and making sure its buyers (who find the best products for customers) are well compensated: In fact, the company pays its buyers *double* what they would make anywhere else.[54]

Another CEO who believes in investing in his business is David Zaslav, CEO of television company Discovery Communications. Zaslav puts creative leaders rather than a business leader in charge of each channel and prioritizes brand building, audience building, and great content. His thinking is that quality content is always going to be in demand. Zaslav sees the company as two halves: "On the right half is better content, better shows, better characters: *Deadliest Catch* and *Oprah*. The left side is everything else. If we can take $2 out of the left side and invest $1 or $1.50 more in our content and brands, that gives the trajectory of our growth a push."[55]

Watch also for the *type* of costs a business cuts. When Starbucks CEO Howard Schultz cut costs during 2009 and 2010, he avoided cuts that would directly affect the customer. Instead, he reduced costs by eliminating supply chain inefficiencies, waste, and certain parts of the support structure. Starbucks also reduced expenses, but at the same time, it kept investing in the things that mattered most: For example, maintaining employee benefits and committing more resources to employee training. During 2010, Schultz said that his customer-satisfaction scores actually rose, reaching their highest levels ever because, "We reinvested in our people, we reinvested in innovation, and we reinvested in the values of the company."[56]

Also, think about this: If the management team is continually announcing cost-cutting programs, this is a sign that they are not focused on continually cutting unnecessary costs. These types of businesses are often serial restructurers as well. For example, during his Hewlett-Packard tenure (2005 to 2010), CEO Mark Hurd took $3.2 billion in restructuring charges and $3.3 billion in write-downs for amortization of intangible assets related to acquisitions. This buy-and-restructure strategy helped HP deliver annual revenue growth of 7.5 percent and 22 percent growth in earnings per share during Hurd's tenure. However, Hurd was constantly restructuring the workforce by increasing the use of contract manufacturing and other cost-cutting measures. He also acquired companies (such as Electronic Data Systems, 3Com, and Palm) to grow markets in services, networking, and mobile devices—acquisitions that, combined with ongoing restructurings, made "one-time charges" recurring. The problem is that once these large costs have been taken so quickly, it becomes more difficult for the business to cut costs further without the quality of the product declining.[57]

❐ 46. Are the CEO and CFO disciplined in making capital allocation decisions?

Capital allocation is the manner in which the management team invests the excess free-cash flows that the business generates.

Management decides when and where these excess free-cash flows should be invested or distributed. There are five actions management can take with excess free-cash flow:

1. Reinvest the capital back in the business in new projects.
2. Hold cash on the balance sheet.
3. Pay dividends.
4. Buy back stock.
5. Make acquisitions.

It is difficult to find CEOs who are both good at operating the business and at allocating capital. The main reason for this is that operating a business and allocating capital are two completely different skill sets; being proficient at one of these functions has no correlation to being competent with the other. As a group, CEOs possess varying degrees of competence when it comes to capital allocation.

The best capital allocators are those who are removed from the day-to-day operations of a business—for example, Warren Buffett, CEO of Berkshire Hathaway; Peter Carlino, CEO of Penn National Gaming; and Bruce Flatt, CEO of Brookfield Asset Management. The best capital allocators delegate the day-to-day operations to other managers within the business; for example, Carlino delegates the day-to-day operations to COO Tim Wilmott. This allows these CEOs to see the big picture and not get bogged down in the details.

One of the best capital allocators in corporate history was Henry Singleton, longtime CEO of Teledyne, who cofounded the business in 1960 and served as CEO until 1986. In John Train's book *The Money Masters*, Warren Buffett reported that he believes "Henry Singleton has the best operating and capital-deployment record in American business." When Teledyne's stock was trading at extremely high prices in the 1960s, Singleton used the high-priced stock as currency to make acquisitions. Singleton made more than 130 acquisitions of small, high-margin manufacturing and technology businesses that operated in defensible niches managed by strong management. When the price-to-earnings ratio of Teledyne fell sharply starting in the 1970s, he repurchased stock. Between 1972 and 1984, he reduced the share count by more than 90 percent. He repurchased stock for as low as $6 per share in 1972, which by 1987 traded at more than $400 per share.[58]

The best way to determine if managers are good at allocating capital is to review their historical decisions, whether they are buying back stock or making new investments. You can identify a good capital allocator by looking for examples where they are disciplined.

For example, in a fourth quarter 2008 conference call, Penn National Gaming CEO Peter Carlino discussed why the company did not build a hotel next to its successful casino site in Hobbs, New Mexico. A hotel would help the casino generate more cash flow as it would encourage visitors to stay overnight. Carlino said that preliminary estimates to construct the hotel came in at $30 million, yet he felt that it would not make sense to build the hotel until the construction costs came in closer to $20 million. This $10 million difference is not a large amount, considering Penn National Gaming generated more than $300 million in distributable free-cash flow in 2009.[59] Even though a hotel would add to cash flows, Carlino demonstrated that he is disciplined in waiting for the right deal before proceeding with any capital investments.

In contrast, the majority of CEOs would probably build the hotel and hope that the extra cash flows from overnight visitors would make up the $10 million difference. But Carlino's capital discipline has helped Penn National Gaming become one of the greatest compounding stocks in the last 15 years, compounding at more than 27 percent from its May 1994 initial public offering (IPO) to its stock price at the end of 2010 of more than $27 per share.[60]

☐ 47. Do the CEO and CFO buy back stock opportunistically?

Earnings per share is the most important measure in determining what a share of stock in the business is worth. Because stock repurchases decrease the number of shares outstanding, they have the effect of increasing earnings per share. If the stock is undervalued, these stock repurchases can add materially to the value of the business. The timing of buybacks will depend on the value of the stock, on how much cash the business has, and how much cash it needs. Management may decide to buy back stock as a one-time act, or you may see management lay out predetermined amounts each year that it plans to use for buybacks.

There are a couple of common motivations behind stock repurchases:

- Management may believe the stock is undervalued, so it takes advantage of the opportunity to potentially add value.

- Management may want to offset dilution from issuing stock options.

Let's review the two reasons for buybacks in more detail.

Adding Value By Buying Back Stock Opportunistically

By making buybacks when the stock is undervalued, management can materially add to the value of the business. For example, if a business is worth $50 per share and management buys 10 percent of the stock at $25 per share, then management has automatically increased the value of the business to $52.50 per share ($25 per share multiplied by 10 percent equals $2.50 per share plus $50 per share). If it instead pays $100 per share, then it is reducing shareholder value. The lower the price it pays for the stock, the more value management will create for shareholders.

The best way to determine if the management team is opportunistic in its stock repurchases is to examine its history. Western Union, for example, generates a lot of excess free-cash flow, so stock buybacks make sense. When Western Union was spun off from First Data Corporation in 2006, management announced it would invest $1 billion per year in stock buybacks. In 2008, when the stock was trading at more than $23 per share, Western Union repurchased $1.3 billion in stock. However, as the stock price *declined* to below $14 per share in 2009, management pulled back, saying the recession had limited its ability to repurchase shares, and that it would only repurchase $400 million in stock. With stable cash flows and a strong balance sheet, Western Union had more than enough cash to buy the stock. Instead, as the stock price *increased*, Western Union began repurchasing stock, announcing it was reinstating its plan to buy back $1 billion in stock each year. Although conserving cash is important, in this case, it was unwarranted given the strong cash flows, and clearly illustrated that Western Union's management team was not opportunistic in its stock repurchases.[61]

An example of a business whose management team has made many opportunistic purchases in the past is AutoZone, an automotive-parts retailer. AutoZone's earnings per share (EPS) grew at a rate of 15.7 percent from August 2002 to August 2010, while its net income grew at a rate of 6.23 percent over the same period. The main reason for the difference was due to the share repurchases that AutoZone made, which reduced the number of shares outstanding from 104.4 million shares to 48.5 million, or by 53 percent.[62] The share repurchases have clearly added value: EPS grew 15.7 percent during the eight-year period. Had AutoZone not bought back any stock, then the EPS would have grown only 6.23 percent, which would have resulted in a lower stock price.

Table 8.2 examines further how AutoZone's stock repurchases have added value over eight years (with August as year end).

You can use a similar table when you are assessing whether a management team has added value through stock repurchases. The amount and number of shares repurchased are found in the 10-K in a separate section titled Stock Repurchases.

Similarly, when a business issues new shares (e.g., stock options), it destroys value. For example, General Motors reported a 4.82 percent growth rate in net income from 1985 to 1995. However, its EPS over the same period grew at an annual rate of only 2.68 percent because GM increased the number of shares outstanding during that time.[63]

Offsetting Options Dilution

When determining whether the stock repurchases add value, disregard those repurchases made to offset options dilution. Most investors don't think of repurchasing issued options as capital allocation, but this is an area that management controls, and it

Table 8.2   AutoZone Stock's Repurchasing History, from 2002 to 2010

Year	Outstanding (in millions)	Repurchased (in millions)	Avg. Price Paid per Share	Amount Paid (in millions)	EPS with Share Repurchases	EPS without Share Repurchases
2002	104.4	12.6	$55.47	$699.00	$4.10	$4.00
2003	94.9	12.3	$72.44	$891.00	$5.45	$4.84
2004	85	10.2	$83.14	$848.00	$6.66	$5.29
2005	78.5	4.8	$88.96	$427.00	$7.27	$5.33
2006	75.2	6.2	$93.23	$578.00	$7.57	$5.31
2007	69.1	6.0	$127.00	$762.00	$8.62	$5.56
2008	63.3	6.8	$125.00	$849.00	$10.14	$6.00
2009	55.3	9.3	$140.00	$1,300.00	$11.89	$6.13
2010	48.5	6.4	$175.63	$1,124.00	$15.23	$6.89

Source: AutoZone 10K 2002 to 2010 August 25 year end, Basic EPS data is Capital IQ

Table 8.3   Microsoft Option Issuance and Buybacks

	2010	2009	2008
Stock buyback (No. of shares, millions)	380	318	402
Options Issuance (No. of shares, millions)*	101	90	68
Percentage of stock buyback used to offset option dilution	27%	28%	17%

*Includes Stock Awards and Shared Performance Stock Awards: Shared performance stock awards (SPSAs) are a form of Stock Award in which the number of shares ultimately received depends on Microsoft's performance against specified performance targets.[64]

is another form of capital allocation. You can create a table that includes the number of stock options issued in a given year compared to the number of shares bought back in order to understand what percentage of stock buybacks are used to offset options dilution. In the 10-K, there is a section titled Stock Plans, where you can find the total number of options that are issued by the business. Table 8.3 is an example for Microsoft.

As you can see from Table 8.3, the amount of stock buybacks to offset options dilution averages 25 percent, leaving 75 percent of repurchases to potentially add value. When evaluating how effectively management is using buybacks, use this percentage rather than all the repurchases.

Key Points to Keep in Mind

- The best-performing businesses over the long term, as measured by shareholder returns, are managed by CEOs who have a purpose greater than solely generating profits.
- Most successful businesses are built on hundreds of small decisions, instead of on one well-formulated strategic plan.
- Good management teams work on proving a concept before investing a lot of capital. They are not likely to put a lot of money in all at once hoping for a big payoff.
- The strategic plans that are most prone to failure are those that have an overly narrow focus, such as those that set a financial target (e.g. guidance).
- Businesses that are decentralized attract independent thought and a diverse workforce, which encourages innovation.

(continued)

- Many of the best-performing stocks in history—that is, those that have compounded at rates greater than 20 percent over 15 years—have used decentralized operating structures.
- When a business has good employee relations, it typically has many other good attributes, such as good customer relations and the ability to adapt quickly to changing economic circumstances.
- If managers are committed to employee training, this is a great sign that they have a long-term orientation.
- Avoid investing in those management teams that quickly announce layoffs the moment their business encounters a setback.
- If a business culture is admired and respected, the business is able to attract great employees.
- Few management decisions are as important as selecting the right people for the right positions. Good hiring indicates sound judgment.
- The best capital allocators are those who are removed from the day-to-day operations of a business.

9

Assessing the Quality of Management—Positive and Negative Traits

In Chapter 8, we looked at how management operates the business; this chapter shows you how to evaluate the positive and negative traits of the managers themselves. Many investors rely on the personality, education, and technical knowledge of a management team to assess whether they are capable of leading a business. These are important qualities, but there are far more important qualities. If you are going to invest for the long term with a management team, you'd also better think about the character and values of the people on that team. For example:

- Is management passionate about operating the business?
- Does the manager have integrity?
- Would managers fudge accounting numbers to meet guidance?
- Do managers have enough humility to acknowledge when they have made a mistake?

As you begin to evaluate the character of a manager, look for a pattern of behavior that can help you forecast future behavior. When it comes to people, the best predictor of future behavior is past behavior. You want to get an overall sense of what the manager is like. In order to do this, look at what the managers have accomplished in the past and more important, how he or she accomplished them. Published interviews are among the best sources for real insight, as are in-depth articles written about the manager. As you are reading and forming an opinion of a manager, make sure you're getting more than just quick quotes or a few annotated quotes. If the majority of answers are captured, it's a much stronger piece of evidence, and it reduces the likelihood that certain comments were taken out of context.

A manager's habits and values are among the most important factors that determine whether he or she will be a success or a failure in the long term. The questions in this chapter will help you to identify the traits that are common to the best-performing managers, so that you can invest with them for the long term.

☐ 48. Does the CEO love the money or the business?

Most investors spend too much time trying to determine whether management has the right financial-incentive structure to create shareholder value rather than examining if the manager has passion for the business. External incentives, such as a large compensation package, will never be as powerful as internal motivation. Passion motivates more than money. Warren Buffett, chief executive officer (CEO) of Berkshire Hathaway, firmly believes this: When he was asked how he determines which managers to partner with, he said, ". . . the biggest question I ask myself is 'Do they love the money or do they love the business?'"[1]

Why Is Passion Important?

Passion is a necessary ingredient for long-term success in business or any profession. If you have ever asked the advice of successful businesspeople on how to become successful, the most common advice you probably received was that you needed to find something you love to do and then do it. By doing what you love and getting very good at it, you'll be happier, society will likely reward you, and the money will eventually follow. They probably counseled you to not go after a job for the money, and in fact, most people who have made a lot of money didn't make that their primary goal. For example, when entrepreneurs create a business, they are usually following some passion. They do not say to themselves, "I want to be an entrepreneur" and then look for a business to start or acquire.

The same rule of success applies to public company CEOs and other managers: If they are not passionate about the business they are managing, they will likely do a poor job managing the business over the long term. Steve Jobs, founder of Apple, said it plainly in a commencement address to Stanford University students in 2005, "The only way to do great work is to love what you do. If you haven't found it yet, keep looking. Don't settle."

The act of building a business over a number of years is slow and can be boring at times. How can CEOs be effective if they are not genuinely interested in what they are doing? CEOs and other managers who are passionate about their businesses throw themselves into their work, constantly learn from their mistakes, and they find opportunities and solutions to problems that others do not see. Passion turns into tenacity, which is a necessary ingredient for success because the rewards are often far into the future.

How Do You Identify Passion?

You can identify passion by answering the following questions:

- Is the business a career or just a job for the manager?
- Would the CEO refuse to sell the business, no matter what the price?
- Is the manager interested in money or motivated by money?
- Does the manager focus on appearances instead of the business?
- What type of philanthropic endeavors is the manager involved in?
- Are the managers lifelong learners who focus on continuous improvement?

Is the Business a Career or Just a Job for the Manager?

Start by asking whether the business is a career or a job for the manager. When you review the backgrounds of managers (which you can find in the proxy statement or articles written about the managers), determine whether they have remained in the same industry for a long period of time or if they jump from industry to industry. If they have remained in the same industry for a long period of time, then the odds are they enjoy their work. Look at previous positions to understand if there is consistency or a pattern in what they do.

For example, the founders of child-care provider Bright Horizons have always been passionate about helping children have the best start possible to their lives. They figured that millions of U.S. parents wanted and needed to work but could not afford high-quality child care. They decided to fill this need with Bright Horizons. A quick check of the founders' backgrounds tells you that this husband-and-wife team also served as co-country directors in Sudan for Save the Children before founding the company. Because their background was previously in helping children, it was obvious that they were pursuing their passions.[2]

Would the CEO Refuse to Sell the Business, No Matter What the Price?

If someone else offered to buy the business from the CEO, how would that CEO respond? A truly passionate CEO would say the business is not for sale and would decline these overtures. In contrast, most CEOs would sell if the price was right. What if you were offered $1 billion for a business generating an estimated $50 million in revenues? Would you sell it because it was an extremely high offer?

This was the situation faced by Mark Zuckerberg, founder of online social network Facebook, in 2006 when he was courted by managers from Viacom, Yahoo, and others to buy his company. Zuckerberg continually resisted their offers and realized that he did not want to sell the business. He said he was not growing Facebook solely for the money and that no amount of money would buy his business.[3] What is most interesting is not whether Zuckerberg made a good decision or not but rather that such a young person (who was only in his early 20s) was so passionate about his business that he would not sell it for $1 billion, or $10 billion for that matter.[4] Zuckerberg prefers to have tight creative and financial control of the business and wants to play the game his way. The money is secondary. Zuckerberg has been quoted as saying, "We are engaged in something greater than getting rich." This is true passion. Fast forward to 2011 and Facebook is valued between $60 billion and $75 billion.[5]

Is the Manager Interested In Money or Motivated By Money?

How do you determine if a manager is interested in money rather than motivated by money? You simply look at their spending habits and how they live. Passionate leaders make little time for other activities or hobbies, and have few outward signs of wealth. They are narrowly focused on the business at hand. In contrast, some managers seek social approval by having big homes and nice belongings. The difference between the two is that one manager is interested in money and the other type is generally motivated by money. People who are interested in money tend to be conservative in their spending habits, whereas managers who are motivated by money tend to have liberal spending habits.

For example, Warren Buffett's personal spending habits have remained the same, while his net worth has increased enormously through the years. Similarly, Dave and Sherry Gold, founders of dollar store retailer 99 Cent Only Stores, have lived in the same home since 1963 and Dave drives an older Toyota Prius. When I asked Sherry Gold why, she answered, "We had everything we wanted that was achievable through money."[6] Money serves as a score, and it does not significantly change their personal lifestyles.

While spending and lifestyle can be an indicator of motivation, it isn't always definitive. Some high-performing CEOs live in big mansions, such as Leslie Wexner, founder of retailer the Limited (owner of Victoria's Secret). He may have liberal spending habits, but his motivation for running the business is more than just making money. Study the managers in-depth to understand the source of their motivation.

To begin studying a CEO's lifestyle, start by compiling a set of articles that focus on the CEO, using a news-archiving service such as *Dow Jones Factiva*. For example, there were many articles written about Stephen Hilbert, CEO of insurance firm Conseco, and his larger-than-life lifestyle. Articles about Hilbert reported lavish parties in his 23,000-square-foot mansion in Carmel, Indiana. His home included a full-size replica of Indiana University's Assembly Hall, and he and his friends wore Hoosier uniforms when they played basketball. Most investors ignored his personal lifestyle because the stock price rose 46 percent a year, compounded, from 1988 to 1998. However, these aspects of Hilbert's personal lifestyle should have been warning signals because they indicated he was *motivated* by money rather than just interested in money.[7]

What happened to the company? On December 17, 2002, Conseco filed for bankruptcy, and the high returns investors had previously earned were wiped out completely.

If you cannot find articles written about the lifestyle of a manager, you can look up the value of their homes, which will give you a glimpse into how they live. Ownership of certain assets such as residential real estate is generally fairly transparent. You can check for residential real estate at the county level where the manager lives. For example, in Austin, Texas, you can search www.traviscad .org, which is the website for the local taxing jurisdiction. You can usually search for properties by the name of the person. First, find out which city the manager lives in and then determine the name of the county and the taxing jurisdiction. In most cases, the county will list the ownership of properties online and you can see the tax value of the home as well as its size.

For example, suppose you're interested in learning more about Warren Buffett's lifestyle. A simple online search will tell you that the tax assessor for Omaha is in Douglas County. You then go to the Douglas County tax assessor website, and enter "Warren E. Buffett." On the site, it lists that Warren Buffett owns a 1921 home sitting on three quarters of an acre of land, with 5,830 square feet with five bedrooms, and a handball court, valued at $660,200 in 2010.

If you want to try a more comprehensive real estate search, there are public records companies that have combined many of the local public records into national databases, allowing you to search for holdings across different counties and states. This would yield information on second homes, vacation homes, and so on. Keep in mind that these properties may be held in the CEO's name or in the name of a spouse or business entity.

Does the Manager Focus on Appearances Instead of the Business?

Managers who are truly passionate about their business have less time for outside social engagements. Steve Jobs, founder of Apple, did not spend his money lavishly when he was one of the richest people in the world, and he claimed to have little time for a social life. He was on a mission to make computers as common as kitchen appliances, which at the time, was dismissed as hype.

It is important to look for distractions managers have outside of the business. The biography found in the proxy statement is a great starting point because it lists the other activities of the top five executives, such as sitting on the boards of other public companies and non-profit affiliations. You want to gain a basic understanding as to whether they are devoting a large amount of their time to other activities. Do they sit on socially prestigious boards in their community? If so, how much involvement does the organization require? Try to gain insight into what motivated the manager to join the board: Was it for social prestige, or was it because he or she is truly interested in the mission of the non-profit? And keep in mind that just because a manager is dedicated to great causes, such as the community, diversity, or other socially responsible goals, this does not necessarily translate into good ethics. For example:

- Ken Lay, who was then the Chairman of Enron, donated $1.1 million in 1999 to endow the Kenneth L. Lay Chair in Economics at the University of Missouri-Columbia. Lay was later convicted of conspiracy and fraud after Enron failed.
- Alfred Taubman gave significant gifts to the University of Michigan in Ann Arbor, and buildings named for him include the Taubman Medical Library and Taubman Health Care Center. There is even a school within the university named for him, the Taubman College of Architecture & Urban Planning. Yet he spent a year in jail after being convicted in 2001 for price fixing at auction house Sotheby's.
- Dennis Kozlowski, the former CEO of conglomerate Tyco International, donated millions to Seton Hall University, and its Stillman School of Business was housed in an academic building named for Kozlowski. Yet he was convicted of looting Tyco of $600 million.[8]

Many times, you can infer the motivation of managers by the number of large social or charity events they attend. For example, when I searched for information about the CEO at a large Texas oil business, all the articles written about him related to his attendance at high-profile social events. I could not understand how he made time for the actual business! I later interviewed him and asked him why he had so much available time to attend all of these social functions, and he answered that he had capable people running the organization. Although this seems like a rational answer, his absence hurt the business, the stock price fell, and he was eventually fired by his board of directors.

What Type of Philanthropic Endeavors Is the Manager Involved In?

Philanthropy can be a great window into the character of a manager. There is a considerable amount of public disclosure in philanthropy. You want to determine what managers care about. Are they seeking social acceptance in their community? Or are they genuinely passionate about the charities they give to? In the case of philanthropy, it is a warning signal if the manager is overly involved in social scene philanthropy—that is, the kind that's more about the social recognition than the charity itself. This indicates that the manager is externally motivated and tends to seek acceptance of those who are in high social standing. Many times, these managers will direct corporate assets to support their social climbing. When you see a business contributing money to the most elite social functions, then it is likely that the manager is using the corporation to improve his or her social standing in the community. These types of donations typically do not pertain to the company but are instead used for social leverage.

To counter a common assumption that philanthropists always have the greater good at heart, consider a few examples:

- All of Enron's key officers were active philanthropists, with a great number of nonprofit organizations in the Houston area benefiting from their contributions.
- WorldCom and Bernie Ebbers were well known as donors to charities and universities in Mississippi, and were respected in the community.
- Adelphia, once one of the biggest cable television companies in the United States, used to sponsor Christmas pageants and flew cancer patients to health facilities for treatment.

Yet all of these businesses are now defunct and many of their executive officers have served jail time.

What can you really tell by studying a manager's charitable giving or philanthropic patterns? Where can you find how and how much a business or person donates? Look for articles about gifts in some of the news stories you read about your company or management. Most corporate and personal giving is direct and isn't reported in any uniform way, though some giving may be through a foundation. If the manager or company has created a foundation, you should be able to scan the foundation's tax return because it is a public record. You can request it from the IRS or just check an online provider, such as *GuideStar*. Look for Form 990, which will detail which groups received gifts, the location and the amount of the gifts, future gift commitments the foundation has made, and contributor names and amounts. Companies will publicize some of this on their websites, but not all of it. Look at more than a year or two, and you can see what the general pattern and focus of their giving is.

Some other ways to turn up additional information include checking websites and regional newspapers by adding the CEO's spouse to your search. You can also check publications and websites of non-profits where you know the CEO serves on the board or giving lists or honor rolls of their alma mater or universities with which they are affiliated. There are also companies that collect and cumulate donation records that have been made public at one time or another. All these can offer a glimpse into the social priorities of the manager you are evaluating.

Are the Managers Lifelong Learners Who Focus on Continuous Improvement?

Lifelong learners are managers who are never satisfied and continually find ways to improve the way they run a business. This drive comes from their passion for the business. It is extremely important for management to constantly improve, especially if a business has been successful for a long period of time. Look for managers who regard success as a base from which they continue to grow, rather than as a final accomplishment.

For example, Michael Bloomberg, eponymous founder of the financial information and media company, wrote, "We've got to improve just to stay even. Each of us at Bloomberg has to enhance his or her skills. Every element of all our products must be improved. . .Most companies never upgrade until they are forced."[9]

The opposite of those who improve are those who are complacent. Complacent managers tend to think everything is okay and often lack passion for the business. They are satisfied, sometimes indifferent, and usually fall into mediocrity as a result. They often remain invested in the way they have done business in the past, such as when Eastman Kodak refused to acknowledge the threat to its film business from digital photography in the 1990s.

Another example is mobile phone manufacturer Nokia, which was one of the most successful European companies: In fact, in 1998, it was the world's biggest mobile phone manufacturer. Nokia was able to get to the top of the industry quickly, but once there, it became complacent. Nokia CEO Olli-Pekka Kallasvuo tended to focus on hanging onto market share instead of creating new products. He ignored the trend of mobile phones merging with computing when Apple introduced the iPhone in January 2007, and he continued to focus on making cellphones that were about calling people instead of about checking e-mail, getting directions, or checking the weather. After the introduction of the iPhone, Nokia's stock price fell 49 percent, and Kallasvuo was eventually replaced as CEO.[10]

☐ 49. Can you identify a moment of integrity for the manager?

Basically, if CEOs have integrity, they are honest. They don't say something to a group of people just because that's what the group wants to hear. When you ask a question, they tell you what they really think. In contrast, if a CEO often says, "We'll go in this direction," but acts differently, be cautious. If the CEO sets certain standards of behavior or expectations of performance, yet violates them personally, then you should perceive that the manager lacks integrity.

How can you learn if the CEO has integrity? One indicator is consistency between what they say and what they do. For example, Warren Buffett, CEO of Berkshire Hathaway, says the same things over and over again, and he follows through in his actions. In contrast, politicians are typically not consistent in what they say or do, which is why so many people are suspicious of them. They often say one thing in order to get elected and then do another.

Another way to observe consistency in behavior is to see how people act under different circumstances. You never truly know someone's character until you have seen it tested by stress, adversity, or a crisis, because a crisis produces extremes in behavior. A billionaire Chinese entrepreneur once told me that he would not do business with a person unless he had seen them encounter a moment of integrity, which he explained as "how you act when you are confronted with a crisis or an ethical situation." He then said that if it took him 20 years to wait for a person to encounter this moment of integrity, he was more than willing to wait in order to do business with them. He had a hard-and-fast rule that has served him well, and he was rarely disappointed by his business partners.

One of the best ways to determine whether a manager has integrity is to identify a moment where he or she faced a difficult situation and see what action he or she took. If you are unable to identify a moment of demonstrated integrity, then you are taking the risk that you do not know how that person will act when faced with a difficult situation. You may want to wait to increase the amount you invest until after you have seen management encounter such a moment.

There are many examples (many already covered in this book) of CEOs who have presented false results through accounting fraud. These CEOs are often concerned with losing access to new capital, defaulting on loan covenants, or they may be worried about how Wall Street views them. Such CEOs typically fail to consider the broader implications of their actions. You want to know if the manager you are evaluating will follow the right path when faced with adverse scenarios.

For example, I once attended an annual meeting of a bank in Texas. The morning before the meeting began, the bank put out a news release announcing it had finalized a deal with a Texas billionaire, whereby he would give them a large capital infusion that diluted existing stockholders. Our firm believed this deal was detrimental to existing stockholders, but I wanted to verify this with company management at the meeting. The annual meeting lasted half an hour, and when it came time for the CEO to take questions from the audience, I raised my hand. Within moments, the CEO stepped down from the podium and declared that the meeting had ended. Surprised, I walked over to the CEO and again tried to ask him a question, but he said that he had to attend the board meeting. I recognized most of the board members, who were still socializing in the room. In that moment, the CEO had failed to demonstrate integrity. In other circumstances, I had had a more favorable assessment of this CEO because he was typically straightforward with information, but in this small act, he demonstrated a lack of integrity. This particular bank eventually went bankrupt due to aggressive lending.

In contrast, when I was researching the background of Dave Gold, co-founder of retailer 99 Cent Only Stores, I was searching for articles that would give me insight into his character. I ran across an article that described how Gold had admitted to making a mistake in purchasing a business for 99 Cent Only Stores. Instead of writing off this investment (as most other CEOs would have), Gold acquired it back from the company *with his personal funds*—in the amount of $34 million, no less!—which was twice what his company had paid for it previously. I had never heard of a CEO buying back a mistake in order to benefit shareholders, especially at two times the price. I felt I had a deep insight into Gold and knew this was the type of CEO I wanted to partner with, and I made an investment in the business when the stock price fell.[11]

The most difficult time to assess a manager is during normal times. You gain more insight into management when conditions are adverse than you do when circumstances are ideal. As you read historical articles written about the business or SEC filings, begin to identify those periods when the business encountered a difficult situation, such as an economic downturn, product recall, negative media coverage that was inaccurate or overblown, or a lawsuit. Read articles, press releases, and transcripts of quarterly conference calls that were written during this time, and note how the management team responded to these difficult situations. If you are assessing a manager with limited tenure at the business, review articles and conference call transcripts at the prior business. Did the manager disclose more information to shareholders, or did the manager clam up?

For example, during the recession that began in 2007, some managers disclosed more information so their shareholders could better understand the operations of the business and what the management team was doing to cope with the difficult economic situation, whereas others did not want to disclose information, citing a lack of visibility as the reason. This was a weak excuse, however, because managers do not need to forecast the future, but they do need to disclose how they are reacting to a difficult situation. You need to determine how a manager responds to a difficult situation and then evaluate the action they took. Were they calm and intentional in dealing with a negative situation, or were they reactive instead? Ideally, you should seek to partner with those managers who solve problems for the long term.

There are a few ways that management typically responds to difficult situations; identifying which actions these managers take will help you decide whether they are an ideal partner or not.

- Some managers allow current adversity to overwhelm them completely. In this type of situation, management is trying to evade the problem rather than confront it. For example, when Bear Stearns was nearing bankruptcy, then-CEO James Cayne could be found playing golf or playing in bridge tournaments. He ignored the risks the firm was facing.[12]
- Some managers attempt to blame the problems on others or on events beyond their control. In this scenario, you will typically see heavily lawyered press releases or releases carefully crafted by public relations firms. The managers will make statements that they are assessing, reviewing, or analyzing a problem. These are indicators that senior managers are not *acting*—which is what they *should* be doing.
- Some managers strike back quickly without thinking things through and often end up going in the wrong direction. These are the managers who announce layoffs in order to quickly cut costs the moment their business faces distress.
- Some managers are determined to get over their setbacks but do not solve the problem; instead, they apply a quick remedy, which only solves the problem in the short run. For example, a retailer I was analyzing discovered that the reason some of its sales had dropped was that it did not have enough shopping carts in the stores. The management team quickly sent in new shopping carts but then failed to follow up later when the supply was depleted again, so of course the retailer found itself in the same situation a few months later.
- The best managers are those who quickly and openly communicate how they are thinking about the problem and outline how they are going to solve it. Again, you are looking for those stories where managers acted with integrity. For example, Robert Silberman, CEO of Strayer Education, disclosed that new-student enrollments had dropped 20 percent in the 2010 winter term, the largest drop that Silberman had seen in his 10-year tenure as CEO. Even though Silberman did not know the exact reasons for the drop, he reported this negative news to shareholders the moment he had the information, and then he held a special conference call first thing the next morning to answer shareholder questions. He gave shareholders as much information as he could, and he explained how he was reacting to it.

- Similarly, on the day of the 2001 terrorist attacks on the World Trade Center, Bruce Flatt, then-CEO of Brookfield Properties, had to deal with several kinds of problems. The media was circulating false reports that Brookfield's four office buildings next to the World Trade Center were not stable and about to collapse, even though engineers had already concluded they were structurally sound. Flatt hired a car to take him from Brookfield's headquarters in Toronto to Manhattan (because no planes were flying that day after the attacks), and he surveyed the four office towers Brookfield owned. After seeing the buildings himself and confirming with engineers that they were sound, Flatt was better able to make corrections with the media and give good information to tenants. He immediately had truckloads of plywood sent in, and he was the first landlord to start repairs in Lower Manhattan. He then promised tenants they could return in eight weeks.[13] Flatt said, "We felt it was important to return to the premises as soon as possible. It was a calculated risk, but we needed to evaluate the situation, make decisions, and help our tenants." Flatt delivered on his promise, and within eight weeks, the tenants were able to return to their offices.[14]

☐ **50. Are managers clear and consistent in their communications and actions with stakeholders?**

The best management teams are clear and consistent in their communications with customers, employees, suppliers, and shareholders. They communicate things as they are and do not attempt to manipulate the information.

You will find that the more transparent management is about the business, the more accountable they are. In contrast, whenever managers make something complex, they may be concealing risk taking or bad judgment. Incomplete disclosure also makes it difficult for you to assess the competence of the managers. Although this may be good for the manager, reducing his or her chances of being replaced, it obviously makes your evaluation of the business more difficult.

The following sections describe a few ways you can (and should!) determine whether management is clear and consistent in its communications.

Read the Company's Annual Report Shareholder Letter

You can start learning how a CEO communicates with shareholders by reading shareholder letters written by the CEO. By reading them sequentially, rather than reading only one shareholder letter, you will gain greater insights into the CEO and the business. You are looking for letters where the CEO communicates clearly about how the business is performing; these letters should describe and explain:

- What is important at their business.
- What is driving their decisions.
- The issues they have encountered.
- The metrics that are important to monitor the health of the business.
- How the CEO plans to resolve issues faced by the business: This is one of the most important pieces of information to look for.

If, instead, the shareholder letter looks like it has been written by a public relations firm or is a carbon copy of the information disclosed in the Management, Discussion, and Analysis section (MD&A) found in the 10-K, then it is likely the CEO is not interested in giving investors insight into how he or she is thinking.

For example, if you read a shareholder letter written by Warren Buffett, CEO of Berkshire Hathaway, you might note how easy it is to understand what he writes and how authentic he is in his communications. When Buffett writes, he says exactly what he means.

In contrast, in The Coca-Cola Company's 2003 annual shareholder letter report, former CEO Douglas Daft wrote, "I am pleased to report that our Company earned a record $1.77 per share in 2003." This good news was coming just after the company had announced a $197 million charge, with the stock down 20 percent since Daft had been named CEO. Daft then went on to explain that this was a "particularly challenging business environment"—in other words, blaming the outside environment for the results. Daft retired from The Coca-Cola Company shortly thereafter.

Read Conference Call Transcripts

Once you feel you have a good understanding of the business, read transcripts from the most recent as well as historical conference calls.

These are a great information source because if you do not have access to the management team, this is the best place to see how they communicate. You can obtain clear insight into how management thinks and acts by reading these conference call transcripts.

Watch how managers address business issues in the conference call. There is almost always a recent issue the business has encountered, and most questions are directed toward such recent issues. Are the managers open and honest in their communications? Or do they attempt to avoid the issue? Monitor how many questions go unanswered. Note if the managers use excuses, such as saying that the information is proprietary. Many management teams will use the excuse that they cannot share information with shareholders for competitive reasons. This is an extremely useful indicator: I have found that if the strategy of the business is based more on hiding information from competitors rather than outperforming competitors, it is far less likely that the business will have long-term success. If the unanswered questions have to do with specific financial guidance, this is okay. You instead want to monitor how many unanswered questions there are about things that are specific to the business, such as marketing, historical mergers or acquisitions, personnel, or legal issues. Most of the time, this is not proprietary information, and the manager should be able to answer these questions or at least tell you how they are thinking about the issues.

For example, during a conference call on November 4, 2004, with a diversified media company that owns radio stations, an institutional analyst asked if management had near-term plans for format changes at its radio stations. Management responded by saying, ". . .we don't disclose any format changes that we might employ in our radio division. I'm sure you understand." In fact, this is not proprietary and is one of the most important components of a radio company. If management does not want to answer questions about the most important part of its business, investors should view management's actions as a warning signal.

In many cases, you will find that the managers *respond* to questions, rather than *answer* them. In other words, they will respond to the question with a statement that has nothing to do with the question, but it makes the manager look as if he or she is answering the question.

For example, one CEO was asked why the margins of the business had dropped, and he went into a long discussion on how the world was quickly changing around him and said that the economy was uncertain. The CEO could have at least explained that margins dropped because the cost of materials had increased, which was the real reason for the drop.

The first part of the call is usually filled with the CEO or CFO reading from a script that has been prepared in advance. A lot of time on the conference call is spent on this part, and I sometimes think that management does this in order to limit the question-and-answer period.

For that reason, I prefer to invest in businesses such as Penn National Gaming, which skips the script and jumps straight into questions with a few prepared remarks. Peter Carlino, CEO of Penn National Gaming, says "I find most of my shareholders can read, so I believe it is best to spend more time answering questions than reading a script that is found on the company website." Over the years, managers have started to remove these scripted sessions from their conference calls to allow more time for shareholders to ask questions. This is an extremely positive sign because it indicates that managers want to address shareholder questions or concerns. They understand that shareholders receive the most valuable insights during the unscripted format.

For example, in an August 2010 conference call, clothing retailer Urban Outfitters announced that it would release a detailed management commentary so that its earnings call could be more focused. Similarly, in July 2010, disk drive manufacturer Seagate and biopharmaceutical company Gilead Sciences both announced that they would start reducing the time spent with prepared remarks on conference calls, instead posting those a couple of hours before the call so investors would have time to absorb the information and formulate questions. These are all positive signals that management is open with shareholders.

The following sections discuss some questions you can ask to better understand how managers communicate with stockholders, customers, employees, and suppliers: How do the managers communicate when confronted with adversity? And does management only emphasize good news in their communications?

How Do the Managers Communicate When Confronted with Adversity?

The best managers to invest in do not make excuses as to why they cannot communicate with customers, shareholders, employees, or suppliers when they are confronted with adversity. Instead, they communicate openly when the economy is in disarray or competitive pressures are high. In contrast, the worst managers to partner with are those who engage in face-saving behavior when confronted with problems. They usually turn to heavily lawyered news releases that do not address the issues, and they dance around the information instead of being forthcoming.

When Howard Schultz, founder of Starbucks, returned to the company in January 2008, he found that problems both inside and outside the company were causing sales to decline. Upon returning, Schultz promptly stood up to his 180,000 employees and their families and admitted that he had failed them. He told them, "Your leadership has failed you, and even though I wasn't CEO, I have been around as Chairman. I should have known more. I am responsible." Schultz said that once he did this, it was a powerful turning point for his company because the burden was off his shoulders, and he could now move forward. In an interview, he said, "You have to be honest and authentic and not hide. I think the leader today has to demonstrate both transparency and vulnerability, and with that comes truthfulness and humility and obviously the ability to instill confidence in people, and not through some top-down hierarchical approach."[15]

Does Management Only Emphasize Good News in Their Communications?

You need to determine what information management emphasizes. For example, in the 10-K, there is a section titled "Selected Financial Data." This is a pro-forma statement that condenses the income statement and balance sheet. This is where management highlights certain financial items it finds important, such as earnings before interest, taxes, depreciation, and amortization (EBITDA) adjusted for some type of charge. This section may give you some insight into management regarding what it reports and doesn't report.

For example, Internet company InfoSpace, one of the few profitable dot-coms (according to its pro-forma statement) during 2000, reported that it had earned $46 million in pro-forma profits during that year. Naveen Jain, then CEO, was touting the stock on CNN's financial network in late 2000, proclaiming, "Our wireless business is on fire!" The truth was that by GAAP standards (instead of pro-forma), InfoSpace lost $282 million in 2000. But the CEO was emphasizing pro-forma targets, which did not realistically represent the true earnings of the business. Eventually, InfoSpace's stock cratered, and a dollar invested at its peak price was worth only three cents by 2005.[16]

The following sections discuss some questions to ask yourself as you either listen to or read what a manager says:

- Is the manager easy to listen to?
- Do you learn from the manager?
- Does the manager use corporate speak?
- Does the manager use double speak?

Is the Manager Easy to Listen to?

Chris Lozano, who was an intern at my firm, attended a lecture at the University of Texas at Austin with talks given by two entrepreneurs. One was the founding partner of a venture capital firm and the other was the founder of Southwest Airlines, Herb Kelleher. It was an interesting contrast according to Lozano, who said the venture capitalist was talking to the audience, whereas Kelleher was engaged in a conversation with the audience. Lozano said, "When I listened to the venture capitalist, I felt like I was having a boxing match with him." If you find it difficult to listen to managers or read what they write, then it is likely a warning signal.

Do you Learn from the Manager?

After you've read or listened to what managers say, ask yourself if you are learning more effective ways to run a business from them. For example, when I was analyzing retailer 99 Cent Only Stores, I learned a lot about the retail business through both Dave and Sherry Gold, the founders. Their teachings enhanced my understanding of the fundamentals of running a successful retail business. On the other hand, if you find yourself wanting to teach a management team how to run its business, this is probably a signal that you have run into an incompetent management team.

Does the Manager Use Corporate Speak?

Many managers use corporate speak or make generic statements. You may often find yourself running two conversations in your head as you try to discern what they mean. Ask yourself, "Do they use a lot of corporate jargon such as the word strategic or thought leadership"?[17] This may indicate that these managers do not truly understand their business and are more concerned with showing others how smart they are. When managers use corporate jargon, it may be that they are more interested in self-promotion than in clearly explaining to shareholders how the business is operating.

Does the Manager Use Double Speak?

Double speak is when someone says contradictory things, such as "We don't time the market, but we will continue to hold cash until after the middle of the year, when things might get better."

For example, the CEO of Reuters, Tom Glocer, once said this in a statement to the company: "Above all else, we acknowledged things would be tough in 2005, but we confidently set a budget that shows Reuters growing our revenues for the first time in four years." Reuters then added that it was not issuing revenue guidance in the memo, which had been released to staff earlier that week. The statement said, "This statement is not meant to imply that revenues will be positive for 2005 as a whole. The 2005 budget is not yet complete, and no revenue guidance has been issued for 2005."[18]

Here's another example: Griffin Mining, a zinc miner, disclosed on February 21, 2006, that "operating costs were higher than envisaged due to inevitable initial teething problems in commissioning the plant."[19] The key question you should ask is, if the teething problems were inevitable, why weren't they in the budget?

And another example: At a conference on October 3, 2001, Joseph Nacchio, CEO of Qwest Communications, stated that instead of trying to convince the audience that Qwest was doing well, he would "just let the numbers speak for themselves on October 31." When October 31 came, the company missed expectations, and Nacchio stated, "Some of you will recall that at a recent conference I said the results will speak for themselves. The reality is, they do not speak clearly for themselves without some interpretation, given the current economic conditions and the effects of merger and other one-time charges." Nacchio quit in June 2002 amid an SEC probe into alleged accounting manipulation.[20]

☐ 51. Does management think independently and remain unswayed by what others in their industry are doing?

One of the toughest challenges a manager faces is to look at all of the profits that competitors are earning and not be tempted to copy that success. Sometimes these profits may be earned from unsustainable sources.

For example, Jamie Dimon, CEO of J.P. Morgan, did not follow his reckless competitors as they chased poor-quality mortgage-backed securities in search of higher fees. At the time, most of J.P. Morgan's shareholders complained that Dimon was being too conservative and that he was passing up the chance to make millions of dollars in profits. However, when the financial crisis of 2009 put some of his competitors out of business, Dimon was one of few CEOs who managed to both weather the storm and strengthen his business during this time of distress.

Shareholders will often attempt to influence managers to maximize short-term profits. The best managers always maintain a long-term focus, which means that they are often building for years before they see concrete results. For example, in 2009, Jeff Bezos, founder of online retailer Amazon.com, talked about the way that some investors congratulate Amazon.com on success in a single reporting period. "I always tell people, if we have a good quarter, it's because of the work we did three, four, and five years ago. It's not because we did a good job this quarter."[21]

Another example of long-term thinking is how Howard Schultz runs Starbucks. For many years, investors have said that Starbucks should undo its company-owned stores and franchise them instead, because this would significantly increase the amount of free-cash flow that Starbucks could generate and would improve the return on capital. Although it is a good argument economically, Schultz has continually refused to franchise Starbuck's stores. He believes that this act would fracture the customer-service culture of the company, which is central to Starbuck's success. He is therefore managing the business for its long-term interests and has demonstrated the ability to think independently.[22]

Another way to determine if managers think independently is to see if they continually benchmark themselves against their competitors or if they try to copy the past success of competitors. It is difficult to copy someone else's success, and when a business tries to copy what it believes makes a competitor successful, it may be a sign that the management team does not have a sound plan for the business.

For example, during the tech boom of 1998 to 2000, I remember people trying to come up with tech-based concepts that would make them rich. Most of these people did not think about meeting customer needs; instead, they were trying to copy the success of others. More recently, investors have started hedge funds in hopes of hitting it big. What they fail to realize is that many of the billionaire hedge fund managers today did not explicitly set out to create large funds. It was an unintended consequence of being at the right place at the right time, which is something that cannot be fabricated.

Similarly, when a Las Vegas casino had a great degree of success luring Japanese gamblers to its baccarat room, competitors tried to copy what they thought was the reason for the success: They spent millions of dollars building larger and more elaborate baccarat rooms and offered more services to lure these Japanese gamblers. For a short while, the Japanese gamblers visited the rival casinos, but they always came back to the original casino. The competitors became even more frustrated and continued to invest millions more, without any success. The reason that particular casino was successful is that the manager took the time to learn the language and culture of these Japanese gamblers. He was in the best position to understand how they thought and what they wanted. The rival casino businesses could not duplicate this because they had only copied what they could see. This should have served as a warning signal that the rival casinos did not have a sound plan of their own focusing on what they did best. Therefore, look out for those businesses that are announcing similar products or services just because their competitors have been successful.

☐ 52. Is the CEO self-promoting?

You need to be careful about investing in businesses run by CEOs who are self-promoting or those with larger-than-life personalities. These are CEOs who are often popularized in the media and consistently show up on business magazine covers because they are announcing headline-grabbing growth projections or transformational news. These CEOs make themselves the brand rather than the business.

You can identify these CEOs easily because they brag about their accomplishments and are often well-rehearsed, articulate, and enthusiastic. In other words, they focus on a great pitch. They also are usually:

- Flamboyant.
- Have lots of charisma.
- Engage in aggressive salesmanship.
- Tend to command the center of attention.
- Take over discussions.
- Have an attitude that they are smarter than everybody else.

Most of the time, these traits mask underlying issues.

Most corporate boards choose these strong-willed, egotistical CEOs because they believe that this type of CEO will be able to meet difficult challenges. However, although these CEOs are good at selling themselves, they often bring many problems to a business because they spend an inordinate amount of time managing to Wall Street's expectations, at the expense of the company's day-to-day business.

Another way to identify these types of CEOs is to monitor how much time they spend attending investor conferences that are sponsored by Wall Street sell-side research firms to promote their businesses. Look on the website of the business in the investor relations section, and identify how many Wall Street events the CEO, chief financial officer (CFO), or other managers are attending. If they are present more than two to four times per month, then you are likely dealing with a promotional CEO who is trying to increase the company's stock price.

As always, there are exceptions for CEOs promoting the business. If the business is dependent on Wall Street to finance its expansion, then it is necessary to generate investor interest. Many businesses issue debt or equity to expand their business or for acquisitions. For example, if they are attending high-yield conferences to generate investor interest in a debt offering, then this is a necessary function for the management team. Instead, watch out for those CEOs that are touting the stock and who do not need Wall Street to finance their businesses.

Other ways CEOs can promote their stock is by spending a lot of time talking with TV outlets and other press. If you see CEOs who are constantly in the financial press, then it is highly likely they are just there to bring attention to their companies' stock. Be cautious of CEOs who focus solely on the stock price. Most investors believe this is a good sign, but it is not.

For example, in telecommunications company WorldCom's 1998 annual report, CEO Bernard Ebbers bragged about a 132 percent increase in income and a 137 percent increase in stock price, and he promised to continue both trends. In 1997, Ebbers told a reporter, "Our goal is not to capture market share or be global. Our goal is to be the No. 1 stock on Wall Street."[23] This statement alone should have caused you to sell your stock. Ebbers was using his company's high stock price to make multiple acquisitions, such as telecommunications company MCI; in fact, he made more than 75 acquisitions. How prominent did WorldCom become? WorldCom eventually (and famously) went bankrupt, and Ebbers was convicted of fraud and conspiracy related to accounting fraud.

Some of the Best-Performing CEOs Are Unknown and Do Not Promote

Some of the best CEOs are collegial, team oriented, and soft spoken, and they are able to gain the confidence of their employees. In fact, many CEOs who have compiled the greatest long-term records of creating wealth are relatively unknown and don't self-promote, such as Yun Jong-Yong, who was CEO of South Korea's Samsung Electronics from 1996 to 2008. Yun transformed Samsung from a maker of commoditized memory chips and other commoditized products to a company that designed innovative digital products, such as cutting-edge cell phones. The opposite of the self-promoter, Yun refused many interviews. Instead, he let the results speak for themselves as Samsung Electronics gained $127 billion in market value under his tenure.[24]

The management teams of some of the best-compounding stocks from 2000 to 2010 spend very little time meeting with Wall Street—for example, Four Seasons Hotels, Strayer Education, Whole Foods Market, Morningstar, and Expeditors International. Instead of simply meeting with analysts each quarter, the management teams at Expeditors International and Morningstar ask shareholders to email or write their questions, and then they answer these questions in a publicly released form 8-K so all the shareholders can read their responses. Issadore Sharp, founder of

Four Seasons Hotels, did not typically meet with analysts and was not available on the quarterly conference call. I once tracked him down at a hotel and asked him why he did not meet with analysts, and he said that he would rather spend time with his employees. He said, "I can spend an hour with you and you might own my stock for a year and then sell it, or I can use that time with the house-keeping staff who could potentially stay at this business for more than 20 years."

Key Points to Keep in Mind

- When it comes to people, the best predictor of future behavior is past behavior.
- Passion motivates more than money.
- You gain more insight into management when conditions are adverse than you do when circumstances are ideal.
- The best managers to invest with are those who quickly and openly communicate how they are thinking about problems and outline how they are going to solve them. They communicate things as they are and do not attempt to manipulate information.
- The more transparent management is about the business, the more accountable they are. In contrast, whenever managers make something complex, they may be concealing risk taking or bad judgment.
- CEOs that focus on their stock price aren't focused on their business.
- Some of the best CEOs are collegial, team oriented, and soft spoken.

10

Evaluating Growth Opportunities

Businesses that are growing profitably create a lot of value. The main advantage of investing in a growing business is that you can receive the benefits of tax-deferred compounding. This is due to the fact that you can hold onto the stock for a long period of time without having to sell it. This advantage has formed the basis of success for many long-term investors, most notably Warren Buffett.

Growth does carry many risks. There is uncertainty about any company's future, but when you purchase growing companies, you are generally paying for future growth as well as current cash flow and profitability. This requires you to determine whether growth can continue, for how long, and at what rate.

This chapter is intended to help you reduce the uncertainty of investing in businesses that are growing. Let's begin by looking at *how* a company is growing.

☐ 53. Does the business grow through mergers and acquisitions (M&A), or does it grow organically?

You can answer this question by viewing the cash flow statement found in the 10-K. In the Investing section of the cash flow statement, there is a subsection titled Acquisitions. Calculate the percentage of cash flow from operations spent on acquisitions for the last 5 to 10 years. Depending on the percentage spent on acquisitions, a business can be classified along a continuum of growth styles. On one end would be those businesses that grow organically. On the other end would be serial acquirers. Selective acquirers belong somewhere in the middle. For example, compare the following companies:

- For-profit education business Strayer Education has not made any acquisitions, but has been growing steadily for many years. Businesses that grow organically are typically not paying a premium price to acquire additional customers. They also don't have to worry about spending their time integrating a new business and its employees into their own operations.
- Medtronic, a medical-device manufacturer, made acquisitions in 2002, 2008, and 2009 and is considered a *selective acquirer.* Selective acquirers typically are not growing to achieve scale, but make purchases to expand their existing product lines. This way they do not have to spend valuable time attempting to gain expertise in new areas.
- Stericycle, a medical-disposal business, is a *serial acquirer* that regularly spends from 30 percent to 150 percent of its cash flow from operations on acquisitions each year. The potential risks to a serial acquirer are paying too much for a business or putting too much debt on the balance sheet.

These are the three basic ways that management can grow the business, and each can be successful. But there is decidedly more risk associated with acquisitions, including taking on too much debt, overpaying for an acquisition, or difficulty integrating the target company.

Make Sure You Place Growth in Context to Revenues

You must always place growth in context to the existing revenues of a business. Many management teams will highlight the growth of a certain division, such as one that is growing 50 percent a year, yet that division may represent only 1 percent of the company's *total* revenues. Therefore, this high growth rate will not materially increase the intrinsic value of the business.

☐ 54. What is the management team's motivation to grow the business?

There is often pressure on management teams to grow their business, because top-line growth can increase the stock price. This pressure can cause senior managers to make mistakes, especially if the growth of the core business slows and they seek growth by launching new initiatives or by making acquisitions in unrelated business lines. Many of these new ventures and acquisitions may fail, and management will spend valuable time selling or closing them. You should become especially concerned whenever management launches new growth initiatives outside of its core business, which increases the probability that management is about to make a mistake.

For example, when Jack Greenberg became the fourth CEO of McDonald's in 1999, growth at McDonald's began to slow as international markets matured and concerns about fatty foods in the United States hurt consumption. Greenberg announced that he would focus on improving the core business, but at the same time, he would pursue new platforms for growth by acquiring other restaurant businesses such as Chipotle, the Mexican food restaurant chain. The result of this growth initiative was that in 2001, McDonald's announced a quarterly loss for the first time in its history. With the core business still deteriorating, Greenberg resigned. During Greenberg's tenure, the stock price dropped from $45 per share when he joined the business in May 1999 to $15 per share on December 31, 2002, when he announced his retirement.[1]

McDonald's then announced that James Cantalupo, who had spent 28 years at McDonald's, would become CEO. Cantalupo's first announcement was that McDonald's was trying to do too many things, and he sold or closed most of the prior acquisitions that were made under Greenberg's tenure. The stock price has since increased from $15 per share at the end of 2002 to more than $70 per share on December 31, 2010, as McDonald's has renewed its focus on its core business.[2]

☐ 55. Has historical growth been profitable and will it continue?

In order for growth to add value to a business, it must be profitable. Growth often fails to translate into profits.

For example, the solar energy industry is growing quickly, but as of 2009, solar panels that are made of silicone produce energy at a much higher cost than conventional methods. Therefore, even though the industry is growing, it is not growing *profitably*.

Similarly, when the Internet industry first evolved, it also grew extremely rapidly, yet most of the businesses were not profitable.

It was extremely difficult to predict which businesses would come out winners.

To evaluate whether historical growth has been profitable, compare gross and operating income margins to *unit* growth over a three- to five-year period. As the number of units sold increases, do the gross and operating profit margins remain the same, or do they increase or decrease?

For example, as the number of transactions increased at money transfer business Western Union, the gross profit margin decreased from 46.9 percent in 2005 to 43.4 percent in 2009. In addition, the operating income margin decreased from 31.8 percent in 2005 to 25.2 percent in 2009.[3]

Then, compare operating income growth to unit growth, again over a three- to five-year period. The operating profit per transaction at Western Union decreased from $9.44 per transaction in 2003 to $6.51 per transaction in 2008. For Western Union, you can conclude that the growth in transactions over the last five years has been less profitable, and you need to determine whether this is a trend that will continue.

☐ 56. What are the future growth prospects for the business?

Begin by reading the business description section and the Management, Discussion and Analysis (MD&A) section found in the 10-K, where management often discusses the growth opportunities for the business.

For example, let's look at the 2010 MD&A section of the 10-K for Intuitive Surgical, which manufactures the *da Vinci*™ Surgical Systems, which provide minimally invasive alternatives to complex surgical procedures. In the 10-K, Intuitive Surgical's management discloses that the installed base of *da Vinci* Surgical Systems has grown from 795 systems as of the end of 2007 to 1,395 systems as of the end of 2009. Clearly, the business is growing quickly and could represent a great investment opportunity. If, instead, you saw the installed base growing from 795 systems to 800 systems, then this may indicate that the business lacks future growth prospects, and you should pay a lower price for the stock.

As Strayer's CEO Robert Silberman says, "What makes a business attractive is not the rate it can grow *in any single year*, but the number of years it can grow *at any rate.*"[4] The destiny of any fast-growing business is to experience a growth rate that slows down at some point. Therefore, you need to determine how long growth can be sustained. To start, you must ask if the business model can be replicated broadly, or if it can be replicated in only certain geographic locations.

For example, hotel franchisor Choice Hotels can license its Comfort Inn hotel brand throughout the entire United States or beyond. A clothing manufacturer, such as Polo Ralph Lauren, has similar potential.

Be careful when forming your future growth expectations from the past successes of the business. Remember, *you do not profit from yesterday's growth.* For example, if you learn that doughnut maker Krispy Kreme is successful selling doughnuts in display cases found in Exxon gas stations, do not assume that strategy will work in *all* Exxon gas stations. The danger lies in taking one instance of success and projecting it. Things may change: For example, more competition may enter the market, or Krispy Kreme may begin to cannibalize its own sales as it begins to open new locations near Exxon gas stations.

Sometimes, it is easy to determine the future growth prospects of a business. For example, let's take a look at Build-A-Bear, the niche mall-based retailer that lets kids build their own stuffed animal. From 2004 to 2009, the management team stated in the company's 10-K that it believed it could open stores in 350 locations, primarily malls, in North America. At the end of 2009, Build-A-Bear had already opened 291 stores, so its growth prospects were limited. Future growth would have to come from increases in sales at existing stores or growth through its franchise business. Build-A-Bear was near its saturation point in terms of possible locations that met its requirements, indicating growth from new stores would be marginal at best.

In other cases, it is more difficult to discern the future growth prospects of a business. In the case of homebuilders, for example, it is not easy to forecast future demand, interest rates, and supply cost increases. You would need to have a handle on all those elements before you could forecast growth for a business in this industry.

To understand the source of earnings growth, compare it to another relevant metric at the business. For example, the earnings of a railroad business may be increasing, but if revenue ton-miles (basically a calculation of total cargo weight times number of miles shipped)

Table 10.1 Comparison of Operating Metric to EPS

Norfolk Southern	2005	2006	2007	2008	2009
Revenue ton-miles (millions)	203,000	204,000	196,000	195,000	159,000
EPS (diluted)	$3.11	$3.57	$3.68	$4.52	$2.76

is not increasing, this would imply there are other sources of earnings growth. Place earnings growth next to the specific metric of a business, as shown in Table 10.1, for railroad company Norfolk Southern.[5]

In this case, we are comparing revenue ton-miles to earnings per share (EPS). You can generally see from Table 10.1 that as revenue ton-miles drop, so does EPS. If instead, EPS increased when revenue ton-miles decreased, then this might indicate that the business is resorting to other things such as cost cutting to increase EPS. These are less sustainable sources of earnings growth.

To forecast potential growth, you must understand if there are secular trends that will help a business prosper by fueling demand. You must also know if the business invests in innovation to develop new products or services. A growing business is one that expands its customer base or sells more to existing customers.

Is the Business Growing Because of Secular Trends?

Secular growth trends are sustained trends driven by demographic or social changes. These demographic or social changes can create an extended period of demand for products or services. For example, think of the growth in the number of women entering the workforce: From 1948 to 2000, women grew from 29 percent of the workforce in 1948 to about 50 percent by 2000.[6] This was a social change, and it drove the secular trends of women purchasing more workplace clothing, the growth in popularity of frozen foods (because there was limited time to cook a meal), and other social changes caused by women having less available time.

Be certain to distinguish between this kind of long-term growth and shorter-term cyclical changes. These short-term changes are also called business cycle changes: these are the ups and downs that are associated with growth and contraction in the wider economy. The earnings of a cyclical business, such as a steel manufacturer, are especially sensitive to business cycles, and change with swings in the economy. (Non-cyclical businesses don't tend to go up and down with the economy.)

If a business benefits from a secular growth trend, its growth is longer lasting than a single business cycle. Secular growth continues through a business cycle. In fact, earnings-per-share of businesses riding secular growth trends tend to peak at each succeeding major business cycle.

Also, be careful to distinguish rising commodity prices from secular growth trends. For example, an oil and gas firm may show revenue growth due to the rise in *the price of oil* rather than *an increase in the amount of products sold.* Study the price of the underlying commodity for the industry over at least three to five years in order to determine the percentage of revenue increases or decreases that are coming from changes in commodity prices versus changes in unit growth.

To better understand investing in growing businesses, I studied the investors who have been most successful at identifying important trends early on. Ron Baron, founder of Baron Funds, has been very successful at recognizing and profiting from the early identification of secular trends. Baron has been an early investor in many successful businesses, including nursing home operator Manor Care; casino Wynn Resorts; for-profit education providers DeVry and Strayer Education; staffing company Robert Half; and online diamond retailer Blue Nile. What is particularly impressive is that he not only invested in these businesses in their infancy, but he continued to hold these stocks over long periods of time—in fact, for decades, in several instances. He discovered most of these businesses long before they began their extended growth phase. He was able to identify most of these businesses because they were run by entrepreneurs who had a clear vision for the opportunities of their businesses, whereas skeptics did not see opportunity. As Baron often says, "We invest in people not just buildings."

For example, Baron invested early on with Mark Vadon, founder of Blue Nile. Vadon believed that not only would wholesale diamond distributors place their inventory on his online retail site, but also that consumers would purchase these high-end products online. Other investors were skeptical, but as Vadon bypassed traditional retail channels and decreased the price consumers paid, Blue Nile became part of the first wave of successful Internet retailers.

To identify secular growth trends, Baron asks whether an industry is one where your children or grandchildren will work, or if it is one where your parents and grandparents worked. His firm looks for those industries that are positioned to have strong job growth over the next 5, 10, or 20 years, and then his firm searches for the best companies in those industries. Today, his firm is investing in innovative businesses that are addressing the biggest challenges on the horizon, such as battery-powered transportation and alternative energy.

Other examples of secular growth trends include:

- The shift in advertising dollars from traditional media (such as cable TV) to online channels has helped fuel the growth of Internet search business Google.
- An increasing number of young professionals are deferring having children and instead purchasing pets, which benefits businesses that sell products for animals, such as pet store retailers PetSmart and PETCO.
- More than ever, people need a college degree to get good jobs. This has benefited for-profit education providers, such as Strayer Education and Apollo Group.

You need to identify and measure the secular growth trends that potentially support the growth of the business in which you are considering investing. Begin by researching the underlying trends supporting secular growth. Try to draw specific insights rather than focusing on broad themes such as "an aging baby boomer population will fuel the demand for nursing homes." For example, if a business sells to 20- to 25-year-old males, then you would research this group to understand how they think and shop. There are various sources you can turn to, such as the research products from:

- Market research firms Euromonitor or Mintel
- Polling firms Harris and Maritz
- Websites such as trendwatching.com
- Regional demographic sources such as ESRI Business Information Solutions
- Magazines such as *Advertising Age*

You can view *Market Research World's* website to locate substantial summaries of these kinds of reports and other studies conducted by leading market research firms. For example, in *Who's Buying Groceries* from the *Who's Buying* series, you will find such information as the fact that household spending on tea rose 28 percent between 2000 and 2005. You can also get a breakdown of the buying patterns of each different age group: people 25–34 years old spent $16.44 on tea in 2005, while people 35 to 44 years old spent $28.08.[7] Most of these sources extrapolate information from government data: For instance, the tea calculations are based on data from the Bureau of Labor Statistics Consumer Expenditure Survey.

Any business school's library will give you current links to market research and demographics content sites.

Innovation

A growth business must always look for new ways to supplement its growth. For example, eight years after its DOS operating system came out, Microsoft supplemented that growth by introducing Windows Office, which in 2009 accounted for 40 percent of its earnings.[8]

Is Innovation a Management Priority?

Monitor management's commitment to Research and Development (R&D) by observing R&D expenses over time. Calculate the percentage of sales spent on R&D expenses.

For example, IDEXX Laboratories (a leading provider of veterinary testing and diagnostic products) has spent more than 6 percent of its revenues on R&D since 1992, to improve its existing products and develop new ones. From 2007 to 2009, IDEXX invested close to $70 million in R&D—which is *12 times more* than its nearest competitor and nearly seven times more than all of its competitors *combined*. This enables the business to continually improve the quality of its veterinary diagnostics and to continually widen its competitive advantage. In fact, IDEXX controls more than 65 percent of its market, and it's now the largest global player in the reference lab market.[9]

Are R&D Efforts Successful?

Just because a business spends a large percentage of revenue on R&D does not mean that it will create successful products. Clayton

Christensen, a professor at Harvard who has studied innovation extensively, reminds us of two rather subtle things about R&D spending. First, most innovation starts out in the wrong direction: Therefore, spending more money upfront can mean more wasted money. Second, breakthroughs tend to happen when resources are most scarce. Christensen estimates that 93 percent of ultimately successful innovations actually start out in the wrong direction:

> The probability that you'll get it right the first time out of the gate is very low. So, if you give people a lot of money, it gives them the privilege of pursuing the wrong strategy for a very long time.[10]

So, rather than just looking at how much is spent, you will need to evaluate how successful past R&D investments have been. The best way to do this is to calculate the percentage of sales that come from new innovations. For example, Graco, a pump manufacturer, spends 3 percent to 4 percent of its revenues annually on R&D expenses. It strives to generate 30 percent of its annual sales from products introduced in the previous three years, and comes very close to achieving those goals: In 2007, 2008, and 2009, Graco generated 21 percent, 26 percent, and 26 percent of its sales from new products.[11]

Medical device maker Medtronic has spent an average of 10 percent of its sales dollars on R&D programs since 1990,[12] which is comparable to most of its competitors that spend between 8 percent and 12 percent of their sales dollars on R&D programs. However, the company's success in creating new medical products differs markedly. For example, Medtronic has consistently controlled close to 50 percent of the cardiac pacemaker market by constantly investing in new technologies and being the first to market with new products. As a result, most of Medtronic's competitors have not been able to take market share away. Medtronic has also spent a large portion of its historical R&D on emerging technologies in neuromodulation, diabetes, and spinal products. The investments made from the middle to late 1990s in these three areas have increased Medtronic's revenue from these areas from 25 percent of total sales in FY 2000 to 40 percent in FY 2010, and has given Medtronic a dominant market position in these three areas. Medtronic's bone-graft product, for example, dominates the spinal market. Clearly, Medtronic has a successful R&D pipeline that leads to new products.[13] By examining the percentage of sales generated by new products and services, you can understand whether management has successfully invested in R&D.

Does the Business Grow By Developing Transformational Products and Services?

It is extremely difficult to project demand for new products. The main difficulty is that you have no existing pattern to extrapolate from. Even if you have very early sales data, it is common to under- or over-estimate it. As you do attempt to estimate demand for new products, keep in mind that most new product launches fail.

Innovators such as Apple or Google are the toughest businesses to forecast, because their products and services are *transformative.* These businesses came to dominate their industries very quickly. Because these businesses created entirely new markets, there was no precedent to use as a basis for a reasonable forecast.

For example, it was difficult for most investors to estimate what the future sales of the Apple iPhone would be. By the end of 2010, Apple had sold nearly 90 million iPhones according to both Apple and Gartner Research. Apple also sold more than three million iPad tablets in less than three months, which is the fastest consumer electronics product in history to reach the $1 billion revenue mark. Most Wall Street forecasts were substantially lower.

To further illustrate the forecasting problem, even Nintendo failed to anticipate the success of its own gaming console Wii in November 2006, which created product shortages. So how can you evaluate whether these companies are worth investing in, when so little is known about the transformative products they're coming out with?

First, you can survey target customers, by calling up friends who use the products or finding message boards where customers discuss the product to understand what they think about the new product or service. Be sure you survey them after they have tried out the product or service for at least three months or so. Had you talked with early iPhone or Wii purchasers, you would have heard extremely positive responses. When the Wii first came out, I spoke with 15 parents of teenage kids I knew throughout the country. I asked them if their kids were requesting the Wii and whether their kids' friends were buying them too. I also interviewed salespeople at five different electronics stores located in Austin, Texas, where the products were sold to ask them if the products were selling well. The answers were consistent that the Wii was a hit product and would likely generate increased sales at Nintendo, making it a potentially good investment opportunity.

Using Market Share Figures to Extrapolate a Company's Potential Growth

To evaluate a company's growth prospects, many analysts and industry associations make some estimate of the total size of the market and then determine the target company's percentage of it. They then determine if a business has substantial growth prospects based on its market share.

To do this, start by reading the section of the 10-K report titled Industry or Market Size. The management team will often disclose the size of the market and its share of the market in this section.

For example, Immucor, a blood testing-instrument maker, estimated in its 10-K report (dated May 31, 2010) that the worldwide blood banking reagent and instrument market generates $1.2 billion in sales each year. Immucor's sales at that time were $329 million, indicating that Immucor had 27 percent share of the market. This indicates that Immucor has plenty of opportunities to grow and increase its earnings in future years, which potentially makes it a good investment opportunity.

However, you also need to be cautious about accepting at face value the market share estimates that are provided by the management team or industry associations. It is always best to assume that businesses have an incentive to report a market size that is larger than it really is. Instead, figure out how market share figures are calculated. Read how competitors estimate the size of the market and whether they are using the same yardstick and the same market definition.

In the case of mature markets, there are several things to be aware of. First, make sure the market size hasn't magically expanded. Read at least 5 to 10 years of 10-Ks to understand if a business has changed the way it calculates its market share or defines its market. For example, one business-services company that had effectively saturated the universe of large business customers began to include *mid-sized* businesses as part of its potential market size, even though these smaller businesses had less incentive to buy and use this company's product.

In another example, I noticed that a medical waste business that I followed reported less market share one year, even as it had grown to be the dominant U.S. medical waste disposal company. As the company had expanded into international markets, it began to report a smaller number that reflected its global market share, and by doing so, they showed significantly more opportunity for growth. New markets, however, are different markets, and must be evaluated separately in terms of potential to grow revenues and in terms of potential profits.

You also want to watch out for shrinking effective markets, which may increase the market share of incumbents. For example, Darling International is the largest U.S. rendering company, which collects and processes animal by-products to create the ingredients for things like soap, chemicals, and rubber. When my firm calculated Darling's market share, we noted that it increased every year. What we found was the effective market size was shrinking. There was just as much rendering going on, but as smaller ranches and slaughterhouses were bought by larger companies (which do their own rendering in-house), there were simply fewer small operations left to choose between Darling International and its competitors. Darling International was increasing its market share, but it did so within *a shrinking market* with fewer total customers.

You also need to watch out for overlapping segments, distribution, and geography. For example, when my firm was analyzing the market share size of Western Union, there were several confounding factors in play. After finding several different estimates and measures of how much money actually crosses international borders, my firm looked in depth at the sources of the estimates: We compared information from national banks, U.S. government agencies, the International Monetary Fund, the World Bank, think tanks, and scholarly studies. We discovered that underreporting in this industry is a predictable norm, making it difficult to estimate the true size of the market. In one case, what first appeared to be an increase in overall market size turned out to be a change in the way Western Union's own data was incorporated into the national estimate. In other words, *nothing had changed*, but because the new market size estimates were bigger, it appeared Western Union's market share had shrunk—which might have led investors to avoid Western Union. Yet the main complicating factor is the large black market for money transfer, or the informal segment. We now think of the informal segment as another competitor, and note that Western Union's growth often comes from taking market share from this segment.

Watch for Signs That Growth Is Slowing

There are many signs that a business's growth may be slowing, including these:

- Targeting a new customer base.
- Attempting to change its business model.
- Paying out a larger percentage of its earnings in the form of a dividend.

Let's look at each of these signs in more detail.

When a business targets a new customer base   When a business begins to target a new customer base, this is often a tell-tale sign that its core business is starting to slow. For example, Apollo Group, a for-profit university, piloted a new program in 2004 to target a new customer when the growth of its core business, the University of Phoenix, began to slow. It created a national online community college named Axia College to target students seeking associates degrees. Instead of serving its core customer of working adults in their late 20s to early 30s who seek bachelor degrees, Axia targeted students who were 18 to 23 years old.[15] By the end of 2010, Axia college students represented nearly 50 percent of the total student population at Apollo Group.

However, even though Axia has been a fast-growing division of Apollo Group, *Axia generates less profits* for Apollo Group than the University of Phoenix because the students at Axia represent half the credit hours compared to bachelor-degree students. Furthermore, Apollo had lower receivables collection rates from Axia students. The increase in receivables from associate-level students constituted the majority of the bad-debt expense at Apollo. This is because Axia students tend to drop out at a higher rate than the traditional bachelor students.[16] From August 2005 to August 2010, the operating margin dropped from 31 percent to 27.9 percent.[17] Therefore, even though Apollo Group has been able to offset some of its slowing growth with growth from a new customer base, this new customer base contributes substantially less to profits than its traditional core customer.

When a business changes its core business model   Another way to recognize if growth is slowing is when a business begins to change its core business model. For example, computer manufacturer Dell has been changing its business model from manufacturing computers to providing computer services. Dell has made several acquisitions in this area, such as its $3.9 billion purchase of Perot Systems. This new business strategy indicates that Dell's core business of selling computer hardware is declining.

When a business begins paying out higher dividends   Another signal a business has limited growth prospects is a high dividend-payout ratio, such as when a business pays out more than 30 percent of its earnings in the form of a dividend. You can calculate a dividend-payout ratio by taking the dividends paid by a business and dividing that number by the earnings of the business.

For example, chocolate maker Hershey Company paid out 50 percent of its earnings in dividends in 2010, which is a typical payout ratio for businesses in the consumer staples industry. Reynolds American, a cigarette manufacturer, paid out more than 75 percent of its earnings in 2010 and increased its payout to more than 80 percent of earnings in 2011. Clearly, the growth prospects of both of these businesses are not as high as they were in the past, and both companies' management teams believe they do not need to reinvest the earnings back into the business.

Beware of Paying Too High a Price for Growth

A growth company usually has a premium price-to-earnings ratio (P/E) attached to it. The reason is that when investors expect growth in earnings, they are willing to pay more, which increases the P/E. For example, you might buy a business that trades at a P/E ratio of 20 times that earns $1 per share. If it is able to double its earnings in the next year, then you are effectively only paying 10 times next year's earnings.

Avoid paying a high multiple for a business, because if expected earnings growth slows, the stock price will drop. For example, the stock price of Internet search business Google was flat from October 2007 to October 2010, even though earnings per share (EPS) grew from $13.50 per share to $25 per share during those three years. The main reason the stock price stayed flat was that investors were concerned that growth was slowing, and they were unwilling to pay a higher price for slowed growth. In Google's case, the P/E multiple dropped from 45 times to 21 times during this period.[18] Now that Google trades at a lower P/E multiple it may be a good investment opportunity, especially if you believe that Google can continue to grow its EPS at historical rates. If you believe that Google's EPS will not grow in the next several years, then you need to pay a lower P/E multiple.

On the other hand, if you pay a high price, and the business continues to grow its earnings at a rapid rate, then the growth will eventually bail you out. When my firm first began buying grocer Whole Foods Market, we paid 20 times adjusted EPS for our initial purchases, at $40 per share. We believed that the high growth rate of Whole Foods Market would increase the earnings of the business and we were effectively paying a lower multiple for the business. For the next two years, the earnings growth slowed down as we entered the recession in 2007 and the stock price decreased to as low as $8 per share. The earnings then resumed their historical growth rate and the stock price rose to more than $50 per share by the end of 2010. Even though it was delayed, the earnings growth made up for the high price we paid for our initial purchases.

Is the Management Team That Was Responsible for Historical Growth Still Leading the Business?

If a business has grown for many years, it is important to make sure that the management team that was responsible for that growth is still intact. When forecasting growth, some investors make the mistake of assuming that the business is generating the growth regardless of the management team. If the management team changes in a material way, then there is a risk in extrapolating from past growth. For example, in the case of Apple, investors are clearly interested in exactly who is running the company, and concern about Steve Job's health directly affects the price of the stock.

☐ 57. Is the management team growing the business too quickly or at a steady pace?

Investors often mistake fast-growing businesses for good investments. In fact, businesses growing too quickly are among the riskiest investments, because the growth is not controlled. Furthermore, a business or industry that has steep rather than gradual growth characteristics attracts more competition, which can also drive down profitability.

You need to determine if the management team is following a *disciplined* or *undisciplined* growth strategy. A high rate of growth does not guarantee profitability, especially if the management team follows an undisciplined growth strategy. If the company is growing in a disciplined way, then the management team will be able to control the growth, creating more value. The following sections describe indicators you can use to determine whether a business is growing in a disciplined manner or if it is growing too quickly.

Is the Business Growing within Its Means?

Businesses that use their own cash to grow have more sustainable growth compared to those that finance growth by issuing debt or equity. First, internally generated cash flow is a cheaper source of capital compared to debt and equity. Second, a business is not exposed to the vagaries of the capital markets, such as when the debt markets froze up in 2008. You can estimate how quickly a business can grow using internal funds by calculating the length of time a business's cash is tied up in working capital.

To do this, calculate the cash-conversion cycle (CCC) for the business. The CCC measures the length of time money is tied up in a business before that money is finally returned when customers pay for the products. It is calculated by adding and subtracting the following:

- The number of days that inventory is outstanding (DIO)
- Plus the number of days that sales are outstanding (DSO)
- Minus the number of days that payables are outstanding (DPO)

The lower the number of days in the CCC, the faster a business can redeploy its internal free cash flows into growth because less capital is tied up in inventory or capital equipment.

For example, homebuilders have to continually borrow money because they typically do not have cash on hand to grow their business because their CCC cycles range from 200 to 400 days. On the other hand, a software business typically has a CCC of 10 days, which allows it to collect and fund a large part of its growth with internal free-cash flow. As a result, a software business has lower risk because it can finance its growth internally and is not dependent on outside sources of capital to grow its business.

Warren Eisenberg and Leonard Feinstein, the founders of housewares retailer Bed Bath & Beyond, had a golden rule that they would never use debt to finance their expansion. They would only open a new store when they had the capital to do it. As a result, during the first decade, growth was slow: The company started with one store in 1971 and grew to 37 stores in 1992, when Bed Bath & Beyond went public. By the end of the ninth year after going public, the store count increased 10-fold without the use of debt, and the market value increased 20-fold.[19]

Is the Business Growing at the Expense of Short-Term Earnings?

When a business is growing, expenses typically grow at a faster rate than revenues, which negatively impacts short-term earnings. For example, when a cable business first enters a new market, it has to make large front-end investments to install the cable. Most of these expenditures are made before the cable company is able to sign up subscribers and generate revenue. As a result, in the first couple of years, depreciation and interest expenses represent a high percentage of revenues, and the business will operate at a loss. However, as the cable business adds subscribers, by the third or fifth year, the profit margins begin to increase, and cash flows turn positive. Therefore, when a business is growing, it may mask the true underlying free-cash flows of the business.

For example, Whole Foods Market invested the majority of its discretionary free-cash flow in new store openings. These expenditures in new stores masked the strong free-cash flows that Whole Foods Market's core business was generating. As a result, it appeared that Whole Foods Market was trading at a high price-to-earnings multiple, when effectively, it was trading at a lower multiple. When new store openings slowed, the high free-cash flows were revealed. For example, in September 2008, cash flow from operations was $335 million; one year later, in September 2009, when new store openings slowed, cash flow from operations had increased to $587 million.

When evaluating the earnings of a growing business, you need to determine if the management team is investing for the long-term at the expense of short-term earnings. To do this, you must understand when profitability is reached with new investments. For example, at Strayer Education (the for-profit university for working adults), a new campus reaches profitability by the end of the second year. Therefore, investments in new campuses made in 2010 will not be profitable until 2013. By understanding how long it takes an investment to become profitable, you will know that the start-up losses from new campuses will negatively impact earnings for a two- to three-year period, and you can adjust the earnings. As the base of campuses that are profitable grows larger and larger, the start-up losses from new campuses have less effect on earnings. For example, in 2003, Strayer opened three new campuses on a base of 14, so these new campuses had a greater impact on the earnings of the business than when it opened 11 new campuses off a base of 60.

Therefore, when evaluating a business that is growing you need to adjust the earnings of the business to account for the impact of higher short-term expenses in order to calculate the true earnings of a business.

Is the Business Growing within the Limits of Its Human Capital?

How fast a business grows can be limited by how fast it can add employees. If revenues grow at a rate of 30 percent or more a year, and a business needs to grow the number of employees at the same rate, a business would have to double its employee count every 2.5 years. Not only would the business have to retain existing employees, but it would also need to hire and train new employees. This can create many risks. It is therefore critical for a business to grow at a rate where it does not outstrip its ability to hire qualified employees.

Spirit Airlines was known for offering low fares in the Florida market, offering fares as low as $9 one-way. Spirit grew quickly, adding as many as 13 destinations in one year. Unfortunately, Spirit also grew beyond the capacity of its employee base, with customers complaining that Spirit lacked enough people to staff its ticket counters, reservations, and customer-service centers. At one point, Spirit had more complaints than any other airline. In this case, the customers were, of course, right. If you checked U.S. Department of Transportation data from 2006 and compared employee counts to numbers of aircraft, you would see that Spirit's low-fare competitors had 77 employees per aircraft, whereas Spirit had only 61 employees per aircraft. Clearly, Spirit Airlines attempted to grow too quickly, without making sure it had the personnel to grow.[20]

It is critical for a business to have enough talented employees to execute its growth strategies. This provides a strong foundation for the growth and makes it more sustainable. At Strayer Education, the number of campuses that it opens is limited by the number of leadership teams it has internally that can staff them. Strayer does not rely on hiring outsiders to grow; instead, Strayer promotes from within. It looks at its internal staff and determines which people have the leadership skills to take on higher-level assignments. Once management figures out how many leaders it has, then it determines the number of campuses it should open in a given year.[21] This strategy frustrates many investors who believe that Strayer can grow at a faster pace; nevertheless, this strategy ensures the sustainability of Strayer's growth.

Does the Business Have the Proper Infrastructure to Grow?

You can think about a corporate infrastructure as all the things that are necessary to support the growth of adding new employees, increasing inventory, or building new sites. There are four broad types of corporate infrastructure that support growth:

1. The *finance area* manages the flow of money through accounting, treasury, tax, and regulatory departments.
2. The *operations area* controls the sales, distribution systems, call center, ordering systems, manufacturing facilities, legal, communications, policy and planning, administration, project management, and health and safety. For example, if a retail store is having difficulty obtaining inventory, it will contact people within the operations area.
3. *Human resources* handles recruiting, payroll, and benefits for employees.
4. *Technology* handles all of the information technology for the business, such as networking and computing systems.

In 1987, airline company USAir bought Pacific Southwest Air for $385 million in order to expand its routes to the West coast.

Shortly thereafter, USAir bought Piedmont for $1.6 billion, which tripled the size of USAir. After acquiring both businesses, USAir learned that its information systems could not handle the increased traffic that came from acquiring Piedmont. Computers broke down regularly, customer service suffered, and even flight crews were scheduled on the wrong days. USAir had clearly outgrown its corporate infrastructure. This caused profitability at USAir to drop from 6 to 7 percentage points *higher* than the industry average before the merger to 2.6 points *below* the industry average after the merger.[22] So if you were considering investing in an airline in the 1980s, you should probably have passed on USAir because it was growing beyond its infrastructure.

Is the Business Finding the Right Locations?

The best management teams in the retail industry expand their store base *opportunistically* rather than setting a specific goal to open a certain number of stores within a certain amount of time. When the management team follows an opportunistic strategy, management waits for the right location, such as a corner on a busy intersection, instead of instructing its real estate department to find a certain number of locations in a city.

In contrast, when a management team sets a specific goal of finding a certain number of locations, the real estate department will look for locations that are available instead of looking for ideal locations. By following this strategy, the management team is creating problems because a few years down the road, the company may have to devote time and significant expenses to closing unproductive locations. This is equivalent to taking two steps forward and one step backward.

Tilman Fertitta, Chairman and founder of restaurant chain Landry's, confirms this idea:

> "You need to grow, but you can't grow at such a pace that you start having secondary locations. And that is what everybody seems to do." Landry's once opened 40 locations for restaurant chain Joe's Crab Shack in a single year, and later sold the chain. Fertitta admits, "If you look at the performance of those 40 stores, [they represented] ... the worst year of any openings."[23]

Organic grocer Whole Foods Market also follows a disciplined store-opening strategy by not opening a store until it finds an ideal location. For example, it took Whole Foods Market 10 years to find a suitable site for its first store in San Francisco, California. As a result of its careful expansion strategy, Whole Foods Market has not closed any stores that it has opened since it was founded. Jim Sud, Vice President of Store Development at Whole Foods Market, summed up the company's strategy during a fourth quarter 2010 conference call:

> We're not going to just sign stores to hit some kind of growth number or some kind of percentage or some kind of target. We're going to sign stores if we find good locations that we think are going to deliver good returns on capital for us. And we're not going to do it artificially just to hit some kind of expectation. Now it's a question of really finding locations that meet our very strict criteria. We're still very proud of the fact that in our 30-plus year history, we've never had a store that we opened ourselves ever fail. So we're really determined to keep that track record alive.

Key Points to Keep in Mind

- The main advantage of investing in a growing business is that you can receive the benefits of tax-deferred compounding.
- What makes a business attractive is not the rate it can grow in any single year, but the number of years it can grow at any rate.
- Businesses that use their own cash to grow have more sustainable growth compared to those that finance growth by issuing debt or equity.
- Businesses that grow organically carry less risk than those that depend on acquisitions in order to grow.
- Be concerned when management is under pressure to grow. Signs of pressure include launching new initiatives and buying businesses outside of the company's area of expertise.
- Growth is more sustainable if it is supported by innovations or secular industry trends. To help you identify secular growth, think about the industry's job-growth potential. Ask yourself if the industry is one where your children or grandchildren will work.

(continued)

- You need to be careful when forming your future growth expectations from the past success of the business. Remember, you do not profit from yesterday's growth.
- Avoid paying a high multiple for a growing business, because if expected earnings growth slows, the stock price will drop.
- You can identify a business whose growth is slowing by learning if the business is targeting a new customer base, changing its business model, or paying out a larger percentage of its earnings in the form of a dividend.
- Growing businesses have higher short-term expenses: Adjust earnings accordingly to get a true picture of underlying earnings.

CHAPTER

11

Evaluating Mergers & Acquisitions

In the quest for greater growth and profits, many management teams see mergers and acquisitions (M&A) as a surefire way to expand their business empires. And they are often willing to pay any price to secure a short-term victory. M&A activity can represent serious risks to a business because poorly executed or undisciplined M&A has proven to be one of the fastest ways a business can destroy value. As an investor, how do you evaluate whether a company's M&A activities are creating or destroying value?

One way of evaluating M&A activity is to understand the motivation of management: *Why* is senior management merging with or acquiring another company? Another is to evaluate whether past acquisitions were successful by using a list of seven questions (discussed in this chapter) to gain insight into management's rationale for making acquisitions. This way you can forecast whether future M&A decisions will add value to the business— and therefore, whether that business is a worthwhile investment for you.

☐ 58. How does management make M&A decisions?

It is critical to understand how management makes merger and acquisition decisions. Todd Green, senior managing director of investment management firm First Manhattan, suggests it is frequently as important to understand *how* acquisition decisions are made as it is to understand *why* they are made. Green says understanding how management *thinks* about acquisitions is one of the few concrete ways for investors to reduce uncertainty in assessing a company's chances of success.

Green believes that, with so many variables in trying to predict where a company is going to be five years from now (such as where the economy is going to be, where future interest rates will be, and what input costs will be) the one tangible factor where you can decrease the uncertainty in the process is in understanding how a management team thinks about acquisitions. In other words, what were they thinking: What did they see as potential benefits?

Green learned this valuable lesson at one of the first meetings he attended after joining First Manhattan in 1981 out of Columbia Business School. The meeting was with the chief executive officer (CEO) and chief financial officer (CFO) of a newspaper publishing and TV broadcasting business. There were 15 people gathered around a conference table, ready to ask questions. Green had done his homework on the company and was eager to learn more. Art Zankel, senior partner at First Manhattan, proceeded to question management about an earlier acquisition that was relatively small. Zankel spent an hour and a half asking management about the merits, prospects, costs, and the risks of the acquisition. Green was surprised that Zankel did not spend any time talking about the publishing business, which represented the bulk of the value of the company.

After the meeting, Green asked Zankel why he would spend an hour and a half asking about such a small acquisition. Zankel said, "If you can understand the rationale behind a $30 million acquisition today, you'll probably be in a better position to predict or understand the rationale behind a $300 million acquisition they make next year or a $3 billion acquisition that they make five years from now." This taught Green that one of the most important parts of the research process is to put oneself in the shoes of the people making the acquisition or capital-allocation decisions. By understanding their thinking in the past, he could evaluate how they might act in the future.

Green used this lesson to evaluate a new CEO of one of his core holdings. As Green got to know the new CEO, he was able to understand how the CEO thought about acquisitions. The CEO had a history of extensive M&A activity and Green understood that the company he was now invested in was going to be a lot bigger in five years, mainly as a result of new acquisitions. Because he understood the CEO's thinking and rationale regarding the prospects, costs, and risks associated with acquiring new companies, Green believed these acquisitions had a high probability of failure, so he sold that company's stock.[1]

What Is the Motivation Behind an Acquisition?

By understanding the motivation behind an acquisition, you can often identify problems in management's process or thinking. There are two common motives or reasons behind an acquisition.

The first is simply to *increase the size of the business.* Often, you will find management teams with big egos who want to be in charge of a larger business. As they consider growing, CEOs and CFOs often become enamored with the acquisition process itself. These CEOs and CFOs may be bored or out of touch with the day-to-day details involved in running their business. They may be insulated, spending most of their time in corporate offices. These CEOs and CFOs often hire investment bankers to find acquisition targets and will then drift into making acquisitions in unrelated business lines. Once begun, the process of buying a business is difficult for them to stop as they become caught up in the excitement of something new. For example, as surprising as it may sound, the Coca-Cola Company once went so far afield as to buy a shrimp farm. Gillette once bought an oil business. These types of acquisitions generally destroy shareholder value because they tend to distract management from the core business. Later on, management often divests these same businesses for less than they bought them for.

Sometimes, of course, it makes sense to grow the business through acquisitions. It is often easier and a more effective use of the company's time to gain a large set of customers by acquiring an entire business rather than acquiring customers one at a time. There is usually less risk in this strategy if the management team is acquiring a customer base that is similar to its existing one.

The second reason management claims to make acquisitions is *when they believe they can improve the operations of the acquired business.* Management often believes that it can improve the operations of the acquired business through synergies, which are supposed to work by making both companies more efficient together. There are typically two main types of synergies:

- Revenue synergies include cross selling to the combined firm's customers, potential access to new markets, or increased pricing power due to reduced competition.

- Cost synergies include improvements in margins by making the acquired firm more efficient; reduction of duplicate costs such as corporate overhead; reduction in procurement costs due to increased buying power; and tax benefits. Cost synergies are usually easier to realize when compared to revenue synergies.

For example, here's how Caterpillar disclosed its motivation behind acquiring Bucyrus, a mining-equipment company:

> The acquisition is based on Caterpillar's key strategic imperative to expand its leadership in the mining equipment industry, and positions Caterpillar to capitalize on the robust long-term outlook for commodities driven by the trend of rapid growth in emerging markets which are improving infrastructure, rapidly developing urban areas, and industrializing their economies. A driving motivation for the transaction is Caterpillar's estimate of more than $400 million in annual synergies beginning in 2015 derived from the combined financial strength and complementary product offerings of the combined mining-equipment businesses.[2]

As promising as it sounds, when you hear managers utter the word *synergy* when they make an acquisition, you should be extremely skeptical that the cost savings or revenue increases they promise will materialize. There are many examples of synergies that have failed to materialize, such as when United Airlines acquired Hertz car rental and Westin Hotels in the 1980s. These acquisitions were based on the idea that United would cross-sell airlines, rental cars, and hotels to travel customers. The intended revenue synergies of cross-selling never materialized however, because most customers chose their hotel based on convenience, not because it was offered as part of a package.

Synergy estimates typically grow during boom markets as the acquiring company forecasts higher revenues due to cross-selling or increased cost reductions. Many times, synergy is invoked when management wants to rationalize a higher price to win a deal. The problem is that it is far easier to put numbers on a spreadsheet than it is to actually realize these cost savings or revenue opportunities in the real world.

For example, when amusement park business Cedar Fair acquired Paramount Parks in 2006 for $1.24 billion, it paid 10.6 times trailing 12 months' earnings before interest, taxes, depreciation, and amortization (EBITDA), which seemed high. Cedar Fair justified this high multiple by citing that it had identified $20 to $30 million in synergies that would materialize from the deal. These synergies would decrease the multiple paid for Paramount Parks from 10.6 times to 8.5 times EBITDA. By February 2009, during his Q4 earnings call, Cedar Fair's CFO told investors that $16 million in impairment charges were entirely due to the acquisition of Paramount Parks. By February 2010, CEO Dick Kinzel was again telling investors during his Q4 earnings call that the performance of "certain acquired parks" would result in impairment charges. He said that though Paramount was cash-flow positive, the performance of Paramount and other acquired parks was "below expectation." The synergies management thought it could achieve turned out to be much more difficult to realize in the real world.[3]

Synergies are least likely to materialize when the two merged businesses serve different customers or are in unrelated areas. For example, in 1999, disability insurers Unum and Provident merged. Unum operated in the group insurance market, and Provident served individuals. Executives of both companies thought that each company's salespeople would be able to sell the other's products, thus creating synergies. Unfortunately, after the two companies merged, the salespeople from each organization did not want to collaborate on cross-selling. The merger also had the unintended consequence of increasing prices for both group and individual customers, which caused customers to move to competitors. Unum eventually undid the merger and exited the individual market in 2007. From the date of the merger (in 1999) to 2007, the stock price of the merged entities *dropped by half.*[4]

Some businesses combine many small businesses in the same industry into a larger one, which is known as a *roll-up*. The reason management teams engage in roll-ups is they believe they can cut duplicate overhead costs, increase purchasing power with suppliers, lower debt interest costs, and combine advertising. However, most roll-ups in industries such as funeral homes, medical practices, auto dealerships, food-service companies, and waste-disposal businesses have failed to create value for investors, and many that used lots of debt went bankrupt.

For example, Loewen Group is a Canadian funeral home company that consolidated many funeral homes during the 1970s and 1980s. During this time, the stock price of Loewen was bid up by investors, due to its constantly increasing earnings. By 1989, Loewen owned 131 funeral homes, and in 1990, it acquired an additional 130 funeral homes. As Loewen began to struggle with its earnings, investors began to realize that the synergies that Loewen had based its acquisition binge on were not being realized. For example, Loewen found that customers did not value the name of a national brand; instead, most customers chose a funeral home based on referrals and previous experience. As a result, Loewen kept the names of its local funeral homes. The only efficiencies realized were that Loewen could cut some costs from embalming and acquiring hearses, but apparently, this was not enough of a benefit: In 1999, Loewen filed for bankruptcy.[5]

Of course, some synergies do materialize. The common element in these is that the customer base is the same, such as when Kraft acquired General Foods. Another example is Pool Corporation (Pool), a distributor of pool supplies. Pool realized that pool contractors were not well served by plumbing or building-products distributors. Pool recognized that customers valued local service and more important, the availability of supplies. Rather than pursuing a strategy of rolling up all firms in the pool-supplies-distribution business, Pool instead focused on strengthening its market position city by city through a combination of *focused acquisitions* and organic growth. Pool's success can be attributed to the fact that it focused on building strong market share in each of the local markets where it operated, which gave it pricing power. In 1990, Pool had eight sales centers and by 2010, Pool had grown to 291 sales centers according to its 2010 10-K.

❐ 59. Have past acquisitions been successful?

Most M&As fail. A few of the reasons are as follows:

- Acquisition candidates are not always available at good prices; as a result, management typically overpays for acquisitions.
- Most businesses that are for sale are not very good, and an acquirer typically ends up buying lots of problems.
- Cultural differences between businesses result in the defection of valuable employees.

There are seven ways to evaluate whether an acquisition has been successful. The following sections look at these (and other) factors in more detail.

Do Acquisitions Fit into the Core Competencies of the Business?

When a business acquires another business, the odds that it will be a successful acquisition improve if it is done within the same industry—such as when Hewlett-Packard (H-P) bought Compaq (both were computer manufacturers) in 2002. After the acquisition was announced, H-P's management set an objective to realize $2.4 billion in cost reductions in one year after the merger. They exceeded this objective by achieving $3.7 billion in annualized savings within a year of the merger. In contrast, whenever a management team acquires another business outside of its core competencies, it risks becoming distracted as it attempts to understand the acquired business and begins to neglect its core operations. Things such as improving the customer experience in the core business get placed on the back burner and instead, time is spent on integrating the acquisition. Furthermore, if the management team begins to run into problems at the acquired business, it may not have the internal resources to solve them.

For example, in 1997, John Mackey, the co-founder of Whole Foods Market, acquired a catalog vitamin business, which he thought would fit in with Whole Foods Market. But when the vitamin business encountered problems, Whole Foods Market did not have anyone who knew how to fix those problems. The lesson Mackey learned was that Whole Foods Market's core competence was in *retail* sales. The company's management team did not know what to do or have the people resources to solve problems stemming from *catalog* sales. In other words, it wasn't just the *type of product* that was important to the success of the acquisition; the *method of distribution and sales* was also critical. Eventually, the vitamin business was liquidated.[6]

When you see a business make an acquisition outside of its core business, this may be a signal that the profitability or sales of the original business are declining or maturing. Other times, management egos may be involved. For example, at one time, energy giant Enron controlled large portions of the gas and electricity markets in the United States. Then it began to expand outside of its core business by attempting to corner the market on broadband capacity; Enron even attempted to become the world's largest water company. Enron lost billions of dollars on these ventures, and the company began to manipulate its accounting numbers to shield these losses, eventually filing for bankruptcy in 2001. Enron may be an extreme cautionary tale of a company acquiring other businesses outside of its core competency, but it's a great example to keep in mind when you're considering investing in companies that are starting to do so.

Does the Management Team Intimately Understand the Business It Is Acquiring?

Companies that acquire related businesses—or at least businesses that the management team knows how to manage—are more likely to be successful in their M&A strategies and therefore better potential investments. For example, Danaher is a conglomerate that has grown mainly through acquisitions, acquiring up to one business a month throughout its history. The company owns a variety of industrial businesses that make dental-surgery implements, hand tools, testing instruments, and other medical and diagnostic equipment. Over the last 20 years (up to 2010), Danaher's stock has returned 25 percent annually. Danaher is successful at acquiring businesses because they are able to reduce many potential risks. They do this by becoming intimately familiar with the operations of the businesses they are about to acquire. For example, before Danaher began to acquire medical-technology businesses, its management team studied the industry for about three years, conducting more than 400 customer interviews, as well as numerous interviews with industry experts and competitors.[7]

To further reduce risk, Danaher executives tour plants and search for ways to improve the performance of the target company *before* they acquire that company. They estimate how much they can improve the profit margins of the firm by implementing what they call the "Danaher Business System," which is a set of management tools used to identify potential efficiencies. This system requires that all employees, from the janitor to the CEO, find ways to improve the way that work is done.[8]

In most of its acquisitions, Danaher leaves the existing management in place and provides them with incentives to improve performance in the form of stock and bonuses. As a result of taking its time to understand an industry before making an acquisition and by learning how it can potentially improve a business before acquiring it, Danaher has been successful at acquisitions.

Cisco follows a similar strategy by routinely developing products in-house before acquiring another company. Cisco attempts to answer the question of whether it is cheaper to develop a product itself or if it is better to acquire another business. This way, the company develops the advantage of understanding how a product works and an in-depth understanding of whether it can compete with the products of a potential acquisition candidate.[9]

Does the Business Retain Its Customers After an Acquisition?

One of the best ways to assess whether an acquisition is successful is to monitor the retention rate of customers after an acquisition. If a business is able to retain the majority of customers three years after an acquisition, then this is a positive indicator that it is making good acquisitions.

Some industries simply have better customer retention regardless of ownership change. Medical-disposal businesses, for example have high customer-retention rates. Stericycle, a medical-disposal company, successfully retains its customers after buying another company. Contrast this to an advertising agency where, on average, customer contracts come up for renewal every two years and there is high customer turnover. If an advertising agency acquires another agency, take into consideration that customers may not renew their contracts with the acquired agency. This increases the likelihood that the acquisition may fail as the earnings of the acquired agency decrease, due to customer defections.

Does the Business Retain Its Employees After an Acquisition?

Acquisitions often destroy a company culture. When a business acquires another business, it typically tries to standardize the acquired business, which can damage the entrepreneurial spirit of the acquired business, making it less valuable. For example, when Lehman Brothers bought money-management firm Neuberger Berman, it stifled the culture, and many of the talented asset managers left the business to start their own firms. The departure of many of these asset managers contributed to value destruction at Lehman.

Attempt to understand the attitude that management has toward the employees of the acquired business. For example, Whole Foods

Market always respects the people who work for the companies it acquires. In fact, Whole Foods Market often promotes some of the employees from the acquired business to create a climate of trust. There is not an attitude of arrogance on the part of the acquirer, which often causes the most talented employees of an acquired firm to leave.

Cisco learned the importance of retaining talented employees after acquiring StrataCom. After the acquisition, Cisco tried to speed up sales and ended up losing not just sales but 30 percent of the employees as well. Since its first acquisition in 1993, Cisco has acquired almost 150 companies and has developed a set of principles and practices that make the acquisitions successful: Buy small, buy early in the product's life cycle, and most important, put the people you're acquiring above everything else. Since 2002, more than 90 percent of the employees acquired by Cisco have stayed with the company.

When Cisco buys a business today, it largely leaves the practices of the acquired businesses in place in order to retain employees. To transfer its values to the acquired business, it uses a mentoring system, in which Cisco managers support managers at the newly acquired company.[10] Early on, Cisco communicates openly with the employees of the acquired firm and gives them essential information about its plans for the business. This gives employees ownership in the process rather than creating uncertainty and a lot of updated resumes as employees look for other jobs. Ned Hooper, vice president of business development at Cisco says they structure the acquisition to retain people through this adjustment period. After that, they can look at Cisco differently. "For us, the people are the strategic asset. . . . We need the expertise."[11]

In 1999 when Cisco acquired Cerent Corporation (a maker of optical networking gear), Cisco made sure its employees were ready to contribute from day one. Employees arriving at work on the morning that Cisco took over the company found new business cards and bonus plans waiting for them. They also found their new health plan information and ready access to Cisco's computer system. In the first six months, Cisco lost only 4 of 400 Cerent employees.[12] Look for acquirers who communicate with employees early so they are not worrying about their jobs and can instead focus on sales and customer satisfaction.

Cisco's Linksys acquisition illustrates why it's important to retain talent for the long-term. When Cisco bought the home and small-business router company in 2003 for $550 million, it wanted to keep the same people who had created the Linksys router. Cisco thought that the market had billion-dollar potential, but that potential existed in marketing future versions of the router that only its creators had envisioned. The product's future was in the employees' heads, so to speak. Watch for those businesses that retain employees after an acquisition as this is often a good sign that the management team is making a good acquisition.[13]

Does Management Have Discipline or Is there a Risk That They Will Overpay?

Management teams, even good ones, usually overpay for acquisitions. This represents a huge source of risk for you as an investor. For example, in October of 2007, online auction house eBay admitted it overpaid when it acquired the Internet phone services company Skype Technologies for $2.6 billion in 2005, and took a $1.4 billion write-down. This write-down represented 53 percent of the total EBITDA generated by eBay in 2007.

Companies overpay because quite simply, they don't know the real value of the target company. They often think they do, which adds to their problem. The seller, of course, is more likely to know the true value and is unlikely to strike a deal on less-than-favorable terms. Here's one more reason that valuation is difficult—excitement. Acquisitions are very exciting and often cause managers to lose objectivity.

It is often difficult to discern whether a business has paid a reasonable price. Also adding to the problem of evaluating the price paid is the fact that it can take at least three to five years to determine if an acquisition has been successful. Johnson & Johnson's management often did post-mortem analyses of its M&As after three years. Former CEO Ralph Larsen said in his 2000 annual report that they also made it a point to weed out acquired companies:

> While the Company actively seeks business-building M&As of companies and product lines, we also have in place a process to continually evaluate those businesses that are under-performing, or which no longer meet our growth objectives and would be

better off in someone else's hands. Over the past 10 years, for example, we have divested 21 businesses or product lines.

There are certain situations where an acquirer is more likely to overpay for an acquisition:

- If there are a lot of competitors bidding, in an auction-type situation, with investment bank pitch books, then the price will likely be high. On the other hand, if the seller cares about who it sells to, then this is a good sign because price becomes a secondary consideration. For example, Berkshire Hathaway has been able to purchase many businesses at good prices because the sellers want to sell to Berkshire Hathaway CEO Warren Buffett. Bill Child, founder of furniture retailer R.C. Willey, sold his business to Berkshire Hathaway on May 29, 1995, for $175 million in stock. Child said, "When I have spoken to students and business people, I have told them that if they ever have a chance to associate with or be a partner with Warren Buffett, to do it and do it fast. It will be the best decision of your life."[14]
- The management team of a business may fear that a competitor is making new inroads into its core business or creating a new market for its customers. For example, because toy manufacturer Mattel feared that the software and games made by the Learning Company threatened its business, it acquired the company—and almost went bankrupt as a result of this acquisition. When Mattel acquired the Learning Company (May 1999) it was suffering from a decline in its core business even though the toy industry was growing in the low single digits. Mattel was not keeping pace. Mattel acquired the Learning Company to transform the business into something beyond a toy company and to spur growth. Management at the time publicly stated that they wanted to grow Mattel's revenue by 10 percent a year. Mattel ended up selling the Learning Company for $27 million at the end of 2000, even though it paid $3.6 billion to acquire it a year and a half earlier. By that time Mattel had replaced the CEO who bought the Learning Company. The new CEO, when asked why they'd sold for so little said, "Because that was the best offer at the time and it was losing about $1 million a day in cash. We needed to stop the bleeding."[15]

- The larger and the more ambitious the deal, the greater the risk that management will overpay. You can recognize these deals when management uses the words "transformational" or "game changing" to describe the merger or acquisition. Steve Case, founder and former chief executive officer and chairman of America Online (AOL), stated, "Now that the AOL Time Warner merger has closed, we have a new company for a new world—one poised to spark a transformation of the media and communications landscape—connecting, informing, and entertaining people in innovative ways that will enrich their lives."[16] Case further explained, "These unmatched assets position AOL Time Warner to speed the development of the interactive medium and capitalize on such transformational opportunities as digital music, interactive television and broadband Internet services."[17] Shortly after the merger, the share price of AOL Time Warner dropped 90 percent from its peak value.[18]
- If the business is healthy, it will usually be able to attract higher offers. On the other hand, if the business is a damaged property, it typically sells for a lower price. The sale price of the Learning Company illustrates as much. Its sales had continued to fall throughout the time it was held by Mattel.
- Acquisitions made when markets are down tend to be at lower prices than those made when markets are up. In 2009, after the United States entered a recession, hotel properties were sold at low prices. According to Lodging Econometrics, the Portsmouth, New Hampshire, hotel-research firm, the average selling price for a hotel room was $58,190 in 2009, which increased 86 percent to $107,988 one year later. Those businesses that bought hotel properties in 2009 paid a lower price than those who acquired hotel companies in 2010.[19]

Successful acquirers have a disciplined acquisition strategy. For example, here are just a few successful acquirers: Brookfield Asset Management; Penn National Gaming; Cisco; Danaher; and Berkshire Hathaway. The CEOs of these businesses are willing to walk away from a deal if they believe they are about to pay too much.

For example, at Penn National Gaming, CEO Peter Carlino did not get into a bidding war with investor Carl Icahn to buy the unfinished Fountainbleau Resort in Las Vegas because he felt he would be paying too much if he offered a higher price. As Carlino said (during a quarterly conference call), "We hit our limit of where we wanted to go and then walked away. Buying properties at full price at high multiples is like treading water. Why use the firepower of our balance sheet on opportunities that will not really increase shareholder value?"

Similarly, Bruce Flatt at Brookfield Asset Management often walks away from deals, even after investing significant amounts of time in them. When a group led by investment bank Morgan Stanley bid $3 billion to buy the famous London-based office development firm Canary Wharf, Flatt offered a rival bid. As the bidding continued, Flatt walked away from the deal when shareholders demanded an estimated $20 million more in cash (a relatively small amount compared to the deal size).[20]

When you are reading historical articles about a business or archived conference calls, look for those examples where the management team walked away from certain acquisition targets due to price or other factors. This is a positive indicator that they are disciplined acquirers.

Evaluating the Price Paid

Write down how much management paid for an acquisition and note whether it used cash or issued stock or debt. What is the multiple paid for the business, such as the enterprise value to earnings before interest and taxes (EBIT), EBITDA, and free cash flow? If the business is paying a high multiple, such as more than 10 times EBITDA, then management expects the EBITDA to grow in the future. The lower the multiple paid for a business, the more room management has to make mistakes in its future projections of the acquired business. The following example illustrates how you would go about determining whether management paid a good price for a business.

Over the last 10 years, Penn National Gaming acquired six casino businesses that generated a combined EBITDA of $454 million for a going-in multiple of 7.2 times EBITDA, which was lower than the average industry multiple competitors were paying of 8.6 times over the same time period. To determine if Penn paid a good price for all of these businesses, you'd need to understand if the EBITDA increased or decreased over the 10-year period. For 2010, the

EBITDA of these six businesses is now slightly above $454 million, which means the multiple that Penn paid on the transactions is still 7.2 times excluding maintenance and development capital expenditures. This indicates that it not only paid a good price, but that Penn has been able to successfully manage these casinos. On the other hand, most of the casinos acquired by Penn's competitors have seen EBITDA decrease by 10 percent to 40 percent over this same time period. Because most of these casinos were acquired at an 8.6 times going-in multiple, they effectively paid a higher multiple because EBITDA dropped, which means they are not successful acquirers. This speaks to Penn's ability to identify, accurately price, and operate casinos more efficiently than their competitors.[21]

When Western Union, a money-transfer business, acquired Custom House (May 2009), an international money-transfer company for businesses, it paid $370 million in cash. Custom House at the time was generating $100 million in revenues. Western Union paid a multiple of close to four times sales. This price makes it difficult for Custom House to yield a high cash-on-cash return on investment for Western Union. In order for Western Union to generate a 10 percent rate of return on this investment in the next five years, the intrinsic value of Custom House would need to increase to $600 million, which means Custom House would need to generate approximately $40 to $60 million in profits by the end of the fifth year. Considering that revenues in 2009 are currently at $100 million this would not be an easy task. At this price, Western Union is betting on the potential that it will be able to significantly increase Custom House's cash flows.

What is the enterprise value to book value paid for the business? If a business is paying a premium to book value for an acquisition, this is an expensive way to grow. It is easier for a business to earn a decent return on book value if it is not paying a high multiple of book at the start. For example, Target builds all of its stores *denovo* (i.e., from the ground up) and therefore builds stores at book value. If instead, Target were to purchase other retailers at a high multiple of book value—for example, if Target paid two times book value—then it would earn a lower return on its investment.

To further illustrate this concept, consider this example: If a stock has a book value of $100 and a market value of $100 and it earns a 12 percent return on book, then you would get a 12 percent rate of return on your purchase. In contrast, if you bought a stock at 150 percent of book value and it earned 12 percent, then you would be receiving only an 8 percent rate of return. Based on valuation alone, which stock would you rather buy?

How Is the Acquisition Financed?

You need to determine how the acquisition is financed, which will give you an insight into the risk tolerance of the management team. In general, there are four ways an acquisition is financed: A business can issue debt, it can use the cash on its balance sheet, it can issue equity, or some combination of all three. Let's look at each of these financing methods in more detail.

Using Cash to Finance Acquisitions   If an acquisition is financed using *cash on the balance sheet*, then management is highly conservative. Most of the acquisitions that Warren Buffett, CEO of Berkshire Hathaway, has made are in cash. These conservative acquisitions have contributed to the excess returns that Berkshire Hathaway has delivered to its shareholders.

Using Debt to Finance Acquisitions   In contrast, if a management team *uses debt* to finance an acquisition, be cautious that it does not take on too much debt. Closely monitor debt coverage ratios and model various scenarios of how the debt might constrict the free-cash flows of the business. For example, create a scenario modeling what would happen if revenues at the combined firm dropped by 10 percent to 40 percent. Determine at what level of free-cash flows it would be difficult for the business to make debt repayments.

For example, for many years, CEMEX, a cement manufacturer based in Mexico, used its strong free-cash flows to issue debt to acquire other cement businesses around the world. CEMEX then slashed expenses and improved the operations of the acquired cement business, which generated even more free-cash flows. CEMEX then used these increased free-cash flows to issue additional debt to make more acquisitions. Each time CEMEX acquired a business, Wall Street analysts questioned whether CEMEX had taken on too much debt. However,

CEMEX continually proved these skeptics wrong and continued to increase the free-cash flows of the acquired business and pay down the debt.

This strategy worked for 20 years, until CEMEX acquired Rinker, an Australian cement company, in 2007. When the real estate industry collapsed in 2008, that collapse compressed CEMEX's free-cash flows, and CEMEX found it difficult to pay back the debt that was coming due from the Rinker acquisition. As a result, in less than 18 months—from June 11, 2007 to November 17, 2008—CEMEX's stock price dropped from $39.25 to only $4 per share.[22] In other words, the stock price was almost one-tenth its price a year earlier, because investors feared that CEMEX would not be able refinance the debt.

Eventually, CEMEX was able to refinance a large portion of the debt coming due, but it was forced to accept a higher interest rate and more onerous terms. This has impaired the free-cash flows of CEMEX. Even though CEMEX will probably survive and even prosper, a lot of shareholder value was destroyed by a debt-fueled acquisition strategy.

Using Stock to Finance Acquisitions   Finally, if a business uses its stock to make acquisitions, make sure the stock is not undervalued, as the acquisition would then dilute the ownership interest of the acquiring business's owners. When a business pays too much, it effectively redistributes wealth from itself to the shareholders of the acquired business. Therefore, you must determine what percentage of the business is being given up to make the acquisition.

For example, when Warren Buffett was on the board of the Coca-Cola Company, he did not let Coca-Cola's management buy Quaker Oats (owner of Gatorade) because "Giving up 10.5 percent of the Coca-Cola Company for Quaker Oats was just too much for what we would get." Buffett estimated that Gatorade would have increased Coke's worldwide case sales less than 2 percent, while saddling Coke with Quakers Oat's slow-growth food business.[23]

If the business can use its overvalued stock to make acquisitions, it favors the acquiring shareholders. For example, many banks have been able to create value by using their high stock prices, such as two times book value, to buy banks priced at substantial discounts to book value, such as 0.5 times book value.

Key Points to Keep in Mind

- Understanding how and why management makes acquisitions is one of the few concrete ways for investors to reduce uncertainty in assessing a company's chances of success.
- As promising as it sounds, when you hear managers utter the word *synergy* when they make an acquisition, you should be extremely skeptical that the cost savings or revenue increases they promise will materialize.
- Acquisitions are most likely to fail when the two merged businesses serve different customers or are in unrelated areas.
- A management team is likely to overpay for an acquisition or buy a business that is not a good operational fit under the following circumstances:
  - The business uses its own undervalued stock to make the acquisition,
  - The target business is sold in an auction-like situation,
  - Management uses debt to finance the acquisition, or
  - Management pays a premium EBITDA multiple, such as 10 times or more, or a premium to book value (two times or more).
- Management is likely to make a successful acquisition if:
  - Management has a history of making successful acquisitions and has shown discipline by walking away from deals in the past,
  - The acquisition fits into the core competency of the business,
  - Management intimately understands the business they are acquiring,
  - The customers and employees remain at the acquired business,
  - The business acquired is bought at a distressed price, and
  - Management uses overvalued stock or cash to finance the acquisition.

Building a Human Intelligence Network

After you have reviewed all of the publicly available information from articles, SEC filings, and industry sources, you may still have unanswered questions. This is the time to go out and interview people who are involved with the business on a day-to-day basis. Doing so will help you fill in the gaps and give you an in-depth view of a business. For example, if the success of your investment is predicated on the business overcoming a specific obstacle, interview sources that have direct experience or have dealt with that particular business first hand. Cross check any assumptions you are making about the business with people who have industry knowledge. This will give you greater confidence in your assumptions and ultimately help you correctly value the business.

A friend once heard an analyst present what appeared to be a well-thought-out case for investing in chip-maker Advanced Micro Devices (AMD), which the analyst believed was undervalued. The analyst told investors in the audience that AMD had just developed a new technology that was going to give it an immediate advantage over its main competitor, Intel. When questioned at the conference about which computer manufacturers would be including the new technology in their products, the analyst had only a blank stare—he didn't know the answer. My friend, who knew the computer industry well, knew that it takes as long as 24 months for manufacturers to incorporate new chips into their products. From that point, my friend knew that the analyst really didn't understand the business, and his investment recommendation was not credible.

This is a perfect example of why it is important to speak with those who have first-hand industry knowledge whenever you make an investment, especially if you are making large assumptions about a business, as this analyst did. It is easy to sit down in front of a computer and dream up various scenarios for a business, but you need to develop an understanding of how a business works from those who have experience operating or dealing with a business. You must make it a priority to speak with people who are involved with the business on a day-to-day basis. This Appendix describes how to locate a variety of sources you might talk to for information, how best to approach them to ensure you'll get the information you're looking for, and how to properly take notes so you'll have the information to go back to in the future.

Evaluating Information Sources

First, you must distinguish whether you are seeking information from a primary source or a secondary source. *Primary sources* are those who have first-hand knowledge about a business, such as management, employees, suppliers, or competitors. *Secondary sources* are those who interpret information from a variety of sources, such as stock analysts or journalists. The problem with relying on secondary sources is that you may not know what information they are using to form their insights. They may simply be voicing an opinion with no factual data to support it. There is nothing wrong with considering these opinions, in fact, secondary sources of information can often be a great source of contrary information to investigate further. The mistake usually lies in accepting and following other people's opinions or advice without investigating the supporting evidence.

How to Locate Human Sources

There are many types of people who can provide valuable information and insight about the company in which you're considering investing. Try to talk to the company's customers, journalists who cover the industry, people at industry conferences, other industry insiders or associates, professors and deans of business schools located near the company you're researching, and even headhunters. The following paragraphs elaborate.

Talk to Customers

Early in my career, one of the first businesses that I researched was Nielsen Media Research, the TV-ratings company. This was and continues to be a monopoly business. Nielsen had been recently spun-off from Dun & Bradstreet, and the stock price had dropped due to the threat of a new competing ratings business, SRI Research, whom Nielsen's customers were funding.

In order to better understand this threat and to understand the stability of Nielsen's business, I interviewed more than 80 percent of Nielsen's customers. I wanted to find out if SRI Research posed a serious risk. I contacted managers in charge of selling advertising time at these stations. Many of the 100 or so sources that I spoke with managed advertising for several stations in a regional market. Nielsen measured 54 cable and network channels (e.g., Fox, CBS, and NBC), located in 44 major markets (and each market had an average of five to six TV stations).

The interview process took me over six months, as I spent about 30 minutes each day contacting these sources. Every time I interviewed a customer, I asked who the customer thought was a good source for me to contact. They told me the same thing over and over: "call Norman Hecht." Hecht ran a research firm that helped Nielsen's customers get fairer ratings, and at one time, he ran Nielsen's primary competitor, Arbitron. When I first contacted Hecht, he was more than happy to talk to me, and in a one-hour conversation, he summarized everything I had learned from interviewing 80 percent of Nielsen's customers. Why had I spent so much time interviewing so many customers when Hecht summarized my research and conclusions in an hour? The only benefit derived from interviewing so many customers was that I knew that Hecht was a credible source.

I now interview and talk to a variety of sources in order to identify who the best sources are in an industry. I am looking for the Norman Hecht of the industry or those who are well connected and know a lot of people in the industry. Ideally, your source's livelihood depends on knowing what is happening at that company, and your source will have done business with the company over a long period of time. It is in the self-interest of those sources to stay abreast of valuable information.

Talk to Journalists Who Cover the Industry

Journalists have a vested interest in seeking good information. As you begin to read articles about a business, you may notice that many of these articles are written by the same journalists. You can research the background of the journalist to learn how long he or she has been reporting about the industry. Look for those journalists who have been reporting on a certain industry for several years. Contact these journalists and ask them who they believe are the best sources to talk to in an industry or, better yet, how they identify the good sources.

Go to Industry Conferences

An industry conference brings together an entire industry under one roof, and it is an excellent way to understand the competitive landscape within an industry. You'll be able to watch presentations from a range of professional perspectives, from CEOs to industry journalists. Find industry conferences where the business is exhibiting. You can often find this information on the website of the business.

For example, if you are studying the television industry, then attending the National Association of Television Program Executives (NATPE) conference will give you valuable insights because most attendees are involved in the creating, developing, and distributing of television programming. You can walk from booth to booth talking to representatives from each company, asking them why their product or service is better than competitors. You will very quickly understand the pros and cons of a product and service by doing this. It would take you a long time to obtain this information otherwise, but you can do this in a few days by attending the conference.

In my visits to conferences, I also like to watch how top management and employees interact. How comfortable are the employees when the top managers are around? Do they change their behavior? I like to ask the employees at the booths what hotel they are staying at and what hotel the managers are staying at. If the managers are staying at a luxury hotel such as the Four Seasons and the employees are staying at a budget motel, this may mean that the business does not value its employees, or at least that management sees itself as different or above the frontline employees.

Other Industry Insiders or Associates

You should also search for tangential sources, not just customers, competitors, employees, and suppliers. Think of other industry insiders or associates, such as those people concerned with manufacturing data, trading data, or people who operate social and professional centers. For example, when my firm was analyzing Western Union, we spoke with individuals who worked at the World Bank whose job was to collect remittance data (when migrant workers send money home, it is called a remittance). We wanted to understand if Western Union's growth potential was high or low based on existing data and whether the existing data underreported the true size of the market. People who work closely with the data were able to give us more detail about market estimates.

For example, we learned that Banco de Mexico, who reports its figures to international groups and the U.S. government, gathered much of its data from Western Union itself. Because they only accumulated data from a few commercial sources, we knew the market size was larger than estimated. This led us to learn more about how the larger market functioned, and eventually gave us greater insight into how remittances work. It also helped us understand that Western Union had more market growth opportunity than was first apparent.

Talk to Professors at Nearby Business Schools

Another great tangential source is college professors and deans of the business school in the area where the business is located, because they probably interact with the local business in some capacity. Also, many prior students of these professors may be working at the business. What is the reputation of the business in the community? Is it a good place to work? Does the university want its students to work there? For example, I sold an investment in one company after I learned from a university dean that the company's management team took advantage of its customers and that many former students complained about an unethical culture.

Talk to Headhunters

Talk to headhunters who work in a particular industry and ask them what businesses they believe are the best places to recruit management from and why. Headhunters are an extremely valuable resource because their job is to find skilled management for a business. You can find headhunters by locating the local office of the larger recruiting firms where the business is located. For example, if a business is located in Atlanta, Georgia, you would search for articles that listed the top 10 headhunters in Atlanta. Then, you can begin to look for individuals in these firms or those who are cited in articles.

How to Contact Human Sources—and Get the Information You Want

One way to start building your human intelligence network is to contact those sources that are quoted in articles written about a business or industry. One of the hardest things to do is to pick up a phone and call someone you have never met. It is called the cold-caller's curse. The stress you feel is produced by a fear of rejection. However, because these people have already spoken to the press, they will likely speak with you, which will increase your confidence in reaching out to other sources. This does not mean that you should talk *only* to readily available sources, but it is a strong start in locating and contacting the best sources.

Try to learn as much as you can about your sources before speaking with them, and then write a letter referencing the article where they were quoted. Ask if they can give you a couple of minutes of their time to further elaborate on their comments. In the letter, let them know why you are calling them and how you will use the information they give you. Sending a letter, instead of an e-mail, will stand out, and you will dramatically improve your chances of speaking with a source.

Also, offer to share your conclusions from your research. This serves two purposes: First, it gives you an opening to maintain a regular contact with a source; second, you will engender goodwill. Be sure to keep in contact with your most valuable sources regularly so that you are not calling them out of the blue when you need them most. You will find that it is tedious to begin this process, but the more you do it, the more momentum you will build, and the easier it will become.

When you contact a source, your goal is to get information on *why* things are happening. The best questions are broad questions rather than direct questions. For example, a direct question is,

"What time is it?" because you get just one answer: *"It is 8:00 pm."* In contrast, a broad question is, *"How do you think this business compares to its competitors, from the customers' point of view?"* You will find that one of the biggest benefits to asking broad questions is that you will uncover many things that you did not know about the business and even things that you didn't realize you *needed* to know.

At the end of the conversation, ask your source who else you should be talking to or who are considered some of the most knowledgeable sources in an industry. You should also tell your sources that you will not quote them in any research reports and that you will protect their identities, even if they give you permission to quote them. There should not be any risks for your source to talk to you, and it is important that you build trust with them.

Don't despair if a source is unwilling to speak with you. I have found that sources who are less willing to speak are the worst sources anyway, as they are often less engaged. People who are open to speaking with you are generally passionate about their subject area, and they will talk at great lengths about it to others who show genuine interest in their knowledge. The more passionate the person, the more open he or she usually is to sharing information.

Create a Database of Your Interviews for Future Reference

Be sure to record all the details from your conversations without adding your own commentary or ideas about what you *think* a source meant. If you are unsure, note this. This way you will not fall into the trap of rationalizing the answers of your source with your assumptions. Remember, great investors see things as they are, rather than as they want them to be. You also want to note whether your source is stating assumptions, a theory, a fact, a question, an idea, or a related point. Do not be in a hurry to write a summary of your conversation, and write down all responses. This way, you can create a collection of interviews that you can turn to later. Many of the answers you receive from your interviews will seem innocuous or unimportant, but this information can be valuable later.

Write a brief synopsis describing your source. Was this person friendly, passionate, and engaged? Or did he or she answer questions quickly and want to get you off the phone? If you include this information in your notes, it may help to provide a context for the source's comments.

You will find that by piecing together a great number of ordinary observations, you end up with unexpected and meaningful insights. As you interview more and more people, you will start to see patterns that help you understand the larger picture.

You want to cultivate your sources and stay in contact with them at least two to three times a year. The main advantage of staying in contact with your sources is that you can turn to them whenever there is a negative news report that causes the stock price to drop. These are the people who can help you interpret the true severity of the news. These sources can also alert you to negative developments and inform you of changes in the business. My firm invested a lot of time over many years identifying reliable people in the industries we were invested in. We have learned that you need to do in-depth work on identifying sources and establishing their credibility in advance, because it is difficult, if not impossible, to do this in a short period of time.

Knowing we could speak to credible, reliable people paid off for us. When the price of our investment holdings suddenly dropped during the economic downturn in 2008, rather than relying on newspapers and other secondary sources for information, we called our customer, supplier, and management contacts to better understand what was going on at the business level at each of our holdings. After speaking with these sources, we learned that things were not as bad as the more sensational news reports suggested. This helped my firm maintain rationality and be opportunistic, because most general news stories were reporting that the U.S. economy was potentially headed into a depression.

B

How to Interview the Management Team

I regard interviewing managers as something of an art, and I admire those who do it well. When you think of the best interviews you have read or watched, you may remember how you were drawn into the conversation. Part of what drew you in was probably the fact that the interview had, at some point, turned into an engaged and meaningful conversation. At their best, management interviews can provide deep personal insight into how managers think.

If you have an opportunity to meet with members of the management team, use your time learning how they got to where they are and ask what lessons they learned along the way. This will put most managers at ease, as you are talking about their favorite subject: themselves! You will also find that the answers you receive are more revealing, and you will gain better insight into their character. Most Wall Street analysts don't ask these questions, so the manager's responses are less likely to be scripted.

The conversation you want to have will be focused on management's view of how the business is run. Ask questions that are open-ended rather than closed-ended:

- An *open-ended question* is, "How did you make the decision to hire the senior vice-president of development?" This type of question requires a detailed, conversational answer.
- A *closed-ended question* is, "What is the tax rate for this quarter?" This type of question can be answered with only a one-word answer, which won't reveal anything about how a manager thinks or makes decisions.

As interviewer, your job is to listen, and then continue to ask questions to clarify what a manager is saying.

Do not ask hypothetical questions, such as, "What would you do if you were confronted with a certain problem?" The answers to these questions do not yield many insights because what managers *think* they will do is often different than what they will *actually* do. Instead, ask questions that will help you learn how the manager thinks and how he or she plans to execute.

Ask Open-Ended Questions

The following are a few open-ended questions you might ask (in no particular sequence). You should focus on the questions that you think will be most revealing to you:

- Why did you join the business?
- How did you rise at the business?
- What skills made you chief executive officer (CEO)?
- What do you believe the job of the CEO is?
- What do you want to be known for?
- How do you measure whether you are successful?
- If you were sitting down with some potential long-term investors, what two or three reasons would you give them to take a look at the business at this time?
- Is there a possibility this business is going to be two to four times as big as it is today, five, or seven years down the road?
- If you were a private business, how would you operate differently?
- What do you like about working here?
- Who are your current and past mentors, and what impact did they have on your life?
- What character traits are needed for your job?
- What character traits do you look for in a successor?
- What three things would you do to *destroy* the business as quickly as possible? Give yourself a one-year time frame.
- What type of people are you looking to hire?
- How do you find quality candidates?
- How are you developing future leaders?
- What is the culture you are trying to instill at your business?

- If we were meeting three years from today, what would need to have happened during that time for you to feel happy about your progress?
- How do you keep the big picture in perspective and not get too bogged down in the everyday details?
- What factors do you consider before you expand into a new market?
- What are the biggest opportunities the business has?
- How many people do you need to hire to grow?
- How do you stay close to your customers?
- What type of information do you need on a weekly basis?
- If you were away for one year, which key metrics would best tell you how the business was doing?
- Why can't other people do what you are doing?

Be Aware of the Danger of Face-to-Face Assessments of Managers

Most investors overestimate their ability to judge a management team based on a face-to-face meeting. They believe they have the ability to judge a person's character by looking him or her in the eye or watching body language. However, there are many problems associated with relying on your gut instincts.

First, you may be unduly influenced by the personality or personal beliefs of the manager. We all like people who are like us, and we tend to dislike people who are not like us or who don't share our beliefs. Perhaps the CEO does not have the same political views as you do, and you therefore dismiss his or her ability. We all overestimate our abilities to be rational, and how much we like someone often affects our judgment.

Another stumbling block is looking at the world through your own perspective rather than through the other person's perspective. Let's say you are a hedge fund manager who likes to push your subordinates to work 20 hour days, 6 days a week. What types of management teams do you think you will admire? You will admire those businesses that push their employees to work long hours. The problem is that this type of culture may not work at certain businesses (or many businesses, for that matter).

Second, managers will tend to share with you the things they think you want to hear. You might sit down with a CEO and listen to what appears to be a well-laid-out plan to create value that increases your confidence in the business. There may be other negative elements that you don't hear about, and in fact, the plan may fail miserably. Part of this is just human nature or optimism and not that the managers intend to deceive you. Adding to this problem is the fact that many managers are simply overconfident in their own abilities.

A third error in assessing management is ignoring situation and context. We often attribute behavior to a person's character rather than to the situation or context. For example, if a person is going through a divorce, this situation may make the person appear to be unstable even though he or she may not be that way on a normal basis.

Fourth, we all have different backgrounds and experiences, which affect how we assess people. If you have spent most of your time in an office, it is likely you will resonate with a manager who has worked in the corporate suite his or her whole life instead of one who spends time in the field.

Fifth, our ability to evaluate people is affected by the company we keep. The more we associate with people with good character, the easier it is for us to recognize those who do not possess good character. Early in my career, I mixed closely with some people with serious character flaws. I found myself constantly making excuses for them. I would say things such as, "I know they have certain flaws, but I am learning a lot from them." Over time, I began to spend less time with these people in both my business and personal life. I found that my ability to make distinctions quickly improved. The more I associated with good people, the quicker I was able to identify those who had serious character flaws that might affect their business.

Your Investment Checklist

Understanding the Business—The Basics

- ☐ Do I want to spend a lot of time learning about this business?
- ☐ How would you evaluate this business if you were to become its CEO?
- ☐ Can you describe how the business operates, in your own words?
- ☐ How does the business make money?
- ☐ How has the business evolved over time?
- ☐ In what foreign markets does the business operate, and what are the risks of operating in these countries?

Understanding the Business—from the Customer Perspective

- ☐ Who is the core customer of the business?
- ☐ Is the customer base concentrated or diversified?
- ☐ Is it easy or difficult to convince customers to buy the products or services?
- ☐ What is the customer retention rate for the business?
- ☐ What are the signs a business is customer oriented?
- ☐ What pain does the business alleviate for the customer?
- ☐ To what degree is the customer dependent on the products or services from the business?
- ☐ If the business disappeared tomorrow, what impact would this have on the customer base?

Evaluating the Strengths and Weaknesses of a Business and Industry

☐ Does the business have a *sustainable* competitive advantage and what is its source?

☐ Does the business possess the ability to raise prices without losing customers?

☐ Does the business operate in a good or bad industry?

☐ How has the industry evolved over time?

☐ What is the competitive landscape, and how intense is the competition?

☐ What type of relationship does the business have with its suppliers?

Measuring the Operating and Financial Health of the Business

☐ What are the fundamentals of the business?

☐ What are the operating metrics of the business that you need to monitor?

☐ What are the key risks the business faces?

☐ How does inflation affect the business?

☐ Is the business's balance sheet strong or weak?

☐ What is the return on invested capital for the business?

Evaluating the Distribution of Earnings (Cash Flows)

☐ Are the accounting standards that management uses conservative or liberal?

☐ Does the business generate revenues that are recurring or from one-off transactions?

☐ To what degree is the business cyclical, countercyclical, or recession-resistant?

☐ To what degree does operating leverage impact the earnings of the business?

☐ How does working capital impact the cash flows of the business?

☐ Does the business have high or low capital-expenditure requirements?

Assessing the Quality of Management—Background and Classification: Who Are They?

☐ What type of manager is leading the company?

❏ What are the effects on the business of bringing in outside management?

❏ Is the manager a lion or a hyena?

❏ How did the manager rise to lead the business?

❏ How are senior managers compensated, and how did they gain their ownership interest?

❏ Have the managers been buying or selling the stock?

Assessing the Quality of Management—Competence: How Management Operates the Business

❏ Does the CEO manage the business to benefit all stakeholders?

❏ Does the management team improve its operations day-to-day or does it use a strategic plan to conduct its business?

❏ Do the CEO and CFO issue guidance regarding earnings?

❏ Is the business managed in a centralized or decentralized way?

❏ Does management value its employees?

❏ Does the management team know how to hire well?

❏ Does the management team focus on cutting unnecessary costs?

❏ Are the CEO and CFO disciplined in making capital-allocation decisions?

❏ Do the CEO and CFO buy back stock opportunistically?

Assessing the Quality of Management—Positive and Negative Traits

❏ Does the CEO love the money or the business?

❏ Can you identify a moment of integrity for the manager?

❏ Are managers clear and consistent in their communications and actions with stakeholders?

❏ Does management think independently and remain unswayed by what others in their industry are doing?

❏ Is the CEO self-promoting?

Evaluating Growth Opportunities

❏ Does the business grow through mergers and acquisitions, or does it grow organically?

❏ What is the management team's motivation to grow the business?

❏ Has historical growth been profitable and will it continue?

❏ What are the future growth prospects for the business?
❏ Is the management team growing the business too quickly or at a steady pace?

Evaluating Mergers & Acquisitions

❏ How does management make M&A decisions?
❏ Have past acquisitions been successful?

Notes

Chapter 1

1. Sobel, Robert. *The Rise and Fall of the Conglomerate Kings.* New York: Stein and Day, 1984.
2. Shepard, Stephen B. "A Talk with Scott McNealy." *BusinessWeek,* April 1, 2002, pp. 66–68.
3. Standard & Poor's Capital IQ.
4. Author's interview with Paul Sonkin in November 2010.
5. Author's interview with Todd Green in March 2011.
6. Author's interview with Paul Sonkin in November 2010.
7. Standard & Poor's Capital IQ; Author's interview with Brad Leonard in March 2011.

Chapter 2

1. Standard & Poor's Capital IQ.
2. VCA Antech 2008 10-K.
3. Ball, Deborah. "Slow and Steady Is Winning the Race and Driving Nestlé." *Wall Street Journal,* September 25, 2002.
4. Gunther, Marc. "The World's New Economic Landscape." *Fortune,* July 26, 2010, pp. 81–82.
5. Arndt, Michael. "Urban Outfitters' Grow-Slow Strategy." *BusinessWeek,* March 1, 2010, p. 56.
6. Gunther, "Economic Landscape," pp. 81–82.
7. Boyle, Matthew. "Wal-Mart's Painful Lessons." *BusinessWeek Online,* October 14, 2009.
8. Mijuk, Goran. "Nestlé Bets on Emerging Markets." *Wall Street Journal,* June 22, 2010.
9. Bevins, Vincent. "Working to a Different Beat." *Financial Times,* December 16, 2010.
10. Browne, Andrew, and Jason Dean. "Business Sours on China: Foreign Executives Say Beijing Creates Fresh Barriers; Broadsides, Patent Rules." *Wall Street Journal,* March 17, 2010.
11. "Pernicious Innovation?" *China Economic Review,* September 2010, p. 10.

12. Kroll, Karen M. "Currency Risk: To Hedge or Hedge Not?" *Business Finance*, June 2007, pp. 35–39.

Chapter 3

1. Boyle, Matthew, Susan M. Kaufman, and Joan L. Levinstein, "Best Buy's Giant Gamble." *Fortune*, April 3, 2006.
2. Porter, Michael. "The Five Competitive Forces That Shape Strategy." *Harvard Business Review*, January 2008.
3. Talley, Karen. "Retailers, Suppliers Tussle." *Wall Street Journal*, February 11, 2009.
4. Rohwedder, Cecilie. "Store of Knowledge." *Wall Street Journal*, June 6, 2006.
5. Dougherty, Dave, and Ajay Murthy. "What Service Customers Really Want." *Harvard Business Review*, September 2009.
6. Bary, Andrew. "Kings of the Jungle." *Barron's*, March 23, 2009.
7. *Ibid.*
8. Southwest Airlines. "Checked Baggage." http://www.southwest.com/html/customer-service/baggage/checked-bags-pol.html. Accessed May 11, 2011.
9. Hart, Christopher. "Beating the Market with Customer Satisfaction." *Harvard Business Review*, March 2007.
10. Cabela, David. *Cabela's: World's Foremost Outfitter, a History*. Middlebury, VT: Paul S. Eriksson, 2001.
11. Shambora, Jessica. "Williams-Sonoma's Secret Sauce." *Fortune*, July 26, 2010.
12. Rust, Roland T., Christine Moorman, and Gaurav Bhalla. "Rethinking Marketing." *Harvard Business Review*, January–February 2010.
13. Meyer, Christopher, and Andre Schwager. "Understanding Customer Experience." *Harvard Business Review*, February 2007.

Chapter 4

1. Author's interview with Pat Dorsey, March 31, 2011.
2. Western Union 2009 10-K and MoneyGram International 2009 10-K.
3. Evans, David S., and Richard Schmalensee, *Paying with Plastic: The Digital Revolution in Buying and Borrowing*, 2nd ed. Cambridge MA: MIT Press, 2005.
4. comScore Media Metrix (U.S. data).
5. Cardona, Mercedes M. "Affluent Shoppers Like their Luxe Goods Cheap." *Advertising Age*, December 1, 2003.

6. Blackhurst, Chris. "La Belle Maison." *The Evening Standard,* May 25, 2010.

7. Standard & Poor's Capital IQ.

8. "Store Brands Surge." *MMR* 27 (2010): 115.

9. "Private Label on the Attack." *Black Book—U.S. Household and Personal Products,* August 2009.

10. LeVine, Steve. "IBM Piles Up Patents, But Quantity Isn't King, "*BusinessWeek,* January 25, 2010.

11. Freedman, David. "Relax. Let Your Guard Down. Why Patents, Trademarks, and Other Intellectual Property Protections are Bad for Business." *Inc.,* August 2006, pp. 109–111.

12. Blackboard 2009 10-K.

13. American Apparel and Footwear Association. *ShoeStats,* 2008. Accessed May 11, 2011. http://www.apparelandfootwear.org.

14. Wubbe, Eileen. "TSL Profile." *Secured Lender,* September 2010, pp. 39.

15. 2004 Four Seasons Annual Report and Time Value of Money, LP interviews with Four Seasons management.

16. Standard & Poor's Capital IQ.

17. *Ibid.*

18. *Ibid.*

19. Steinberg, Richard M. "Merrill Lynch Failed at ERM, and Then Just Failed." *Compliance Week,* August 2009, pp. 42–43.

20. Verschoor, Curtis C. "Who Should Be Blamed the Most for the Subprime Loan Scandal?" *Strategic Finance,* December 2007, pp. 11–12.

21. Tobin, Edward. "Cola Wars Soldiers March Toward Marketing Battle." Reuters News, November 22, 1999; "Canadian Beverage Firm Cott Can't Find Buyer Amid Pricing Pressures." Dow Jones Online News, April 24, 1998.

22. Standard & Poor's Capital IQ; Steverman, Ben. "Netflix Battle with Blockbuster Gets Ugly." *BusinessWeek,* July 24, 2007.

23. Carroll, Paul B., and Chunka Mui. "7 Ways to Fail Big: Lessons from the Most Inexcusable Business Failures of the Past 25 Years." *Harvard Business Review,* September 2008.

24. Standard & Poor's Capital IQ.

25. *Ibid.*

26. Dalton, Matthew. "Risks to BP Revival Center in U.S." *Wall Street Journal,* January 2, 2008.

27. Talley, Karen. "Retailers, Suppliers Tussle." *Wall Street Journal,* February 11, 2009.

28. Porter, Michael E., and Mark R. Kramer. "Creating Shared Value" *Harvard Business Review,* January–February 2011.

29. Standard & Poor's Capital IQ.

30. Hoover, Sandra, and Saul Bromberger. "Supply Chain Challenges: Building Relationships." *Harvard Business Review*, July 2003, p. 70.
31. Schlangenstein, Mary, and Mary Jane Credeur. "Higher U.S. Airfares Loom as Oil Climbs Toward $100." *Bloomberg News*, December 22, 2010.

Chapter 5

1. Standard & Poor's Capital IQ.
2. Wiggins, Jenny. "When Coffee Goes Cold Part 1." *Financial Times*, December 13, 2008; Damian Whitworth (Interview with Howard Schultz), "I Worry About Everybody. I'm Paranoid. You Have to Be." *Times (London)*, March 12, 2011.
3. Standard & Poor's Capital IQ; Ignatius, Adi. "We Had to Own the Mistakes." *Harvard Business Review*, July–August 2010.
4. Standard & Poor's industry reports; Moody's ratings and financial databases, as of July 1, 2006.
5. Moorman, James. "Telecommunications: Wireless." *S&P Industry Surveys*, January 20, 2011.
6. "Domino's Pizza Completes Its Recapitalization Plan and Declares $13.50 per Share Special Dividend." PR Newswire, April 17, 2007.
7. Brookfield Asset Management website.
8. Moody's ratings and financial databases, as of July 1, 2006.
9. Flatt, Bruce. Brookfield Asset Management Conference Call, November 7, 2008.
10. Pruitt, A.D. "Cannery Loan is in Default—Vornado Stopped Making Payments on $18 Million Mortgage on the Landmark." *Wall Street Journal*, May 12, 2010; Kris Hudson and A.D. Pruitt. "'Jingle Mail': Developers Are Giving Up On Properties." *Wall Street Journal*, August 25, 2010.
11. Standard & Poor's Capital IQ.
12. *Ibid.*
13. Goldman Sachs dotCommerce Day Investor Presentation by Williams-Sonoma, June 22, 2010.
14. Constellation Brands at Barclays Capital Back-To-School Conference, *CQ FD Disclosure*, September 10, 2009.
15. *Drug Store News*, Yearbook Issue, April 1, 2010, pp. 26–29.
16. Ball, Jeffrey. "Truck Firms Go on Buying Binge to Circumvent a New EPA Rule." *Wall Street Journal*, May 28, 2002.

Chapter 6

1. Taub, Stephen. "SEC Charges Six with Inflating Revenues." *CFO.com*, October 16, 2006. http://www.cfo.com/article.cfm/8047493.

2. Plunkett, Linda M., and Robert W. Rouse. "Revenue Recognition and the Bausch and Lomb Case." CPA Journal, September 1998; Standard & Poor's Capital IQ.
3. Badawi, Ibrahim M. "Global Corporate Accounting Frauds and Action for Reforms." Review of Business, 26, no. 2 (2005).
4. Lahart, Justin. "Corner Office Thinks Short-Term." *Wall Street Journal,* April 14, 2004.
5. "Waste Management Ex-CEO Says SECs Suit Against Execs Is Biased." *Corporate Officers and Directors Liability Reporter* 17, no. 17 (2002).
6. Byrne, John A. "Chainsaw Al Dunlap Cuts His Last Deal." BusinessWeekOnline, September 6, 2002; Sunbeam 1996 and 1997 10-K.
7. Sysco 2010 10-K.
8. "Break-even Occupancy Declining." *Hotel & Motel Management,* June 16, 2003.
9. Standard & Poor's Capital IQ.
10. Standard & Poor's Capital IQ.

Chapter 7

1. Dell, Michael, speaking to analysts in Round Rock, Texas, April 2, 2008.
2. Lublin, Joann, and Spencer Stuart, "CEO Tenure, Stock Gains Often Go Hand-in-Hand." *Wall Street Journal,* July 6, 2010.
3. Byrnes, Nanette, and David Kiley. "Hello, You Must Be Going." *BusinessWeek,* February 12, 2007, pp. 30–32; "Executives Need More Than 90 Days to Integrate." BusinessWire, March 13, 2006.
4. Interview by Thomas Stewart, "Growth as a Process." *Harvard Business Review,* June 2006.
5. Byrne, John. "Chainsaw Al Cuts His Last Deal." *BusinessWeek Online,* September 6, 2002.
6. Interview with Seng Hock Tan in May 2010 and October 2010.
7. Standard & Poor's Capital IQ as of end of 2000 to 2009.
8. Hawthorne, Fran. *The Merck Druggernaut: The Inside Story of a Pharmaceutical Giant.* Hoboken, N. J. : Wiley, 2003.
9. Foust, Dean. "Where Headhunters Fear to Tread" *BusinessWeek,* September 14, 2009, pp. 42–44.
10. CarMax 2009 Proxy Statement.
11. Schwartz, Nelson D., Doris Burke, and Matthew Schuerman, "Greed-mart." *Fortune,* October 14, 2002.
12. *Ibid.*
13. Dixon, Jennifer. "How Kmart Fell." *Charleston Gazette,* July 14, 2002.
14. Rockoff, Jonathan D. "Merck Names Frazier as CEO." *Wall Street Journal,* December 1, 2010.

15. Foust, Dean. "Where Headhunters Fear to Tread." *BusinessWeek*, September 14, 2009, pp. 42–44.
16. "3M a Lab for Growth?" *BusinessWeek*, January 21, 2002, pp. 50–51.
17. Fastenal Proxy Statements, 2001 to 2009.
18. Standard & Poor's Capital IQ.
19. 99 Cent Only Proxy Statements, 1997 to 2005.
20. 2009 Morningstar Proxy Statement.
21. 2006 Heartland Express Proxy Statement and Standard & Poor's Capital IQ.
22. Standard & Poor's Capital IQ.
23. 2010 Oracle Corporation Proxy Statement.
24. 2010 Whole Foods Market Proxy Statement.
25. Dillon, Karen. "The Coming Battle over Executive Pay." *Harvard Business Review*, September 2009.
26. *Ibid.*
27. Schwartz, Nelson D., Doris Burke, and Matthew Schuerman. "Greedmart." *Fortune*, October 14, 2002.
28. "The Brain Behind Teledyne: A Great American Capitalist." *New York Observer*, April 7, 2003.
29. Byrne, Harlan S. "Dimon in the Rough: A Turnaround at Bank One Won't Be Quick Under Its New CEO." *Barron's*, April 3, 2000.
30. Standard & Poor's Capital IQ.
31. Harris, Craig. "Sweet Deal for Soda Honchos?" *Seattle Post-Intelligencer*, August 14, 2007.
32. Searcey, Dionne, and Kara Scannell. "SEC Now Takes a Hard Look at Insiders' 'Regular' Sales." *Wall Street Journal*, April 4, 2007.
33. Casselman, Ben. "Chesapeake CEO Sells Holdings." *Wall Street Journal*, October 11, 2008.

Chapter 8

1. Mackey, John. "Conscious Capitalism: Creating a New Paradigm for Business." In Michael Strong, ed., *Be the the Solution: How Entrepreneurs and Conscious Capitalists Can Solve All the Worlds Problems*, Hoboken, N. J.: 2009.
2. Horowitz, Jed. "Buffalo's First Empire: Enigmatic Profit Machine Series: 5." *American Banker*, September 14, 1993.
3. Davenport, Todd. "Wilmers: Profitability Plus Community Involvement." *American Banker*, December 1, 2005, pp. 22–27.
4. Standard & Poor's Capital IQ.
5. Collins, Jim. "The 10 Greatest CEOs of All Time." *Fortune*, July 21, 2003.
6. Author's interview with Robert Silberman, Austin, Texas, May 19, 2010.

7. Standard & Poor's Capital IQ; Fuller, Joseph, and Michael C. Jensen. "Just Say No to Wall Street: Putting a Stop to the Earnings Game." *Journal of Applied Corporate Finance* 22 (2010): 59–63.
8. Slywotzky, Adrian J., and John Drzik. "Countering the Biggest Risk of All." *Harvard Business Review*, April 2005, p. 86.
9. Gilbert, Clark G., and Matthew J. Eyring. "Beating the Odds When You Launch a New Venture." *Harvard Business Review*, May 2010.
10. Perkins, Tom. *Valley Boy, The Education of Tom Perkins*. New York: Penguin Group, 2007.
11. Markels, Alex. "The Sky Really Is Falling." *U.S. News and World Report*, November 8, 2004.
12. "The Brain Behind Teledyne: A Great American Capitalist." *New York Observer*, April 7 2003; Henry Singleton at a Teledyne annual meeting.
13. Author's interview with Dave and Sherry Gold in May 2010.
14. Stemberg, Thomas. "Treat People Right and They Will Eat Nails for You, and Other Lessons I Learned Building Staples into a Giant Company." *Inc.*, January 2007.
15. Bob Graham interview by Michael Shearn and Matt Dreith, April 8, 2011.
16. Langreth, Robert, and Andrea Petersen, "Drugs: Stampede Is On for Impotence Pill." *Wall Street Journal*, April 20, 1998.
17. Guilford, Dave. "GM Gives Up on Share Gain." *Automotive News*, November 17, 2003; general press coverage of GM for the period; Business Monitor International. "Market Overview." *U.S. Autos Report*, 2008–2010.
18. More, Roger. "How General Motors Lost Its Focus—and Its Way." *Ivey Business Journal* 73, no. 3 (2009).
19. Author's interview with Paul Larson in November 2010.
20. Frean, Alexandra. "Monsanto hopes the grass will be greener with new crop of products." *Financial Times*, January 8, 2010.
21. Bennett, Robert A. "Continental Illinois Challenge." *New York Times*, August 2, 1982; "Aggressive Banking Pays Off at Continental Illinois Corp." *Wall Street Journal*, October 15, 1981; Bennett, Robert A. "Shaping Chicago's Top Bank" *New York Times*, September 28, 1981; Singer, Mark. *Funny Money*. Boston: Mariner, 2004; Rowe, James L., Jr, "Record Bailout for Continental Bank Launched." *Washington Post*, May 18, 1984.
22. Bonamici, Kate. "Ford Decides to Let the Pinto Explode." *Fortune*, June 27, 2005; Halpern, Paul. "The Corvair, the Pinto and Corporate Behavior." *Policy Studies Review* 1, no. 3 (1982): 540–545.
23. NIRI (National Investor Relations Institute). *Guidance Practices and Preferences-2009*, May 2009 ("2009 NIRI Survey"); *Guidance Practices and Preferences Survey-2008*, May 2008 ("2008 NIRI Survey"); *2007 Earnings Guidance Practices Survey Results*, July 2007 ("2007 NIRI Survey"). http://www.niri.org.

24. Standard & Poor's Capital IQ.
25. Schroeder, Alice. "Please Hold for Mister Buffett." *BusinessWeek*, March 8, 2010.
26. December 2010 LVMH Annual Report.
27. Adams, Susan, and Hannah Elliott. "Master of the Brand, Bernard Arnault." *Forbes*, November 22, 2010.
28. Livingston, Sandra. "Being Different Helps Make Carrier a Success." *Cleveland Plain Dealer*, February 21, 1993.
29. Lublin, Joann. "CEO Tenure, Stock Gains Often Go Hand-in-Hand." *Wall Street Journal*, July 6, 2010.
30. Ignatius, "Mistakes."
31. "Company Interview-Richard Galanti." *Wall Street Transcript*. March 22, 2010, pp. 49–51.
32. Vinnedge, Mary. "From the Corner Office—Herb Kelleher: Beating the Big Boys at Their Own Game." *Success Magazine*, October 3, 2008.
33. Pacelle, Mitchell. "Despite Lawsuits, Enron Bonuses Haven't Been Returned." *Wall Street Journal*, November 3, 2003.
34. Nunes, Paul, and Tim Breene, "Reinvent Your Business Before It's Too Late." *Harvard Business Review*, January–February 2011.
35. Wagner, Rodd, and James Harter. *The 12 Elements of Great Managing*. New York: Gallup Press, 2006.
36. Tindell, Kip (CEO of Container Store), Lecture at 2nd Annual International Conference on Conscious Capitalism, May 2009; Casey Shilling (VP of Marketing Communications) Container Store, April 6, 2011.
37. Buffett, Warren. Letter to Shareholders of Berkshire Hathaway, Inc., 1990.
38. Dade, Corey, and Cari Tuna. "FedEx Joins Other Firms Cutting Pay, Retirement." *Wall Street Journal*, December 19, 2008.
39. Schulz, John D. "A 'Clear Opportunity.'" *Traffic World*, December 8, 2003.
40. Burke, Monty. "Back to Life." *Forbes*, January 20, 2002.
41. Cawood, Scott. "Company Culture: The Intangible Pathway to Profitability." *Employment Relations Today*, Winter 2008.
42. Herskowitz, Mickey, and Ivy McLemore. *People Are The Product, A History of AIM*. Houston: AIM Funds, 2000.
43. Author interview with Lee Valkenar, March 2011.
44. Sisodia, Raj, Jag Sheth, and David Wolfe. *Firms of Endearment*. Upper Saddle River, NJ: Wharton School Publishing, 2007, pp. 33–34.
45. Hymowitz, Carol, and Matt Murray. "Management—Boss Talk: Raises and Praise or Out the Door—How GE's Chief Rates and Spurs His Employees." *Wall Street Journal*, Eastern edition, June 21, 1999.

46. Standard & Poor's Capital IQ.

47. Interview with Casey Hoffman December 2010.

48. Herb Kelleher, speaking at the University of Texas at Austin, October 19, 2006.

49. Erickson, Tamara J., and Lynda Gratton, "What It Means to Work Here." *Harvard Business Review*, March 2007.

50. O'Toole, Jim. "What's Needed Next: A Culture of Candor." *Harvard Business Review*, June 2009.

51. *Ibid.*

52. *Ibid.*

53. Much of the info on board alignment and board conflicts of interest is drawn from Marianne M. Jennings, "Preventing Organizational Ethical Collapse" *Government Accountants Journal* 53, no. 1. (2004).

54. Holt, Nancy D. "Workspaces." *Wall Street Journal*, October 15, 2003.

55. Edgecliffe-Johnson, Andrew. "The Biggest Beat of Non-fiction Television Eyes a Global Prize." *Financial Times*, January 10, 2011.

56. Ignatius, "Mistakes."

57. Jones, Steven D. "In the Money: Hurd's H-P Grew, But Charges Pruned Earnings." Dow Jones News Service, August 10, 2010.

58. "The Brain Behind Teledyne: A Great American Capitalist." *New York Observer*, April 7, 2003.

59. Time Value of Money, LP free cash flow estimate.

60. Standard & Poor's Capital IQ.

61. Western Union 10K reports, 2007 to 2009.

62. Standard & Poor's Capital IQ and AutoZone 10-K reports, 2002 to 2010.

63. General Motors 10-K reports, 1985 to 1995.

64. Microsoft 10-K reports, 2009 to 2010.

Chapter 9

1. Varchaver, Nicholas. "Buffett Goes to Wharton." *CNN Money*. May 2, 2008. http://money.cnn.com.

2. "The Best Advice I Ever Got." Linda Mason, Chairman and Founder Bright Horizons Family Solutions, interviewed by Daisy Wademan Dowling, *Harvard Business Review*, September 2008.

3. Tapscott, Don. "Changing the World, One Friend at a Time." *Globe and Mail*, July 3, 2010.

4. Vascellaro, Jessica. "Facebook CEO in No Rush to 'Friend' Wall Street." *Wall Street Journal*, March 4, 2010.

5. Efrati, Amir, and Pui-Wing Tam. "Facebook Share Clamor Heats Up." *Wall Street Journal*, March 17, 2011.

6. Interview with Dave and Sherry Gold, May 2010.

7. Sparks, Debra. "Conseco's Morning After." *BusinessWeek*, June 5, 2000.

8. Porter, Jane, and Alina Dizik. "Make That 'Dr. Chainsaw,'" *Business-Week*, September 11, 2007.

9. Bloomberg, Michael. *Bloomberg by Bloomberg*. Upper Saddle River, NJ: John Wiley and Sons, 2001, pp. 62–64.

10. Lynn, Matthew. "The Fallen King of Finland." *BusinessWeek*, September 20–26, 2010.

11. Coffey, Brendan. "Every Penny Counts; Selling Everything for 99 Cents Made Dave Gold Rich." *Forbes*, September 30, 2002.

12. Kelly, Kate. "Bear CEO's Handling of Crisis Raises Issues." *Wall Street Journal*, November 1, 2007.

13. McNish, Jacquie. "Brookfield Begins to Rebuild: Firm Mends its Office Towers, Reputation." *Globe and Mail*, September 24, 2001.

14. Daly, John. "The Toughest SOBs in Business." *Globe and Mail*, January 31, 2003.

15. Ignatius, "Mistakes."

16. "Dot-com job: As InfoSpace Stock Collapses, Insiders Cash Out." *Seattle Times, Knight Ridder/Tribune Business News*, March 7, 2005.

17. Rittenhouse, L.J. *Do Business with People You Can Trust: Balancing Profits and Principles*. New York: and Beyond Communications, 2002.

18. "Reuters Shares Rise on Upbeat Revenue Statement." Reuters News, October 8, 2004.

19. Larsen, Peter Thal. "Griffin Mining." *Financial Times*, February 21, 2006.

20. Howell, Martin. *Predators and Profits: 100+ Ways for Investors to Protect Their Nest Eggs*. Upper Saddle River, NJ: Prentice Hall, 2003, pp. 44–45.

21. Lyons, Daniel. "The Interviews: Books (Jeff Bezos)." *Newsweek*, December 28, 2009.

22. Ignatius, "Mistakes."

23. Barrett, Amy, and Peter Elstrom. "Making WorldCom Live Up to Its Name." *BusinessWeek*, July 14, 1997.

24. Hansen, Morten T., Herminia Ibarra, and Urs Peyer. "The Best-Performing CEOs in the World." *Harvard Business Review*, January–February 2010.

Chapter 10

1. Standard and Poor's Capital IQ.

2. *Ibid.*

3. *Ibid.*

4. Strayer Education Annual Report 2009, Robert Silberman.

5. Norfolk Southern 2009 Annual Report.

6. Toossi, Mitra. "A Century of Change: the U.S. Labor Force, 1950–2050." *Monthly Labor Review*, May 2002. Accessed May 11, 2011. http://www.bls.gov/opub/mlr/.

7. "Tea." *Who's Buying Groceries*, 5th ed., Ithaca, NY; New Strategist Publications, Inc. 2007.

8. Copeland, Michael, with Seth Weintraub, "Google's Next Act." *Fortune*, August 16, 2010.

9. Standard & Poor's Capital IQ; IDEXX 10-K reports, 2006 to 2009.

10. Mangelsdorf, Martha E. Interview with Clayton M. Christensen in "Good Days for Disruptors." *MIT Sloan Management Review* 50 (2009): 67–70.

11. Graco 2009 10-K.

12. Standard & Poor's Capital IQ.

13. Medtronic 10-K reports, 1992 to 2010.

14. MoneyGram International 2007 Analyst Day Transcript-Final, Fair Disclosure Wire, March 7, 2007; Ersek, Hikmet (Western Union CEO), Credit Suisse Group Technology Conference Transcript, Fair Disclosure Wire, December 1, 2010.

15. Q4 2006 Apollo Earnings Conference Call, October 18, 2006; Standard & Poor's Capital IQ.

16. March 29, 2010 Apollo Group Conference Call, Fair Disclosure Wire.

17. Standard & Poor's Capital IQ.

18. *Ibid.*

19. Standard & Poor's Capital IQ; Giverny Capital's Francois Rochon; Bed Bath & Beyond 10-K reports, 1995 to 2001.

20. Stieghorst, Tom. "Cheap fares, Short Staff Mean Long Delays for Spirit Airlines." *South Florida Sun-Sentinal*, September 30, 2007.

21. Strayer Annual Reports, from 2001 to 2009.

22. Carroll, Paul B., and Chunka Mui. "7 Ways to Fail Big: Lessons from the Most Inexcusable Business Failures of the Past 25 Years." *Harvard Business Review*, September 2008.

23. Ruggless, Ron. "Having Words with Tilman Fertitta, Chairman and Founder, Landry's Inc." *Nation's Restaurant News*, October 25, 2010, p. 42.

Chapter 11

1. Author's interview with Todd Green, May 28, 2010.

2. Caterpillar press release, November 15, 2010.

3. MacFadyen, Ken. "A Synergy Runup?" *Mergers and Acquisitions Report*, May 10, 2010, p. 37.

4. Carroll and Mui, "7 Ways to Fail Big."

5. Carroll and Mui, "7 Ways to Fail Big."
6. With permission from John Mackey.
7. Danaher Conference Call, Fair Disclosure Wire, December 11, 2003.
8. Hindo, Brian. "A Dynamo Called Danaher." *BusinessWeek*, February 19, 2007.
9. "Mergers—The Cisco System, Secrets of US Computer Giant's Success." *Strategic Direction*, Vol. 20 No. 7, 2004, pp. 25–27.
10. *Ibid.*
11. Ewers, Justin. "Cisco's Connections." *U.S. News & World Report*, June 26, 2006, pp. 49–53.
12. *Ibid.*
13. *Ibid.*
14. Benedict, Jeff. *How to Build a Business Warren Buffett Would Buy: The R.C. Willey Story.* Salt Lake City, UT: Shadow Mountain, 2009.
15. Mattel at Banc of America Securities 33rd Annual Investment Conference, (Robert Eckert, CEO of Mattel), September 17, 2003, Fair Disclosure Wire, September 17, 2003.
16. Case, Stephen. "Thinking Ahead." *Executive Excellence*, June 2001, p. 8.
17. "America Online and Time Warner Complete Merger to Create AOL Time Warner." BusinessWire, January 11, 2001.
18. Standard & Poor's Capital IQ.
19. Stoessel, Eric. "Hotel Sales are Hopping." *National Real Estate Investor.* November-December 2010, p. 15.
20. Marr, Garry. "Brookfield Said Set to Re-open O&Y Bid: 'Pennies' Reported to be Standing in Way of a Deal." *Financial Post*, August 25, 2005.
21. Kontomerkos, Mario (Corporate Vice President of Finance at Penn National Gaming) in discussion with the author, February 2011.
22. Standard & Poor's Capital IQ.
23. Eig, Jonathan. "Behind the Coke Board's Refusal to Let CEO Daft Buy Quaker Oats." *Wall Street Journal*, November 30, 2000.

About the Author

MICHAEL SHEARN founded Time Value of Money, LP, a private investment firm, in 1996 to devote his attention to selecting and researching stocks and private investments. He launched the Compound Money Fund, LP, a concentrated value fund, in 2007. Michael serves on the Investment Committee of Southwestern University, which oversees the school's $270 million endowment. He is also a member of the Advisory Board for the University of Texas MBA Investment Fund. Shearn graduated from Southwestern University, a small liberal arts college in Georgetown, Texas, with a B.A. in Business, *magna cum laude*, with an emphasis in Accounting and Finance.

Index